Photography and Africa

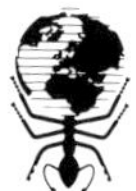

exposures

EXPOSURES is a series of books on photography designed to explore the rich history of the medium from thematic perspectives. Each title presents a striking collection of images and an engaging, accessible text that offers intriguing insights into a specific theme or subject.

Series editors: Mark Haworth-Booth and Peter Hamilton

Also published

Photography and Spirit John Harvey

Photography and Australia Helen Ennis

Photography and Cinema David Campany

Photography and Science Kelley Wilder

Photography and Flight Denis Cosgrove and William L. Fox

Photography and Literature François Brunet

Photography and Egypt Maria Golia

Photography and Italy Maria Antonella Pelizzari

Photography and Africa

Erin Haney

reaktion books

Published by Reaktion Books Ltd
33 Great Sutton Street
London EC1V ODX
www.reaktionbooks.co.uk

First published 2010

Printed and bound in China by Toppan Printing Co. Ltd

British Library Cataloguing in Publication Data
Haney, Erin
    Photography and Africa. – (Exposures)
    1. Photography – Africa – History.
    2. Africa – Pictorial works.
    I. Title
    II. Series
    770.9'6-DC22

ISBN: 978 1 86189 382 6

Contents

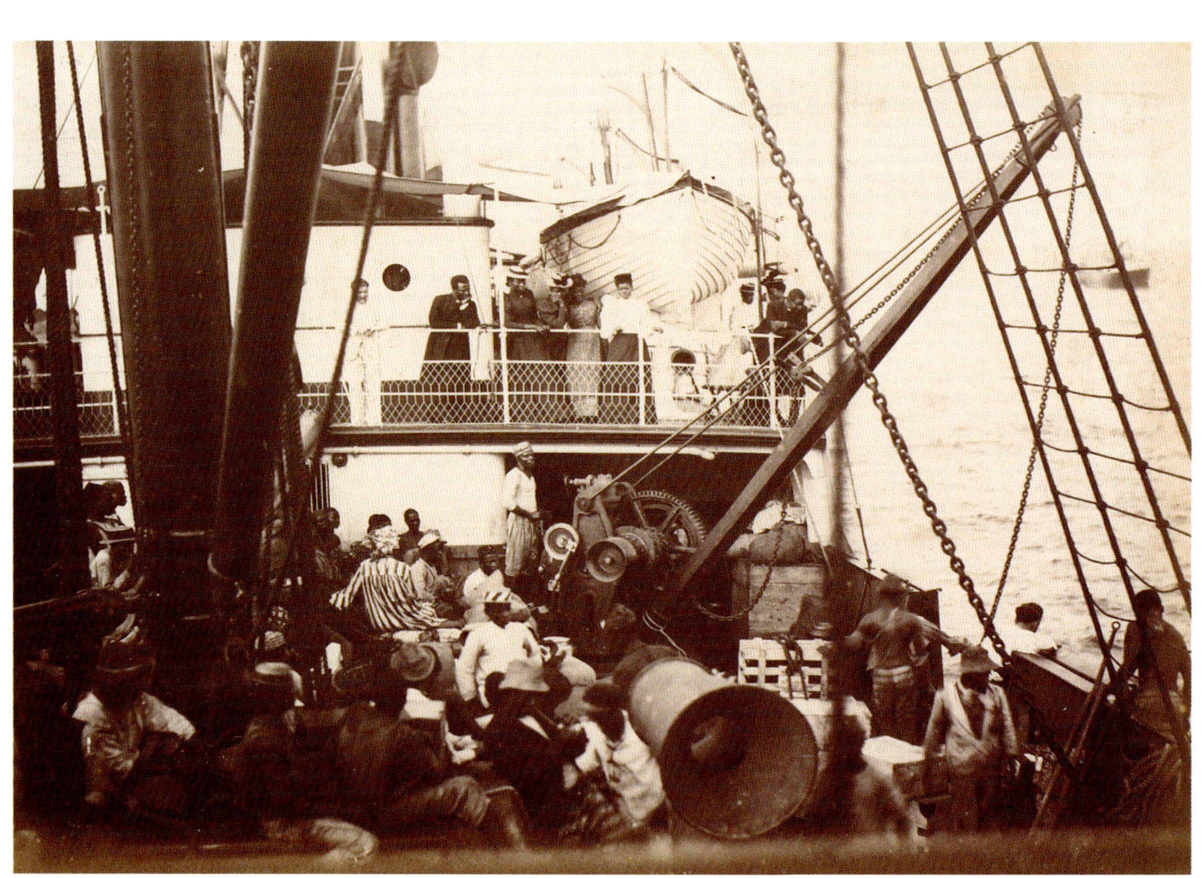

Introduction

In 1894, N. Walwin Holm (b. 1865) offered lessons, theoretical texts and magazines on the art of photography at his Adela Portrait Studios in Lagos, 'for those who wish to go forward with the broad Sunlight'.[1] Looking back, we now know that the earliest photographic efforts in Africa consisted of the labours of roving local, resident and itinerant photographers – these innovators moving with the sun – who have left for us images which survive, even from as early as 1840. Although photography is one of the most formidable creative traditions on the African continent, attention to this medium as seen in exhibitions, critical and scholarly writing, and all manner of up-to-the-minute disseminations, is a rather recent phenomenon. In no small part, this attention has been enlivened by a wealth of contemporary photography coming from the continent and its diasporas. So it is perhaps less surprising that in these intervening years, we find photographic forms interwoven through many Africanist modernist practices, and that they have proliferated across genres and geographic borders.

The 'photographies' considered here are several, encompassing a range of technologies from daguerreotypes to digital photography. The term 'Africa' proves a much trickier question, problematic most of all for the way it is often substituted as a singular term to stand in for a multiplicity of cultural, political, social and artistic experiences.[2] Modernist and contemporary artists have long been wrestling with the received wisdoms of monolithic 'Africanness' as it is currently posed within the remit of world history and present-day creativity. What's more, the geographic expanse of the continent should deter any attempts towards

1 Photographer unknown, *Deck Passengers on an African Steamer*, c. 1890–1900, albumen print.

a cohesive 'African' narrative: we remember the continent has 59 nations and more protectorates, from the Maghreb to South Africa and including the Indian Ocean islands. If this was not enough, these are influenced by the ebb and flow of its diasporas, including those movements dating back to slave trades across the Atlantic, the Sahara and the Indian Ocean. Claims for African identity are contested and various, their frames of reference often couched in terms which are more often personal, rather than ethnic or national. Chinua Achebe's observation to Kwame Anthony Appiah still resonates:

> There isn't a final identity that is African. But, at the same time, there *is* an identity coming into existence. And it has a certain context and a certain meaning. Because if somebody meets me, say, in a shop in Cambridge, he says 'Are you from Africa?' Which means that Africa means something to some people.[3]

'Africanness' registers in relation to one's residence, and to one's momentum. The same seems to hold for African photographs. The concern for 'African photography' has been initially one of diaspora critics, writers, artists and curators. In Paris, the research efforts of the publishers and writers of *Revue Noire* magazines resulted in a large number of publications dedicated to photography by photographers born and/or still resident on the continent, beginning in 1991. The following year *Revue Noire*'s team mounted 300 photographs at the Centre Wallonie Bruxelles in Paris, and their landmark exhibition and catalogue *'L'Afrique par elle-même'* (*A Self-portrait of Africa*, 1998) were launched at the Maison Européenne de la Photographie. The efforts of Simon Njami, Jean-Loup Pivin, Pascal Martin Saint Léon and Pierre-Laurent Sanner also contributed to the Guggenheim Museum's exhibition *In/sight: African Photographers, 1940 to the Present* in New York (1996). Photography's apparent realism made it perhaps a particularly enticing and approachable medium for uninitiated audiences. In 1996, Okwui Enwezor and Octavio Zaya put it this way:

> No medium has been more instrumental in creating a great deal of the visual fictions of the African continent than photography. Yet,

ironically, in attempting to defuse the power of these historicist
fictions, we must rely upon photography and its vast array of signs,
which also stand at the juncture of this refutation.[4]

This activist inclination of these efforts came out of current political
circumstances (racism and misrepresentation, and lacunae representing
African creative production in European and US institutions). Scholarly
writing, at the time of the first publications, directed attention to the
treasures lodged on the continent: family and colonial archives, albums,
commercial repositories, all forgotten sources 'which remain for historians
and archivists to retrieve, catalogue, interpret, and preserve for future
generations'.[5] There is hope for regaining access to a total archive, one
which counters an admittedly, rather unspecified colonial archive; indeed
there is a strong undercurrent in these writings which suggests that most
photographers 'from Africa' were in some way contesting these colonial
visual tropes.

For this reason, among others, all the more is at stake for evidence
of early photography by Africans. Many had assumed that there was
no early record by photographers living on the continent. Olu Oguibe,
following research of the 1980s and early 1990s, listed nineteenth-century
photographers whose names had been presumed to represent European
photographers: N. Walwin and J.A.C. Holm from Accra and Lagos, F.R.C.
Lutterodt from Accra, George S. A. Da Costa from Lagos and Alphonso
Lisk-Carew from Freetown among others. If Nicolas Monti noted in *Africa
Then* (1987) that photography could be a subversive tool for Africans as
a means of expression and for showing their true circumstances, then
photography was rendered a defiant and political act: 'even in the face
of opposition and active discouragement, Africans nevertheless took
possession of the camera and photographic processes.'[6] It may be a
reasonable assertion, but we need to know more. Giving these photographs their due requires moving beyond the fiery narratives that perhaps
drew us to them initially: African/European photographers; imported
technologies/African adaptations; sophisticated photographers/naive
subjects; colonial/post-colonial subjecthood. Things seem subtler
now, more complex. We do well to recall that the advent of African

photographic practices occurred alongside longstanding and novel
artistic traditions, and with crucial changes in the social and economic
landscape across the continent. There was the shift from Atlantic slave
trade to colonial rule, as well as African resistance to these incursions;
the emergence of nation-states and modern ethnicities, and increasing
conversions to Islam and Christianity; and the emergence of black elite
intelligentsia, schooled in Europe.[7] Some of the categorizations that informed early research on photography, primarily the distinction between
imperial versus local photographic projects, are utterly upended by the
intricacy of experience and movement of photographers, patrons and the
objects themselves. Crucially, the awareness of these paradigms intensifies
by considering archives of all kinds, which have moved and continue to
move across the globe.[8]

The study of photography and Africa remains a political question.
What follows in this book is consideration of works made primarily,
though not exclusively, by people who were born or lived on the continent, its visitors, and those of its diasporas. They represent some themes
which will resonate with those who profess interest in the continent, and
also those compelled by a photograph. All the same, these images are
provocative, resonant and powerful gifts. They draw our attention to a
much larger set of conditions, of family and studio and commercial and
colonial archives on the continent and beyond, and many more stories
will emerge from research in – and more sustained consideration of –
African archives and those elsewhere. We cannot fully acknowledge
the depth of photographic history in many parts of Africa because of
disruption, migration, loss and the destruction of civic and personal
archives; though where private or public African collections do remain,
they are often regarded as objects imbued with creative, personal and
historical value.[9] This does not mean preservation is a universal concern.[10]
Photographic objects move into the world, and their material existence
matters and is often updated.[11] The dissemination of postcards, photographs of staged tableaux, landscape, portraits and personal mementos
are things of a massive image circulation; considering these dynamics
requires the viewer to reflect of the local political conditions, economic
opportunities and restraints under which photographers have operated.

This field has lavished attention on outside perceptions of Africa, on photography's connection with European imperialism, the various efforts by explorers, colonizers, missionaries, entrepreneurs and academics. We know much less about the material intricacies, the frames of reference, and the intellectual challenges that photographs and their archives present as they emerge from complex local creative contexts. African photophiles, historians, photographers and collectors abound, and in places across the continent people keep, update and figure out ways of interpreting and disseminating what the photographic past means for local histories, and how such repercussions ripple outward.

I have included works from African, European, American and Middle Eastern collections and archives; commercial, public, civic and private archives; missionary collections, colonial private albums and postcards. These photographs provoke for me what are some of this subject's most compelling and open-ended questions. The works mentioned in these chapters stand more as invitations for further thinking about materiality, the process and experiences of photography, rather than completed and tidily composed discussions; so they are informed by what is omitted as much as anything else. This cannot be a photographic survey of the continent, nor is it historically comprehensive. It is not limited to art photography, colonial photography, the work of missionaries' projects, or popular depictions of Africa and its people. I have not delved into war photography, Hollywood-style depictions, fashion photography, imagery of the National Geographic/Discovery Channel variety, or exoticist treatments. The contemporary artists featured in the final chapter have been to some degree successful in global art markets and have exhibited either in Europe or the USA. And, for the most part, this work relies on research which is accessible in English.

The first chapter on early photographies points to the different conditions of the medium's emergence, and to the conditions of instability, momentum and innovation which characterize early photographic practices and the photographers themselves. Portraiture is touched on in chapter Two, suggesting that there is a realm of diverse and complex practices beyond that of the current superstars. Chapter Three engages with aspects of colonial photography in central Africa and the use of struggle photography as political resistance in South Africa, foregrounding the camera's links to overtly political imagery in different contexts. The fourth chapter draws together examples which demonstrate the porous borders between the mediums of photography and other creative visual and performative practices. The final chapter suggests that contemporary photographers rifle through aspects of earlier photographic traditions, showing themselves to be resolutely connected citizens of the world in ways distinct from the cosmopolitanism of their nineteenth- and twentieth-century predecessors. Through these stories and images, we are pressed to re-imagine and expand the remit of what has largely been presumed to be photography's roots.

Deck Passengers on an African Steamer (illus. 1) reminds us to bear in mind that the movement of African images, objects and artists themselves is an ancient phenomenon: it is one glimpse in the life of those movements (*c.* 1885) on a steamer just off the southern Guinea coast.[12] For readers of all backgrounds, I hope above all that these images will set one wondering, and arouse an intense curiosity. For me, these short stories about photographs and photography evoke the variety and dynamism that underlie and animate the creative traditions from which they come.

one

Towards a Wider History

Shortly after the introduction of the daguerreotype to the world in 1839, several parties ventured out to capture profoundly symbolic sights in Egypt. The monumental landscape, dense with relics of antiquity, drew European commercial photographers tracing the paths of earlier French occupiers. Around the same time, the Ottoman Viceroy of Egypt, Pasha Mehmet Ali, learned the daguerreotype processes from the visiting French painter Horace Vernet in Cairo. Viceroy Ali chose Alexandria's ancient port as the subject for his first image in 1839.[1] The port represented one of several gateways of antiquity connecting the African continent and the Mediterranean world, and was also at that time a front of regional power struggles over control of Egypt. Photography offered people a new way of framing and visualizing the things that mattered to them, but we are just beginning to come to terms with the range of photographic practices by early photographers on the continent.

Early photographers made an art of crossing borders in an era of unprecedented momentum. It will become clear that even their earliest efforts were not simple one-way transmissions of technologies and processes from Europe. Their images were equally transitory. If making 'likenesses' meant bearing a burden of heavy cameras and equipment, the resulting images were comparatively featherweight, easily borne on steamship routes, and so exchanged and proliferated across continents and oceans.[2] Yet the tangible photographic remnants of this earliest period, as it remains in private and public collections on the continent, is scattered about. Although new archives and other documentary evidence are periodically coming to light, African contributions have been largely overlooked as a result of the fragility of the photographic record as it stands on the continent.

Neither Vernet's nor Ali's daguerreotypes have survived from 1839. In many cases, posterity has favoured those early photographic images which were reproduced as aquatints or in other media, or bound in expensive travel books and souvenir albums produced in the Near East and Europe. More broadly, it had long been assumed that the only nineteenth-century photographers in Africa were foreign. Since the 1980s, strands of documentary evidence about early African photographers have surfaced. Vintage images by local photographers survive in small numbers of archives, although in many cases attributions are lost. Many west African studios that were presumed to be European-owned are presently being reconsidered and correct attributions made. Studio stamps, of course, mask the presence of numerous photographer employees. On the continent, African private and civic collections have been disrupted by the migrations of families and communities, humid climates, accidental and deliberate destruction, and the dispersion and loss of studio archives.[3] More recently, poverty speeds up the sale of photographic patrimony to dealers and collectors.

In Egypt, one of the very earliest sites of exploration photography, scholars and romantic travellers with cameras made images that sustained a European mirage of Oriental decadence and monumentality. Simultaneously, west African port towns, teeming with merchants and entrepreneurs, fostered local studios and patronized itinerant sea-going photographers from abroad. Southern African ports sat at the convergence of busy global sea-routes linking the Near and Far East, Australia, other parts of Africa, the Americas and Europe. They hosted a variety of travelling and home-grown photographers amid the waves of European settler migrants. The early studios in east Africa and the Indian Ocean islands came about by way of a multiplicity of Indian, French, British and local entrepreneurs working for colonial and local elite concerns.

From 1839 onwards and throughout photography's first decades, Egypt attracted large numbers of intrepid photographers, in greater quantities than any other part of the continent. Europeans were the first of these, followed by practitioners from the Near East. Egyptian images were so abundant and so widely circulated that these scenes and views were subsumed into the oldest iconography of European photography.[4]

European academic and popular interest in north Africa's wealth of ancient monuments rose on the heels of exploration, colonialism and the drive to obtain a shorter route between Asia and Europe through a Red Sea route. This region's strategic importance made possible the emerging western scholarly interest in antique history and archaeological ruins in Egypt, Asia Minor and Palestine. When Napoleon invaded Egypt in 1798, he brought with him a contingent of scholars, historians, artists and draughtsmen to document the exotic place. French military operations led to the uncovering of the stele known as the Rosetta Stone on 20 August 1799, sparking a wave of exploration such as the Swiss explorer Johan-Ludwig Burckhardt's investigation of the temple of Abu Simbel in 1812.

Egypt's cultural treasury was an ideal subject for the very earliest French proponents of photography. When François Arago presented the introduction of the daguerreotype to the French Academy of Sciences in 1839, he emphasized its descriptive powers. Arago claimed it would have taken dozens of draughtsmen decades to record the hieroglyphs of Thebes, Memphis and Karnak, while the new technology was a tool which would 'surpass . . . the work of the most capable among our painters'.[5]

While the gradual unearthing of such monuments drew scores of scholar-explorers to the Near East, the earliest photographic expedition suggests the explosion of French and British public fascination with Egypt. Artists and commercial pictorialists flocked to Egypt. Among them were the French painters Frédéric Goupil-Fesquet and his teacher Horace Vernet, who travelled to Alexandria with 'two improved daguerreotype' cameras.[6] In Cairo, their party joined the Swiss daguerreotypist Gaspard-Pierre-Gustave Joly de Lotbinière, who was employed by the large commercial firm Lerebours. Their original daguerreotypes of Egyptian ruins and monuments are now lost, but some served as the basis for engravings bound in lavish volumes by Lerebours, *Excursions daguerriennes* (1840–44) and Hector Horeau's *Panorama d'Égypte et de Nubie* (1841). Rather than recording expanses of hieroglyphs recommended by Arago, many early daguerreotypes captured the stillness and saturated shadows of the monumental ruins. Such subjects suited the long exposure times that daguerreotypes required.[7] Broad vistas filled with wondrous architecture rendered the Egyptian landscape static and remote, as other-worldly as it was geographically distant from mid-nineteenth century Europe.

This trio were the first of a multitude of pioneer photographers drawn to north Africa. The French traveller and writer Maxime Du Camp was among the first to produce a great photographic record, and pioneered the first travel book illustrated with calotypes, *Égypt, Nubie, Palestine et Syrie* (1852). Du Camp endeavoured to make scientific recordings of archaeological monuments, which was part of his commission by France's Ministry of Public Education. Du Camp also recorded Egypt's contemporary structures, but these were not published. Equally noteworthy was the accomplishment of Félix Teynard, whose vast photographic survey *Égypte et Nubie* (1854–8) includes many images of great delicacy of shadow and pattern. Teynard's catalogue included images of ancient ruins along with views of the modern Egypt he journeyed through, which complemented in scope and approach the foundational text of French Orientalist scholarship, the 23-volume *Description de l'Egypte* (1808–*c.* 1822).

The dualistic character of the American-French J. B. Greene's project reflects two sides of early photography in north Africa, driven by scholarly inquiry and inflected by a Romantic strain. Greene pioneered the use of photography to record an archaeological dig. Yet his salt prints, with their velvety tones, are intensely atmospheric evocations of the north African landscape. Greene's framing of a partly unearthed statue of a woman at Abu Simbel distils an image of grandeur and decay. Captive to the passage of centuries, the still queen keeps to the shadows; Greene's architectural composition balances a judicious handling of intense sunlight and architectural shade. Her splendour is magnified by the passage of

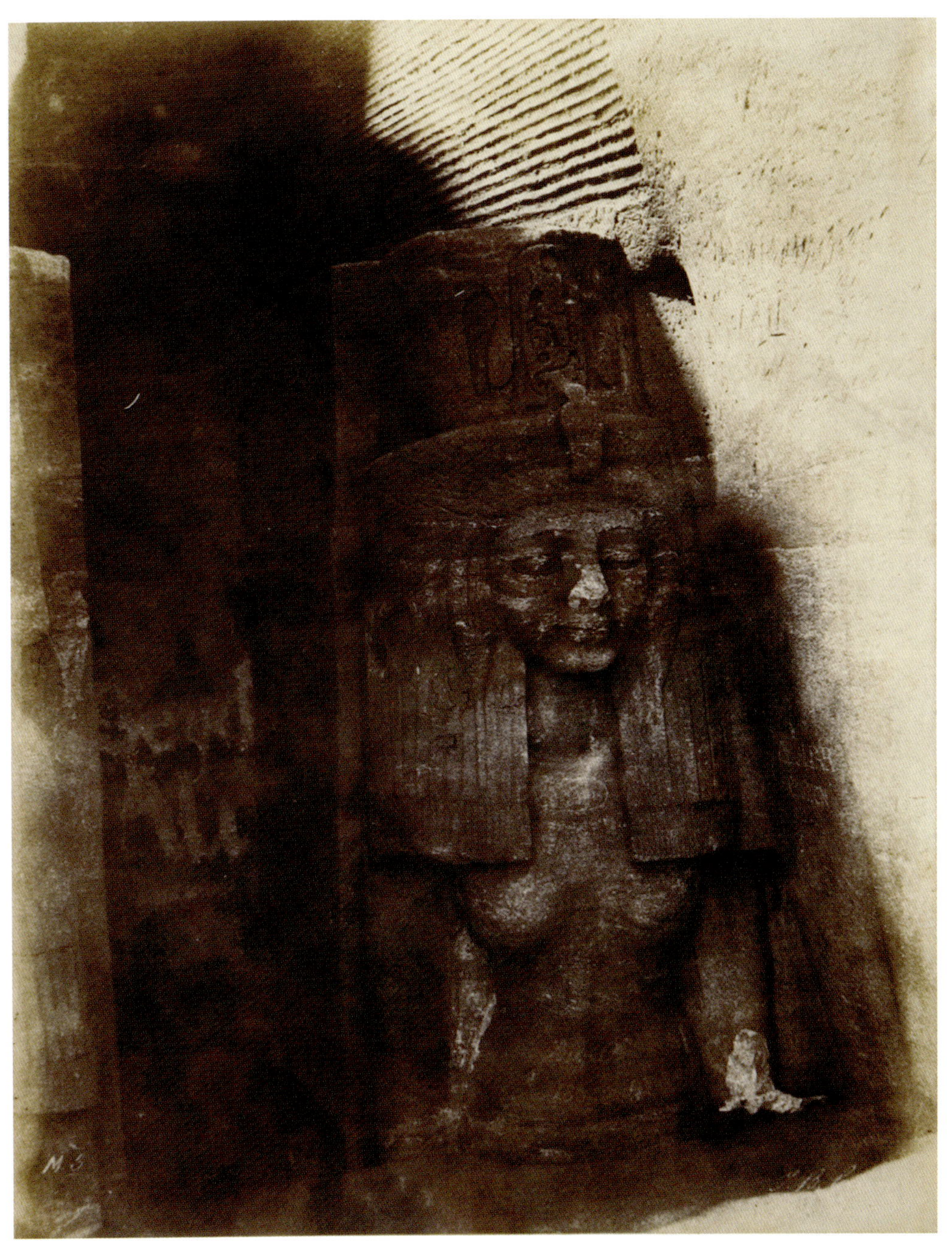

time, an emotional theme in the work of many Romantic artists. The poet
Shelley mused in wistful tones:

Among the ruined temples there . . .
. . . wild images
Of more than man, where marble daemons watch
The Zodiac's brazen mystery, and dead men
Hang their mute thoughts on the mute walls around,
He lingered, poring on memorials
Of the world's youth . . .'[8]

Francis Frith, the English printer, photographer and marketer,
was among the most commercially astute of early travel photographers.
Beginning in 1857, Frith's images review an increasingly standardized
catalogue of Egyptian, Nubian and Near Eastern views. Frith's remarkable successes were a result of his high technical standards and his early
exploitation of the new wet plate collodion process which allowed for
high quality images of large size. His scenes are peopled by contemporary
Egyptians and tourists, and invite the viewer in with this tuning to human

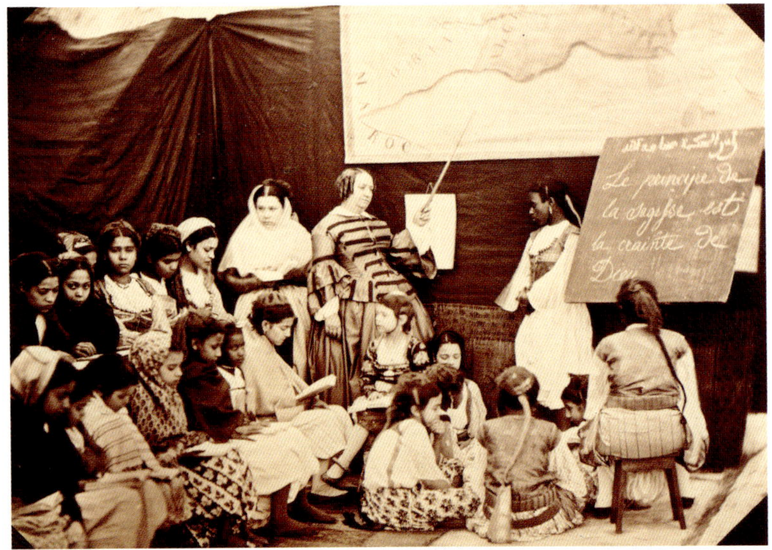

3 Félix Moulin, *Algerian School*, 1856,
albumen print.

scale. Increasingly curious English audiences could immerse themselves in Frith's offerings from the comfort of their drawing rooms. There were stereo-optican slides, lush albumen prints bound in formidably priced portfolios and albums, but there were also the ephemeral enticements of public exhibitions and narrated lantern slide presentations.

Early photography in north Africa took in a wider variety of subjects than has been widely acknowledged. The French photographer Jean-Baptiste Alary was probably the first to open a studio in Algiers, the capital city of the newly conquered colony of Algeria. Alary and compatriot P. H. Delamotte produced the first daguerreotypes in 1850. The exhibition of Algerian views in Paris' Société Française de Photographie in 1857 may have included the new albumen print techniques in works by Alary, Gustave de Beaucorps and Dr Lorent of Venice. Alary's intricate prints included panoramas of Algiers, famous mosques and palaces, Arab cemeteries, studies of local people gathered and houses in Algiers. Hints of the colony's distant history are evoked in Berber and Roman monuments, the ancient towns of Constantine and Médéa, and its Arab cemeteries. Yet Algiers was taken by the French only ten years earlier, in 1847, and this is signalled by photographs of military forts, monuments to the French conquest, and construction sites underway which emphasize the relatively recent dominion.[9] The touring French photographer Félix Jacques-Antoine Moulin (*c.* 1802–1875) created fascinating social tableaux of imagined interior scenes in the late 1850s: a harem composed of women and children casually lounging, a portrait of Superior Muslim Council member Mohammed Largucch, a grouping of dervishes. Another presents a more ambiguous scene: a French teacher points to a map of north Africa, her young female charges study their books while two pupils gaze strikingly at the camera, and most ignore the blackboard which intones *'La principe de la eglise est la crainte de Dieu'* ('The principle of the church is reverence for God').

By the mid-nineteenth century, a dramatic rise in the demand for images of the Orient from European and Near East audiences led to a proliferation of commercial studios. They sold single images and also compiled volumes incorporating the work of many different photographers. The inception of Thomas Cook tours in 1869 cemented an already expanding tourist market, and this in turn encouraged an influx of foreign photographers. Itinerant photographers ensured a steady supply of Egyptian and Near Eastern imagery, many of which were sent to be mass-produced at factories elsewhere. As a growing number of photographs circulated around the region, genres of popular imagery coalesced. There were ethnographic 'type' portraits, at times haphazardly labelled with purported ethnicity, class and occupation by photographers, as well as printers and marketers. Erotic imagery was another popular genre.[10] Many photographers in Egypt relied on prostitutes or slaves for models who posed undressed, enacting the fantasies of harem scenes which echoed Orientalist paintings and staged European erotic photography. Picturesque views, such as the pyramids, were increasingly scattered with tourists, unearthed monuments, the Nile, archaeological excavations and objects from tombs, and were found side-by-side with views of Cairo streets or carefully composed urban tableaux.

That such great numbers of these images were widely disseminated contributes to a sense of a rather homogenous north African image-world, heavy with monument and sights that prevailed on the increasingly well-trod tourist routes. Much rarer are photographs depicting portraits of local individuals, families or groups, or imagery that documents the social and political realities of the day.

Amongst the most noteworthy of resident photographers who settled in Cairo by the 1860s were the German W. Hammerschmidt and the Italian-English Antonio Beato. Another was French photographer Henri Béchard, whose views are composed from unusual vantage points including Cairo views and compelling intimate studies of the city's inhabitants, and whose details surpass the constraints of the staged type images. Likewise, Hammerschmidt's studies of Cairo's merchants invite close inspection in a way that more commonly staged scenes could not; more importantly, they evoke wonder about the relationship he had with the rarely pictured denizens of his adopted city. *Rice Vendors* is a study on balances, with the merchants and their young servant directing their gazes at the camera with a sense of conversational immediacy.

By the 1870s, the most successful studios in north Africa were international in scope, expanding the already thriving market of photographers

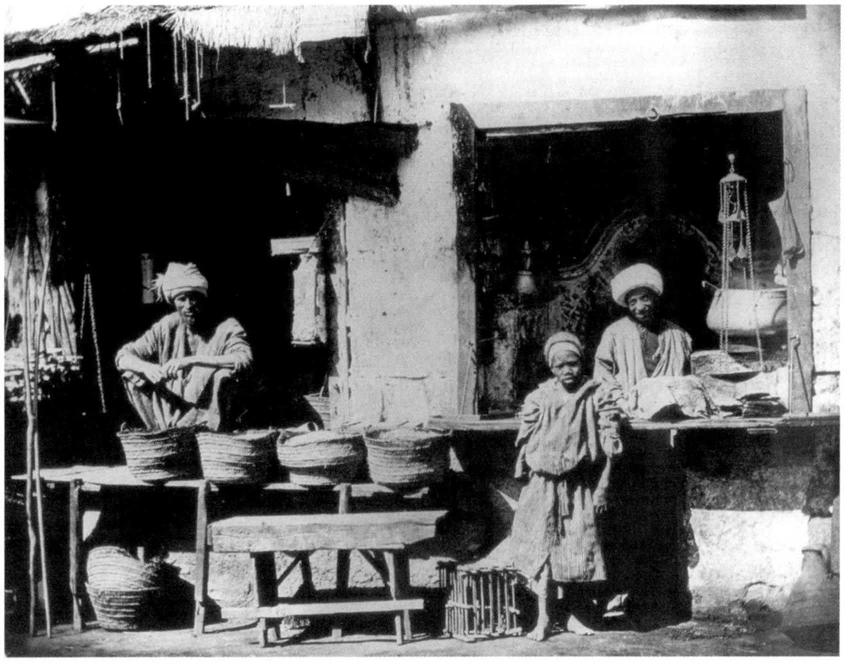

in the region. J. Pascal Sébah was based in progressive Constantinople, the French husband and wife team Bonfils and Cie operated studios from their base in Beirut, the Zangaki brothers came to Cairo from Greece, and three Armenians converted to Islam and operated under the name of Abdullah Frères. The breadth of some of these photographers' activities is surprising, such as that of Armenian photographer G. Lékégian. While his staged tableaux of quotidian Egyptian life were sought after and used as models for visiting Orientalist painters, Lékégian was also employed by the British occupying army. A notable image by Abdullah Frères (and which has been attributed to Lékégian) suggesting the flux of studio glass is an image of Al-Azhar University (illus. 5). The visual effect of the cloistered scene heightens a sense of social and personal spheres rarely seen in the roll-call of travel photography. The occasional images of amateur photographers on tour, religious pilgrims and foreign residents attest to a modernizing region in the throes of rapid change. Hippolyte Arnoux from Port Said set up his darkroom on

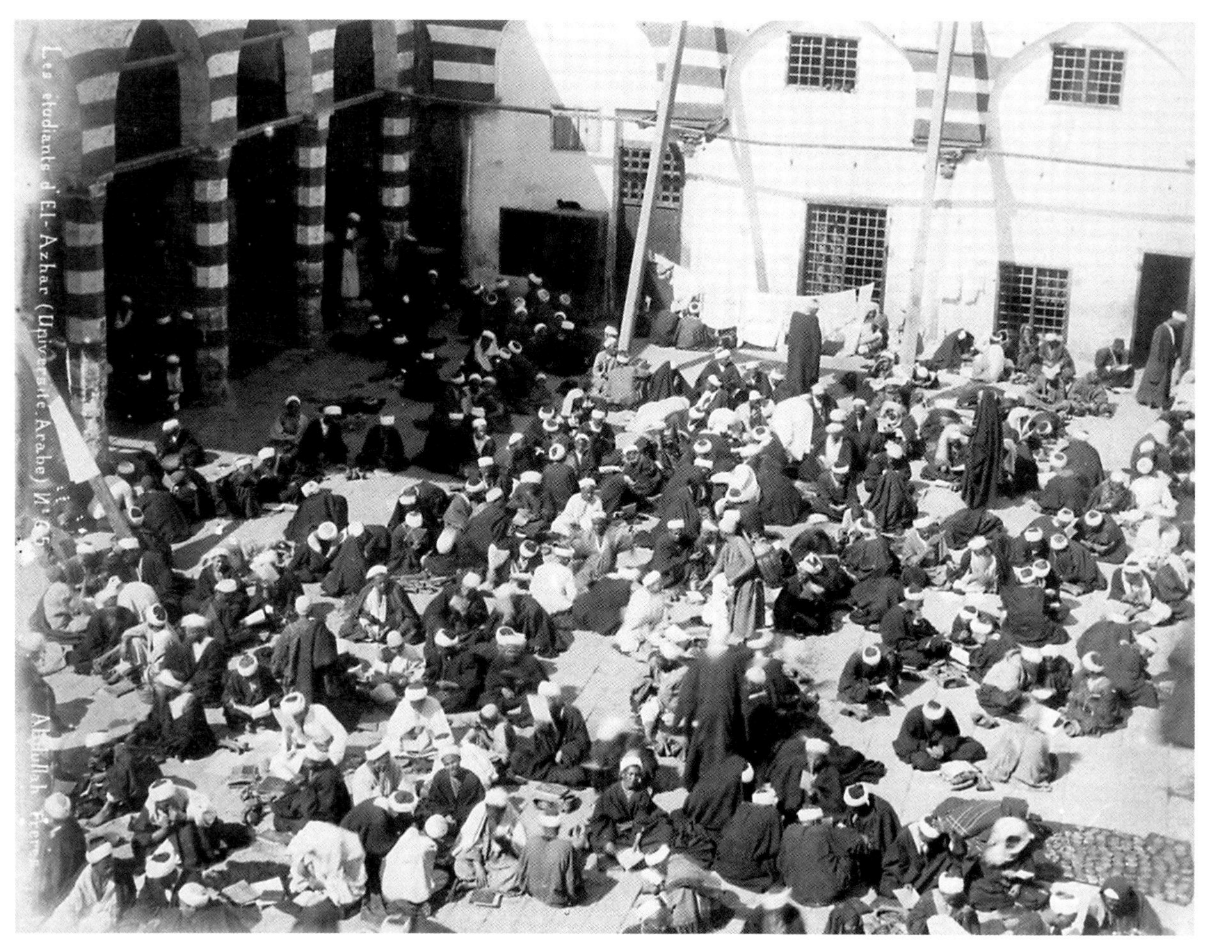

a boat on the Suez Canal, and documented its construction and the industrialization attending it through to the canal's opening in 1869. The resident photographer L. Fiorillo also documented the spaces of landscape in the face of colonial intervention such as the expansion of the Suez Canal and the scene of British army troops resting near the pyramids during the 1882 occupation of the Nile Valley. Fiorillo stayed in Alexandria during the bombing of the city and made a kind of anti-picturesque album of the ruined landscape and the city's destroyed sites during the same year.

5 Abdullah Frères, *Al-Ahzar – The Arab University in Cairo*, 1890, albumen print.

A particularly compelling set of images was taken by a Muslim photographer of note, a colonel in the Egyptian army, Mohammed Sadic (he signed his images 'Sadic Bey'). Charged with the annual escort of the sacred carpet from Egypt that would cover the Kaaba during the pilgrimage to Mecca in 1881, Sadic's photographs indicate the care taken to document the journey from Egypt to Medina and Mecca. Sadic Bey photographed the Kaaba, Hajj pilgrims, and selected significant personages such as the sheik of the Prophet's Tomb and its guards for photographic portraits. The photographer wrote that in the heart of Islam's holiest sites at the time of pilgrimage, religious fervour demanded that he conceal his camera.[11]

To assert that the majority of photographers discussed here contributed only to Western photographic and visual traditions – adding nothing to those of north Africa and the Near East – would be to overlook several possibilities. The visual economy of commercial north African imagery extended not to a solely European audience, but one that included significant markets in the Near and Middle East, India and the Americas. The very ebb and flow of photographers around this region ensured that picture-making was a recognizable and commonplace activity in the cosmopolitan reaches of urban north Africa. And although we know little of the extent to which resident and local commercial photographers catered to local patrons, it is very possible that portraiture, views of cities, and the ubiquitous scenes and types were of interest to a portion of the wealthy and elite groups. For now, the lack of research on material evidence from local studios, private family collections of antiquity and civic archives leaves us with more questions than answers about the early north African photographic traditions in the context of local consumption and patronage.[12] But it is certain that such rich photographic beginnings must have provided inspiration for local as well as international audiences, patrons, artists and casual viewers.

west Africa

In contrast with north Africa, the longstanding photographic traditions found in many urban *entrepôts* of coastal west Africa grew from local interest and patronage from the medium's first years. The particular flavour of cosmopolitanism and wealth found in west African port towns and other centres was shaped in part by the established Atlantic trade and the flows of ideas, goods and people from the fifteenth century. The first travelling photographers hailed from Britain, France, Holland, the USA and Liberia, Sierra Leone and the Gold Coast. To be sure, there was a very early market and international trade in scenes, views and types which would send imagery of west Africa and its people far afield. Even as studies of early photography continue, it is by now certain that west African towns are remarkable sites for some of the earliest African-run studios on the continent and with this, sustained local patronage from the 1850s. Portraiture and recording important civic events are the most prominent of those nascent traditions.[13] Many nineteenth-century photographers appeared to enjoy an audience which was surprisingly wide-ranging. Their local and far-flung patronage included commissions by missionaries, colonial administrations, local and foreign merchants, explorers, travellers and even the occasional academic. The success of the photographers stems in part from their adept mobility.

Coastal west African towns had traded with European companies and residents since the fifteenth century. They were the outlets for trade in raw materials and people flowing by land and sea routes that connected west Africa, Europe, the Americas and Asia. West African royal families and elite routinely sent children to Europe for education; conversely, some young European trading company employees spent the majority of their lives on the coast where they married and raised families. The last gasps of slavery in the Americas gave rise to movements eastward: African-descended freemen and captives, merchants and missionaries left Brazil, the USA, Canada and London to 'return' to Liberia, Sierra Leone, Nigeria and other settlements. In this milieu, nineteenth-century photographers of diverse origins made likenesses of the cosmopolitan swell of urban, royal and migrating patronage of west Africa.

Among the earliest accounts of photography in the region are those from the Gold Coast (present-day Ghana). In January 1840, Captain Bouët anchored at Elmina. At the house of a local Afro-Dutch merchant, the mariner used the camera given to him by the French government; he made

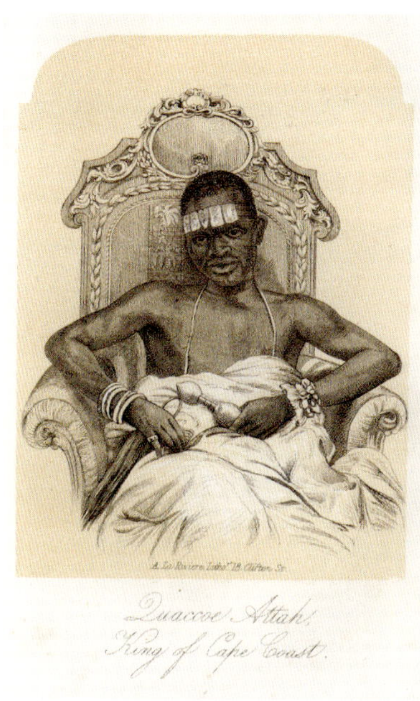

6 *Quaccoe Attah*, lithograph by A. la Riviere after an 1856 daguerreotype by Daniel West.

a daguerreotype of the town and nearby views. The event was recorded by the Dutch fort's governor, though the image no longer survives.

> Although the process is very long and difficult, at two o'clock we had the most beautiful and faithful depiction . . . Even the leaves of some of the palm trees which stand near the fort could be counted with a magnifying glass.[14]

By 1841, technological advances allowed for early commercially available portraits. The humid climate along the west African coast has likely destroyed any of those first fragile images, but a few engraved portraits survive that were pulled from daguerreotypes. One reproduction of an engraving portrays a prominent Elmina merchant, probably taken in 1847, and still in the collection of his descendants. The daguerreotype might have been the work of itinerant photographer Heer Sorin, whose records state he charged Elmina clients – consisting of 'Negroes', 'mulattoes' and 'Europeans' – six dollars a portrait.[15]

Daniel West's 1856 travel journal recorded his surprise when Gold Coast church attendants offered to pay him for daguerreotype portraits. The Scottish missionary noted 'it is impossible to describe the excitement and wonder which the photographic process creates'.[16] On seeing his portrait, the king of Cape Coast, Quaccoe Attah, exclaimed that it should be taken to Great Britain to have an oil painting made of it for him – presumably this medium was more in keeping with his notions of Fante royal display. The daguerreotype has been lost, but the engraving on which the image was based on shows the visage and regalia of the king (illus. 6), omitting the massive entourage of attendants, royal objects and furniture the king brought with him on the occasion of having the portrait made.

Colonies in Sierra Leone and Liberia, and to some extent in Lagos and the island Fernando Po (present-day Bioko Island, Equatorial Guinea), were remarkable in the west African context as they were established to repatriate freed blacks from the New World. These waves of migrants built the capital cities of Freetown and Monrovia, who eventually merged into a distinctive urban Creole (Krio) society, and who had interest in maintaining cultural and personal ties with Great Britain and North

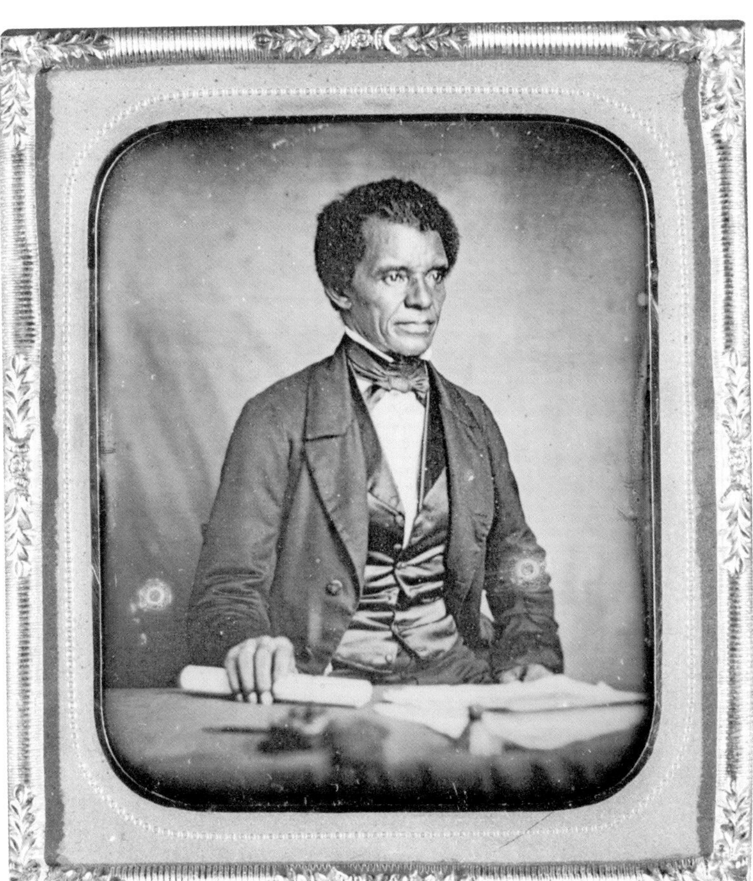

America respectively. A daguerreotype portrait sent from Monrovia to Maryland was a fragile gem, a treasured portrait of settler biography, and became a reminder to distant loved ones across the ocean.

The only known daguerreotype portraits to survive from west Africa come from Liberia's first photographic studio, owned by African-American émigré Augustus Washington. Already a well-known photographer in the USA, he moved to Monrovia and opened a studio in 1853, having brought supplies with him. Washington charged three dollars a portrait and sold $500 worth within five weeks; a number of these portraits, some of which are identified by name, remain in the archives of Liberia's founding organization, the American Colonization Society. One by Augustus Washington shows Beverly Page Yates, the Vice-President of Liberia, taken sometime between 1856 and 1860. The group of distinguished portraits of Senators and government officials appear to have been incorporated into at least one watercolour painting, which arranged them schematically by name and pose in each image. Washington's portrayals are movingly composed and often beautifully lit, his subjects stern, with many of them holding books or indicating their roles as lawmakers and leaders. Washington would go on to create a string of accomplished portraits all along the coast, extending his practice to Sierra Leone and Senegal, and probably the Gambia through at least 1860.[17]

Freetown, Sierra Leone, was a wealthy centre with even more expansive mercantile networks. A cluster of early photography studios flourished there, including the pioneer Washington, who set up shop in 1857; others followed by the late 1860s. Like Washington, many of them worked as travelling photographers as well, such as Freetonian Francis W. Joaque (*c.* 1845–1900). Joaque opened a Freetown studio in the late 1860s, then made his way east to Fernando Po in the early 1870s and later to Gabon. His Fernando Po studio prospered through the 1890s, and during the expanse of his career Joaque passed on his knowledge to many of the next generation of local photographers.[18]

The story of J. P. Decker, a Gambian photographer who emerged amid the Freetown milieu, brings the multi-faceted nature of early photographic practice into focus, and suggests a model that many other photographers may have pursued. Decker portrayed urban elite and European missionaries, produced ethnic type images for sale, and worked on colonial commissions.[19] He moved along the coastal corridor from the 1860s, and his images stamped 'WCA' (West Coast of Africa) demarcate the region with which many later photographers would also identify with themselves. One of his earliest extant images is an albumen print *carte-de-visite* of a Swiss missionary Johann Jakob Weiss with his new wife and two servants taken in Accra around 1869 (illus. 8).[20] The image brims with news for those who knew the family: the position of Mrs Weiss's hand alludes to her early pregnancy, and the inclusion of servants indicates a domestic situation in keeping with elite Accra society. The painted backdrop and carpet, chair and stand draped with cloth were commonplace accoutrements of a worthy travelling studio. Decker was one of many photographers to advertise their offerings in local newspapers before their arrival, listing fees, services offered, testimonials and the best times for portrait sitting.

It was probably Decker's, or possibly Joaque's photographs, which were the basis of engravings of Fante soldiers, women with children, and the like, published as 'Fante types' in the *Illustrated London News* during the 1873–4 Anglo-Asante war.[21] Noting the manifold interest in his images, Decker seems to have marketed his works widely. For example, an 1869 directive from London's Colonial Office to document all the colonial buildings in the Empire led to Freetown's hiring of Decker for the job. The principal buildings, government constructions and military stations of the British West African headquarters at Banjul, the Gambia, Cape Coast, the Gold Coast and Nigeria are Decker's work, and they appear not only in Colonial Office albums but also in specimen books of missionary records.[22]

Another notable example of the era's relentless border-crossing is the Gold Coast photographic dynasty, the Lutterodt family. The pioneer of the family was Gerhardt, born to a notable Accra family.[23] Gerhardt began his work peripatetically in 1870 in the port towns between Freetown and Douala. For the next seven decades, Gerhardt's brothers, nephews and sons opened studios across the region, passing on their knowledge within the family and to others who sought them out, and always emphasized their international credentials. One 1884 journal noted of Gerhardt's arrival:

A variety of views may always be obtained . . . Having had considerable experience at Monrovia and other places through which he has travelled, he hopes to be in a position to give every satisfaction.[24]

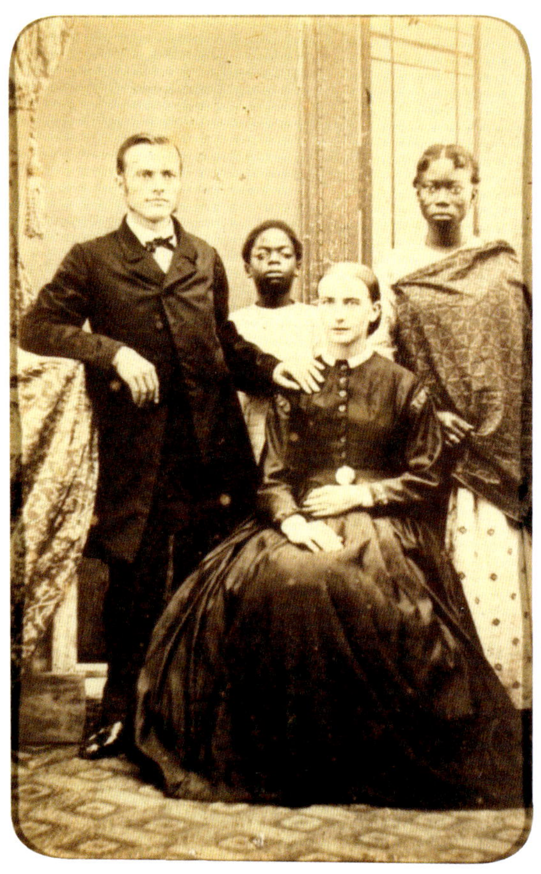

8 J. P. Decker, WCA (West Coast of Africa), *Revd Weiss with his Wife and Servants*, Accra, Ghana, *c.* 1869, *carte-de-visite* albumen print.

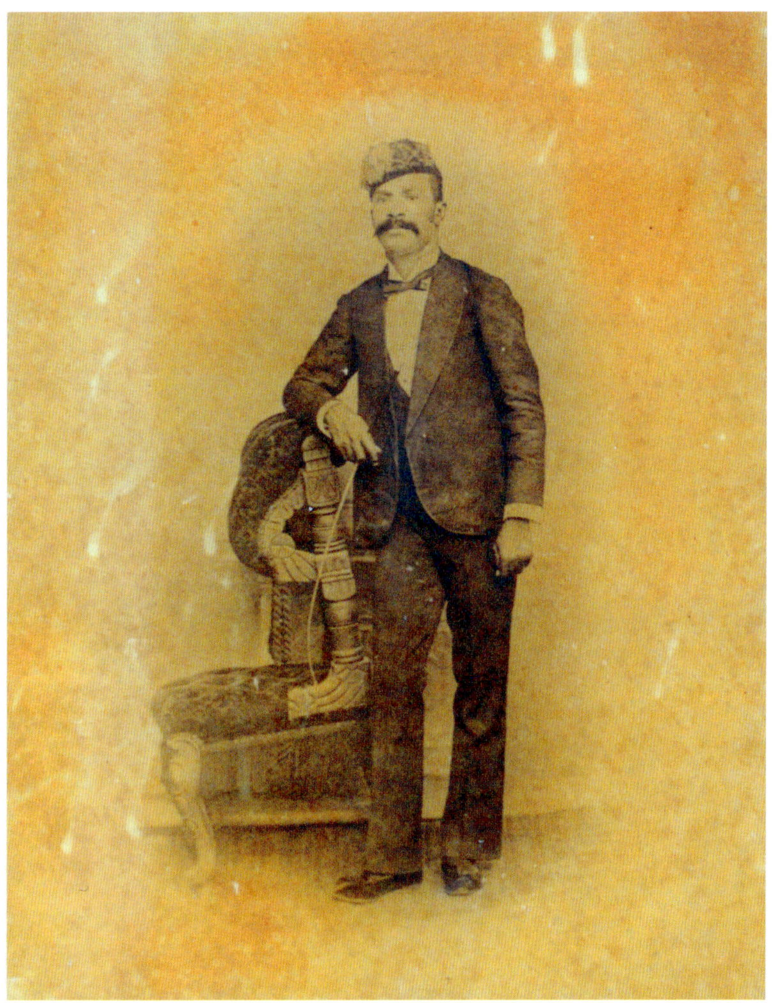

Advertising themselves as 'portrait and landscape' photographers, the bulk of the Lutterodt family's oeuvre seems to have focused on portraiture. These and other works remain scattered in private and civic collections in west Africa as well as in several European and American collections, although not in the quantities of those of their contemporaries (crucially, postcards appear not to have been integral to their commercial success, though a few Lutterodt studio photographs were published in the travel accounts of the day). Frederick G. C. Lutterodt, active from 1883, included among his credentials the awards received for documenting German colonial expeditions, as well as his experience in Victoria, Cameroon, French Gabon, Fernando Po, São Thomé and Principé. From 1870 through to 1945, eleven photographers of the Lutterodt family have been documented, all of whom travelled extensively for family apprenticeship within west Africa and Europe, and worked as studio photographers and owners across the west and central coast of Africa. This formidable string of studios, during the span of seven decades, purveyed new techniques, styles and photographic modes, bringing vast experience to bear within the local demands of elite patrons.[25] Along the way they brought up new generations of family apprentices from childhood as well as admitting eager students from their journeys for tutelage. The Lutterodt family exemplifies a fruitful creativity underpinned by a geographically subtle cosmopolitanism. Though their successes did not manifest in published series or commercial ventures such as postcards, the dynasty's longevity was based on operating and marketing the most up-to-date imagery for a breadth of customers, across linguistic, cultural and emerging colonial boundaries.

In contrast with the British protectorates and colonies of west Africa, little has been written of the earliest photographers who frequented settlements under French control – later Afrique Occidentale Française (AOF). This is particularly the case for the mid-nineteenth century, where wealth accumulated in the fifteenth century Bordelais-settled port of Saint-Louis, and other port towns like Gorée (present-day Senegal). Recent research efforts now support what's best guessed, that commercial daguerreotypists worked in Saint-Louis by the early 1850s, and the wealth of the city soon drew others, like Washington of Monrovia in 1860 and Decampe the following year.[26] Though we only have documentary evidence of their work, portraits by J. P. Decker do remain in Saint-Louis collections, and affirm that the city hosted a number of African and French photographers and postcard printers.[27] From the 1880s onwards, as the capital of Senegal and the AOF were gradually transferred from Saint-Louis to Dakar, photographers marked this shift, migrating southward on the new rail route. This movement included Saint-Louis' wealthy families of prosperous merchants, civil

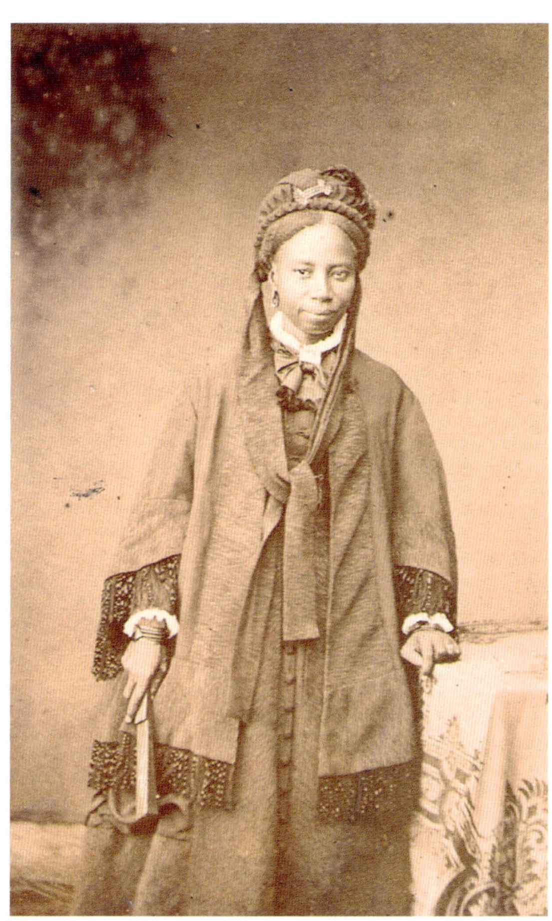

10 Félix or Blaise Bonnevide,
Femme de Saint Louis, Senegal, 1885,
carte-de-visite.

servants and *signarés* (powerful women who married European traders and became influential intermediaries, agents and successful traders themselves, forming *métis* – mixed-race – communities that grew in Saint-Louis over the centuries).

The material record is slowly emerging. Rare *cartes-de-visite* and type images from Félix Bonnevide's Saint-Louis studio (*c.* 1880s) survive, including portraits of finely dressed French residents and Saint-Louisiens. This portrait of a *Femme de Saint Louis* is relatively rare for the era, and represents a powerful fragment in the history of local patronage in the last quarter of the nineteenth century. Studio photographers and postcard producers in Senegal were predominantly French, often from Paris or Bordeaux. Other photographers were travelling through, or hired to record important events, or were with military, religious or commercial missions. Among the many-recorded names there are notables such as Johannes Barbier, the Noal brothers, Louis Hostalier and Pierre Tacher; many studios and their archives were absorbed into later generations of studios and with new partnerships.[28]

On the other hand, Senegal is perhaps the most prolifically represented in postcard form, and for francophone west Africa this comprises the largest and richest body of material for the study of early photography.[29] Through postcards, the prolific photographer and publisher François-Edmond Fortier (1862–1928) effected and disseminated the most comprehensive photographic record of west Africa. Travelling systematically over twenty years, he photographed a vast range of subjects and colonial life in urban and rural Senegal, not to mention the French Soudan, Guinea, Dahomey and Côte d'Ivoire. Fortier favoured nude portrayals – especially of African women – and his cards were among the models for Picasso's *Les Demoiselles d'Avignon* (1907). Other kinds of subject matter, from family portraits to local festivities, political events, important buildings, views and documenting colonial projects were also reprinted as postcards, although it is the representations of African people by colonial photographers which has drawn the most scholarly attention. A wealth of emerging sources in France and former French colonies suggests the enormous range of imagery still to be reckoned with.

West Africa's pioneer studios thus catered to the breadth of clientele, from portraits of elite and local authorities, to missionaries, colonial staff and resident traders, the flux of voyagers and colonial governments. This considerably complicates the story of how imagery circulated and was consumed in the region. The collections originating from nineteenth-century local family collections vastly differs from the west African imagery amassed in souvenir albums of European missionaries, colonial employees, explorers and travellers.[30] Moreover, local photographers appreciated the power of international photo markets as much as other colleagues, one example being the (not yet identified) images of Fred Grant (1892–c. 1905). From 1870, Grant travelled extensively in his native Gold Coast, making views and landscapes, groups and types of people, and undertook what was thought to be the first photographic tour of Asante, 'that country of unenviable reputation' in 1884. It was noted that he sought to sell the images in Europe and publish a sketch of his travels before he would sell them locally.[31]

N. Walwin Holm (b. 1865), a native of Accra, opened his hometown studio in 1882, and later with his son, J.A.C. Holm, maintained a branch in Lagos as well. Studio Photoholm mass-produced albumen souvenir prints and sold portraits which were transformed into type formats for postcards.[32] The elder Holm was also commissioned by the British to record the expansion of colonial rule in the southwest of Nigeria in 1891.[33] In the *Annexation of Ado*, the governor of Lagos, Sir George C. Denton, and his military staff are seated with the Chief of Ado at a ceremony on the signing of the region's annexation to the Lagos colony. Holm's image of the durbar includes little of chiefly regalia or pomp; this is not a day to be remembered fondly (and indeed, Egba traders later blocked routes despite this annexation).[34] The principal subjects are partly obscured by the crowd of supporters; Holm's careful inclusion of attendants' faces suggests a deliberate record of the political participants and local observers of the day. This is far from a straightforward picture of victory or defeat,

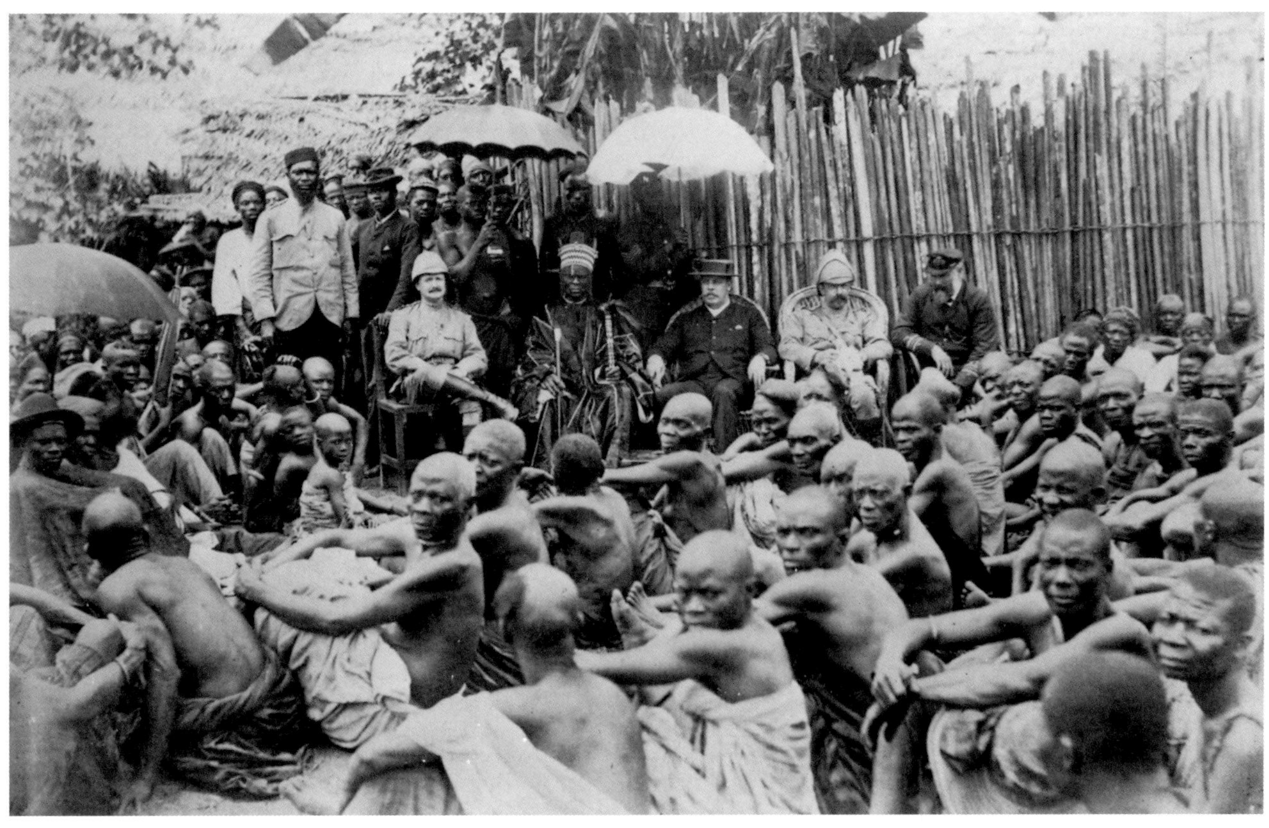

11 N. Walwin Holm, *Annexation of Ado to Lagos Colony*, 1891, albumen print.

and the ambiguities are revealed not only in the self-presentation of the subjects, but also by the photographer's framing, as is true with many images meant to record moments of colonial victory.

Given the peripatetic nature of local photographic enterprise in west Africa, we can easily imagine that there are urban and regional visual traditions, which have their beginnings in the nineteenth century and which are inherently broad and border-crossing in their origins. Portraiture is among the most readily observable of these; this genre's threads and dimensions will be explored in other chapters of this book. We can also surmise that because of trade routes and the relative prosperity of these urban *entrepôts* that people of local extraction, perhaps even more so than colonial residents and other expatriates, were the patrons of the earliest west African photographic commissions. This makes west Africa an exception to the rest of the continent, although new evidence could continue to surprise us.

That said, early photographic traditions were restricted predominantly to the elite: the wealthy merchants and traders, traditional authorities and new 'big men', and communities close to military forts, trading centres and missions. Urban patronage increased as photographs became more affordable and more could buy, keep, give and send a special image, while amateurs soon brought their cameras into the streets alongside their professional colleagues.

southern and central Africa

By the mid-nineteenth century, the first travelling photographers had arrived in southern Africa; elsewhere they rode the waves of commercial prospects, selling views of distant places and bringing new views for sale, and taking portraits of European settlers. Later practitioners worked in tandem with exploration and scientific missions. Southern Africa's initial efforts begin in Cape Town with Sir John Herschel (1792–1871), the son of a noted astronomer, and credited with coining the word 'photography' in 1838. Herschel made several sketches with the camera obscura he owned while resident there in the 1830s, and he was the first to record the effects of hyposulphites on silver.[35] The settlement of Cape Town was a strategic anchorage in the Southern hemisphere, a point on sea routes connecting Europe, the Americas and African coasts with India, Australia and the Far East.

Among the first photographers to have visited Cape Town were those with already-established studios in other colonies. Charles Shepard and Samuel Bourne of Calcutta – who established what is reckoned to be one of the world's first photographic studios – came, as did G. B. Goodman of Sydney. They likely stopped en route to other destinations. Jules Léger came from Paris, zigzagging across the Indian Ocean between India, east African ports and Australia. Léger's relentless voyages, making photo-graphic views and producing hand-coloured portraits, took him along

12 E. Thiésson, *Native Woman of Sofala, Mozambique (said to be Queen Xai Xai)*, 1845, daguerreotype.

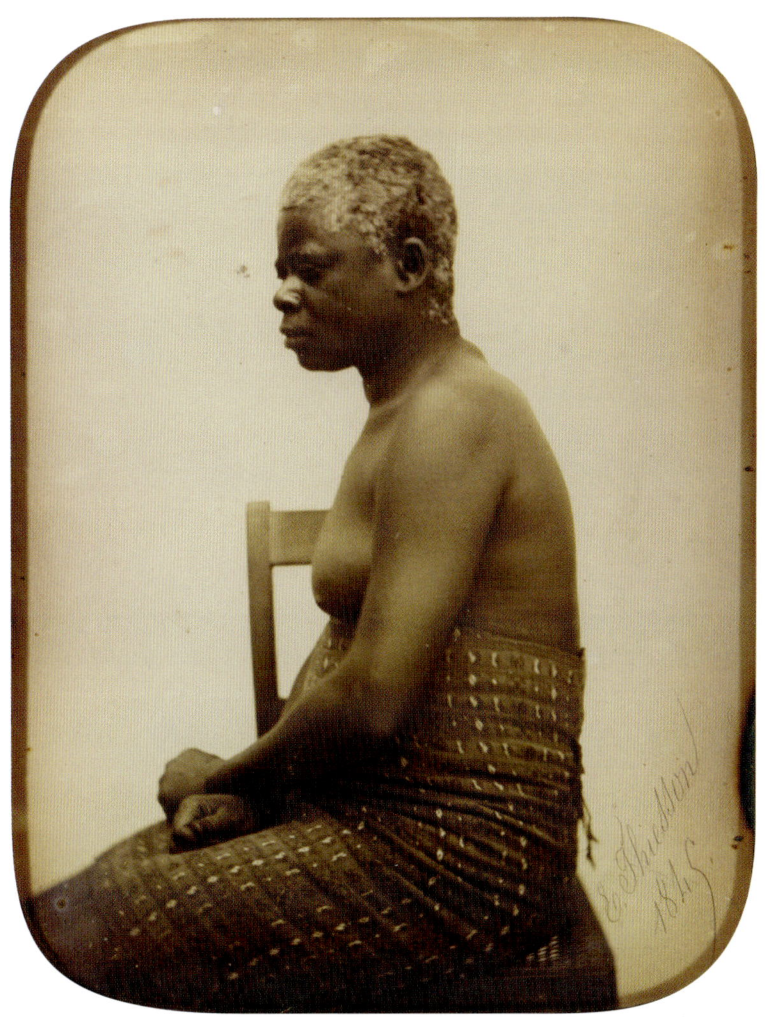

the east African islands and then to Port Elizabeth in South Africa. The earliest photographic object to survive from this region is an 1845 daguerreotype by the French travelling photographer E. Thiésson, said to be of Queen Xai Xai of Sofala, Mozambique. Although a record of the circumstances of their encounter has yet to be found, Thiésson's presentation of this woman of obvious authority, set in profile, passive and with her eyes cast down, is particularly unsettling.

35

New studios in southern Africa's settler towns marked the tenuous footholds of the new colonial arrivals. While Cape Town was an old urban centre populated by waves of immigrants from Europe and slaves from Asia and Madagascar since the mid-seventeenth century, other towns like Grahamstown and Port Elizabeth swelled with colonists from the 1820s Settler movement in Britain. These migrants were among the first eager patrons of photographic portraits in southern Africa. As with settlers in Sydney, Freetown or Hawaii, such images amounted to a precious fact of a person's survival in a new land, and a vivid communication to relatives who remained behind.

Léger was a savvy marketer, and he readily seems to have framed photography's possibilities to people in newly established settlements. After securing his first clients in Port Elizabeth, Léger trained a local assistant William Ring, who moved with him inland to Grahamstown and staged an exhibition in 1846. The topography of these emerging colonial spaces was of practical and symbolical importance, and the pair aimed to produce, as a complement to writings about the colony, views of 'several sections of the town, and which will convey a better idea of it to strangers than those birds-eye views which have usually been given . . .'[36] By 1847, Cape Town and Port Elizabeth photographers and traders offered cameras, chemicals, plates for sale, opportunities to learn the art of making daguerreotypes, and even studios which specialized in photographing children.

Meanwhile, two of Cape Town's most successful studios drew patrons by offering the height of sophistication in the latest techniques and studio accoutrements imported from Britain. The Londoner S. B. Barnard cultivated a studio filled with exotic objects, and offered his customers the most artistically refined of portraits. Another practitioner, F.A.Y. York, circulated views from his home town of London as well as those of local views and public events. York's studio reinforces the urgency of photographing the new colony: he made portraits of people in their homes and also took pictures of their houses for posterity.[37] At the same time, studios proliferated in smaller towns, with photographers from Germany, the USA and South Africa. Very little of this early studio imagery has been yet recovered that could convey the sense of these personal commissions.

Both residents and intrepid voyagers brought cameras to document travels inland, providing some of the only photographic views of southern and central African interior from the mid-to-late nineteenth century. Many eager expedition photographers were stymied by the unwieldy, slow processes, heavy equipment and fragile glass plates the early practices required, particularly those working before the widespread access to dry plate technology in the 1870s. John Kirk was one exception to this rule. Adept with a number of different photographic processes, Kirk produced images of people and sights during his extensive travels in southern Africa, including the daguerreotypes he made as the expedition botanist for David Livingstone's 1859 Zambesi expedition.[38] Kirk's image titled *Murchison Rapids, River Shire, 1859* marks Livingstone's 'discovery' of this river and its falls, considered by explorers as a major obstacle to inland navigation and commercial expansion. It marks one of many moments where exploration efforts on the continent cemented their claim to African topography by means of the camera.[39] Photography stood alongside other forms of artistic production, as seen in the example of Thomas Baine's painting of Victoria Falls, a definitive illustration when compared to James Chapman's 1862 stereo slides of the same scene.[40]

Such expeditions were driven by a range of imperatives: finding navigable rivers, accessing natural resources, setting up religious missions, ending the east coast slave trade and mapping the territory for European incursions inland. Drawings and engravings based on photographs adorned explorers' published accounts and appeared in the European illustrated press. Some expeditions encapsulated their own narrative of explorers' glory and heroism, as was the case with Henry Morton Stanley's 1871–2 expedition in search of Livingstone. In Stanley's voluminous works, he valorized the commercial potential gained by geographic 'exploration'. There are fanciful illustrations of battle scenes and jungle fauna, picturesque views of the great lakes, sculpted bowls and incised calabashes, somewhat incongruously interspersed with photograph-based engravings of stately portraits like those of the Ugandan Kabaka Mtesa the First and the Sultan of Zanzibar, Seyyid Bargash.[41] There are many portraits of Stanley and his entourage of bearers, comprised of men, women and children at the end of their three-year westward trek from Zanzibar,

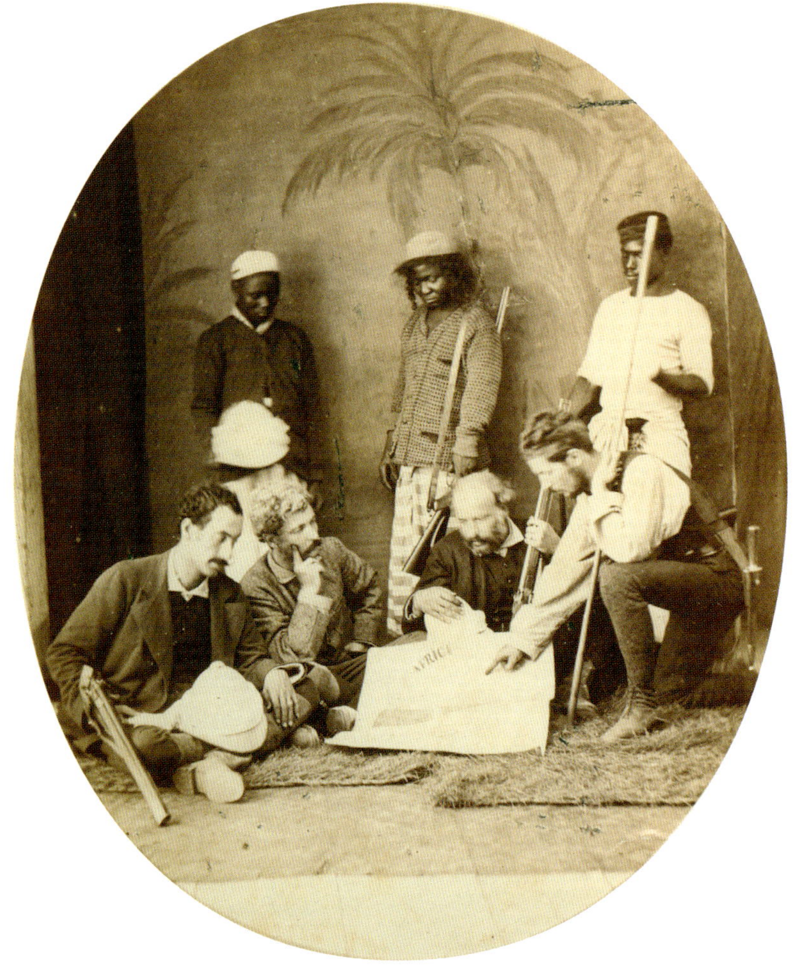

13 Unknown photographer, *Henry Morton Stanley Describing his Travels to the Portuguese Expedition (Ivens Capello Serpa Pinto) at Luanda (August or September, 1877)*, albumen print.

along the Congo River to Boma on the west coast of Congo. Another stage-manages the picturing of European exploration, as seen in one taken with Portuguese explorers and African guides in Luanda.[42] This visual narrative is nicely encapsulated in Patrick Brantlinger's observation: 'Africa grew "dark" as Victorian explorers, missionaries and scientists flooded it with light.'[43] Equally arresting are rare portraits of the African guides who led the expeditions, such as that of the highly esteemed Sidi Mubarak Bombay, who spent his youth enslaved in India,

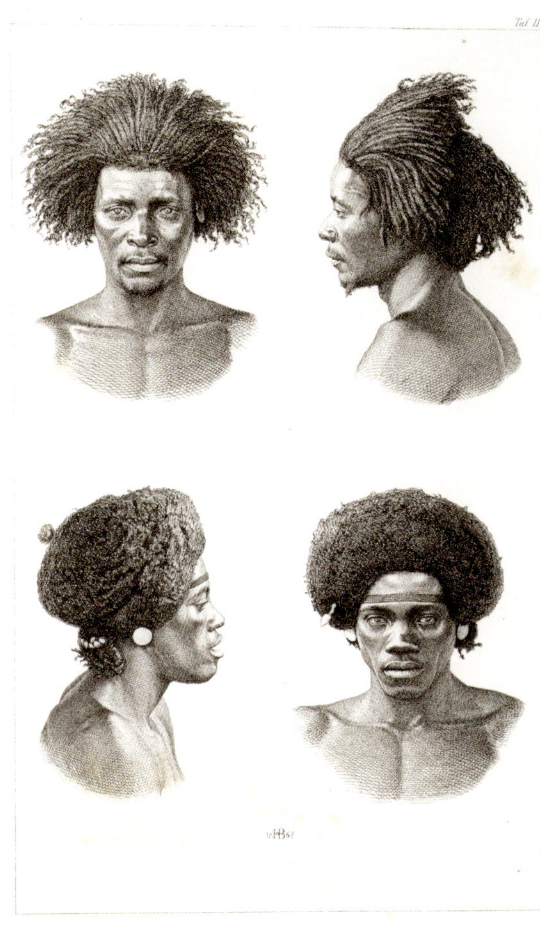

14 Gustav Fritsch, *Portraits of U'ngeke and U'ndewel*, 1872, lithograph based on photographs.

and served on expeditions with European explorers Burton, Speke, Stanley and Cameron.[44] Only a poor reproduction of his portrait has been recovered, but it shows Bombay's direct gaze, his chest lashed with leather holsters holding rifle and swords, a formidable presentation.

Colonial expansion tied into several distinctive strands of anthropological inquiry, mapping and photographic documentation. As Elizabeth Edwards noted, these were part of distinct projects attempting to 'define and classify the physical nature and origin of human races, and by implication their culture'.[45] One of the earliest efforts in southern Africa was Governor Sir George Grey's ethnographic initiatives to photograph indigenous people after the conquest and annexation of their lands into the Cape Colony in the late 1850s.[46] Significant numbers of these 'portrait types' were published, subjects seen facing the camera and in profile against plain backgrounds, each accompanied by the subject's name, place of origin and occupation. Among these were portraits by German anthropologist Gustav Fritsch, such as the fairly direct portraits of two men from Durban, U'ngeke and U'ndewel, published in 1872.[47]

Systematic photographic recording was imagined to be a pressing matter, given the widely held mid-nineteenth century belief that 'pure races' were dying out, intermarrying, or being otherwise modified by a variety of circumstances. Yet these photographic projects could be fascinatingly multivalent. There is much more than a salvage paradigm, or the illustration of ethnic identity, in the portraits by James Chapman in Damaraland (now Namibia), exhibited at the World Exposition in Paris in 1867. A few years later, astonishingly powerful portraits were produced by F. Hodgson, as part of the Palgrave expedition to Namibia in 1876, which presented rulers and other elite in full length, seated, a

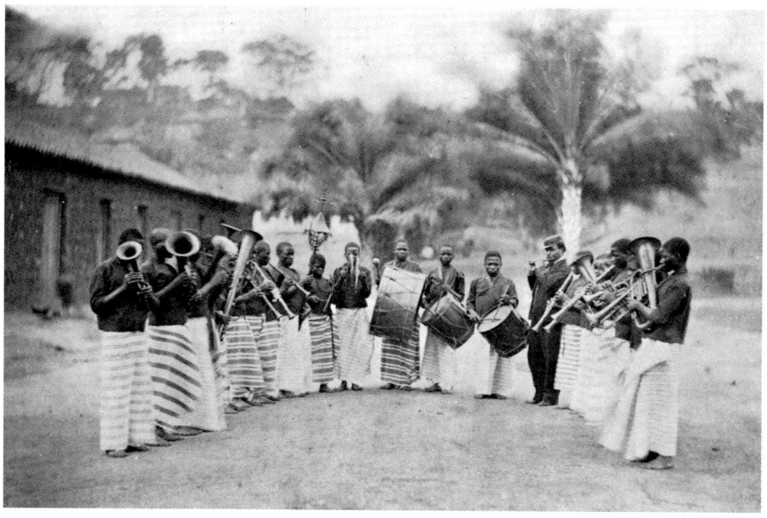

15 J. A. da Cunha Moraes, *Band of a Great Fazenda*, c. 1870, photogravure.

number of them in western dress, all of which may have rendered them more sympathetic, and possibly arranged to suggest to policy makers an easy annexation of their lands by the British.[48]

If there was an ideal of photographing an encyclopaedic and comprehensive catalogue of humanity, the gaps and resistances between individual photographs, collections and the structures they inhabit, provoke a more complex account of interaction. Series of overlapping ideas and visual practices inform a range that included popular displays and the collecting of exotic *carte-de-visite* portraits, and the ordered anthropometric photography geared towards segments of scientific communities. One attempt to collect anthropometric photographs of all 'races' of people in the British Empire by anthropologist Thomas Henry Huxley and which began in 1869, was eventually met with widespread resistance from within local colonial officials and would-be subjects. In the Cape Colony, ethnographer Wilhelm Bleek encountered such resistance to the demand of measured and unclothed figures presented frontally and in profile, that inmates from the Breakwater Prison were pressed into service. In the end, Huxley's project, though conceived of as systematic and centralized, remained an incomplete and heterogeneous mixture of photographic treatments and blank spots.[49]

As the momentum of southern African colonization gathered strength through the nineteenth century, Afrikaner Boer settlers expanded north and east, away from the bounds of British colonial rule. The trekkers' pioneer existence, as solitary agriculturalists, was embodied in portraits and images of wagons on the veld. One of the most well documented of these migrations was Cecil Rhodes's Pioneer Column, peopled by recruits who trekked into Mashonaland to colonize what would become Rhodesia (present-day Zimbabwe). William Ellerton Fry made 154 images of the journey in 1890, including *Incident on the Road to Mashonaland*, where unruly oxen and overturned wagons were perhaps the most picturesque of the settlers' encounters.

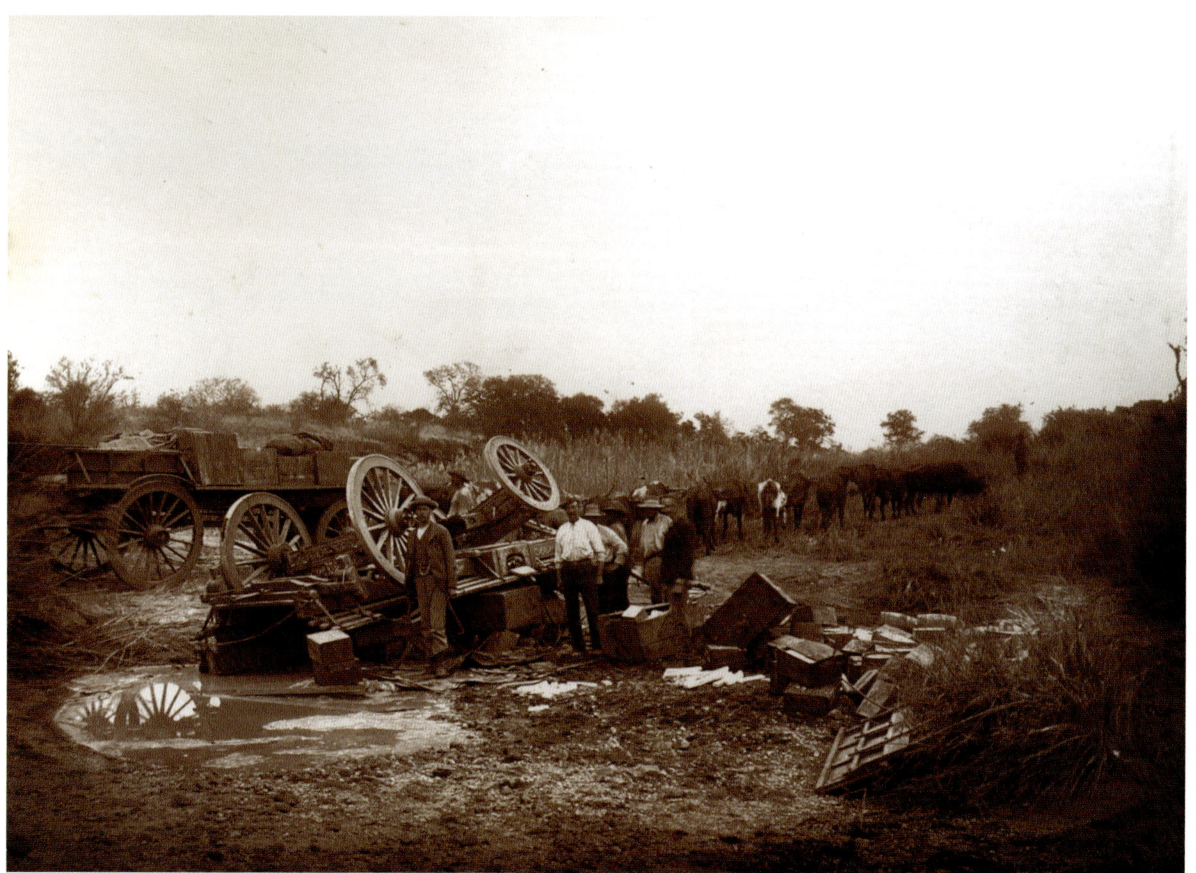

16 William Ellerton Fry, *Incident on the Road to Mashonaland*, 1890, carbon print.

From the 1870s, commercial photographers worked their way from cities on the coasts of central Africa to inland towns through southern Africa. Two studios had opened by 1870: J. N. da Silveira and Widow Moraes & Sons.[50] There is less evidence for early photographers in Mozambique, where J. and M. Lazarus, J. P. Fernandes and J. Wexelson worked in Beira and Lourenço Marques by the 1890s.[51] Of special interest is the large corpus of images of African and Afro-Portuguese elite portrayed by J. A. da Cunha Moraes from the 1870s, including remarkable portraits of African ambassadors from independent kingdoms in the interior who had come to meet with the Luanda governor. Da Cunha Moraes's studio was prolific, preserved in his four-volume *Africa Occidental* (*c.* 1870). Among the images is a corps of musicians of a well-turned-out brass band; they were likely labourers or slaves on this unidentified plantation (illus. 15). The musicians' circle has peeled out to admit the camera, their decorum picked out in fine contrasts, while palm fronds whirl and a row of quarters provide a distant backdrop. The image sparks this evocative absence: a full sonority of horns, musical traditions passing with the ships that traded and migrated, reverberating back and forth across the Atlantic.

Perhaps the most widely circulated imagery of nineteenth-century southern Africans derive from commercial studios. Landscape views were common, and portrait types were often creative exotic tableaux featuring suggestively posed females, or 'warriors' with weapons, sold as popular souvenir images and postcards. George Taylor Ferneyhough's studios in Pietermaritzburg and Kimberley, John Wallace Bradley's in Durban and J. E. Middlebrook's in Kimberley were among those which specialized in commercial images for local markets, and which were later distributed more widely by postcard jobbers.[52]

In contrast to commercial portrayals of 'natives', dramatically staged and at times revealing the reluctant subjects' distress, examples of privately commissioned studio portraits of the nineteenth-century black cosmopolitan elite ocassionally emerge. These urban patrons were often educated in mission schools, but these photos have survived only in small numbers from the 1890s because of the systematic disruption of separatist policies over the past 150 years. Their subjects included members of the political class whose inheritors would protest against apartheid policies. A few

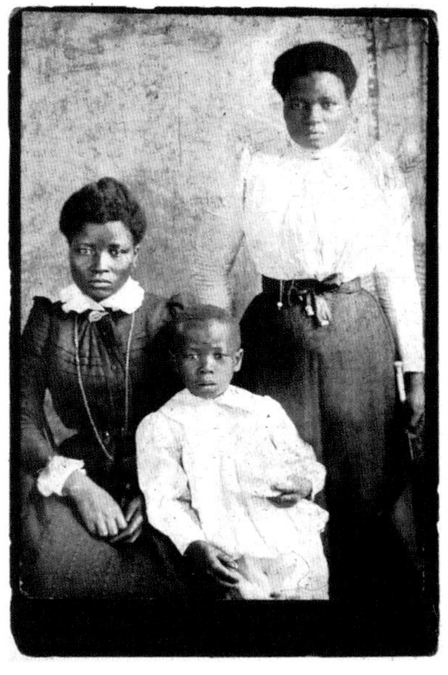

17 Unknown photographer, 'Portrait of Two Women and a Boy', from *The Black Photo Album / Look At Me: 1890–1950*, 1998, albumen print digitally reworked for projection by Santu Mofokeng.

portraits remain in private family collections, and others are kept in official archives such as the South African National Library. The photographic terrain of nineteenth-century southern Africa, marred by the omission and the politically inflected portrayals of non-white people, render these portraits all the more fraught. South African photographer Santu Mofokeng has sought out and presented some of these images as sources of lost narratives and buried photographic histories in his *The Black Photo Album/Look at Me, 1890–1950* (1996).[53] He gathered together portraits from family collections, whose rarity evokes alternative social histories which may have been neglected or kept in familial memory, but have not yet been accounted for in broader social commentary. The portraits flash in a slide show, interspersed with Mofokeng's texts which, by turns, accentuate losses of genealogical and historical context, and point to the photographs as intensely personal and political artefacts. His project is multivalent: the texts tease out assumptions about how portraits are rendered, what we make of appearances, and the self-presentation and dubious labels like 'mentally colonized'. Mofokeng's approach was echoed by several projects roughly contemporary to the *Black Photo Album*, which also sought out alternative histories and techniques of reflecting on the imagery held in colonial and personal archives. If the majority of the surviving (and accessible) photographic record suggests that early photography in southern Africa was the product of settler and colonial projects, and these were the very pictorial traditions that gave rise to early twentieth-century modernist photography depicting Africans in romanticist and preservationist modes, it is becoming clearer that there were other photographic traditions, and other audiences, which demand attention.

The Horn of Africa and the east

The first wave of eastern Africa's photographers brings into focus the Indian Ocean as a crucial thoroughfare of visual and technological influences. The vast region, which for purposes here includes the eastern mainland, the horn of Africa and the Indian Ocean islands, east Africa's early photographers came from France, Britain, India and other points beyond. The islands of Mauritius, the Seychelles and Madagascar were among the very first stopping places for the area's first photographers, partly because of their strategic location in France's expanding colonial economy, and as chief ports on the maritime routes between Europe and Asia before the Suez Canal opened in 1869.

Mauritius' prosperity fostered an ample patronage that drew enterprising photographers, both amateur and professional. Colonized by the French effectively from 1735, its wealth was gathered in sugar plantations owned by French, Franco-Mauritians and Creoles. The island also served as an important French ship-building centre, as well as a key strategic naval base. Locally, its plantations relied on the import of slaves from Madagascar and the mainland, and after the abolition of slavery under British control in 1835, the immigration of masses of indentured servants came from India, through the gates of Coolie Ghat, up until the end of the nineteenth century.

Photographers quickly founded their studios alongside already established artists – portrait-painters and engravers – in the Mauritius capital city of Port-Louis. Accounts in the press evoke the remarkable public spectacle of the first 'demonstration of the daguerreotype process' by civil servant Ferdinand Worhnitz, who had just returned from Europe.[54] A few months later, the engraver J. Dureau announced his plan to use the daguerreotype process for public edification, by publishing a volume of lithographic engravings of 'views of the principal monuments and landscapes of the island'. The notice further claimed 'it is well known that this process affords the highest degree of veracity and precision' . . . and so in this way, 'the wonderful invention of Mr Daguerre is destined to become more than a simple luxury or an amusement for the idle rich'.[55] Indeed, within a few years, competition among new studios meant more affordable images for everyone. While resident painters catered to the wealthy elite on Port-Louis, a painted portrait cost at least three times more than a daguerreotype likeness.

Mauritius' photographers were plentiful enough that there was a spectrum of studio practices. The Emy and Tardieu studio was the first to open in there in 1843, followed by the studios of Evariste Letourneur,

18 Unknown photographer, *Curepipe*, c. 1940, silver gelatin print.

In 1867 a malaria epidemic in Mauritius forced many colonists to retreat to the western highlands, establishing Curepipe, which became a rapidly flourishing town,

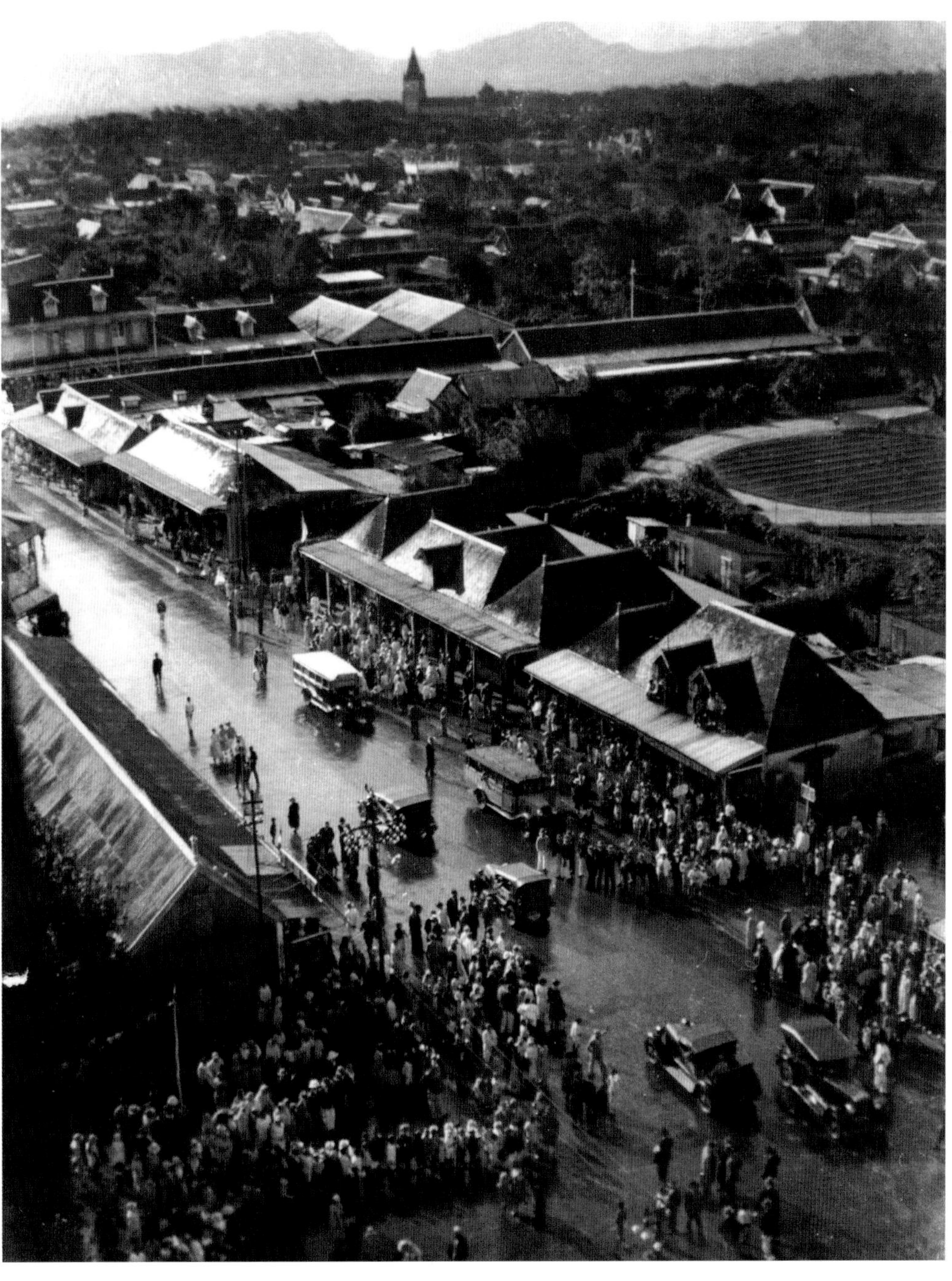

Lemaire, the aptly named Soleil, Baron Séguier, and Giroux in the early years.[56] The Trood Brothers, established in 1844, offered portraits to Port-Louis' less prosperous residents, and also depicted the squalid conditions of the thousands of recently released slaves who had gathered in the capital city, though it is uncertain if their images survive. One of the earliest instances of governmental uses of photographic record-keeping remain in the trove of identity photographs of African, Indian and Chinese immigrants arriving at Coolie Ghat, by photographers Acly and Lecorgne. Another notable pioneer was Modeste Chambay, who ran a very successful studio for nine years, and then, upon pioneering a method of transferring colour to paper positive prints, he left for Paris in 1863, where he opened two studios.[57]

Among the most well-travelled of roving photographers to visit Mauritius was Jules Léger, who arrived from India in 1845. Working frenetically, Léger advertized in local papers in advance, offering hand-coloured portrait daguerreotypes, his extensive Mauritian views, and even daguerreotypes of painted and sculpted portraits.[58] Léger was probably the first photographer to visit the nearby island of Réunion, and he later travelled to Seychelles and Australia, and then back to the mainland to open one of the first studios in Port Elizabeth, South Africa. By the 1870s, such a wealth of photographers had gathered in Port-Louis that the city's offerings were comparable to those in Paris, with practitioners importing the best equipment, and even inventing new techniques to export to Europe.[59]

By comparison, the nearby smaller island Réunion also enjoys an exceptionally rich photographic heritage, but its efflorescence came slightly later, in the 1860s. As is the case with the other Indian Ocean islands, there were a number of professional artists working as painters and engravers by the time Léger stopped for his short tour in 1846. A commercial tour by Parisians Parent and Rondeau in 1861 recorded the island's sights, monuments and sugar mills for a souvenir album marketed to the island's sugar barons.[60] Other photographers who were active from the 1860s include the first local photographer François Cudenet (b. St Pierre, Réunion, 1836) and his contemporary, Louis Antoine Roussin, a prolific lithographer, engraver and painter who worked from his own

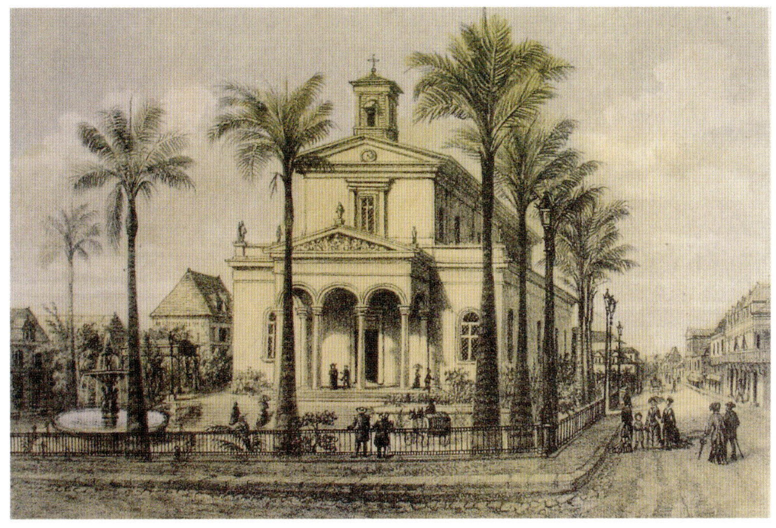

and others' photographs.[61] Roussin produced lithographic series of Réunion's views from 1857, and his subjects varied enormously, some easily captured by the camera and some not: mountain scenes and portrait types, but also labourers laying stone bridges across treacherous ravines, the processions of Indian migrants on festival days, Creole performances and the celebratory dancing in the Place du Gouvernement on the day of slavery's abolition in 1848. One lithograph presents an iconic view of the Rue de L'Église, which was probably partially based on his photograph. The main square features imported architectural prominences and carefully delineated public spaces; it is a paradise of a luxuriously appointed colonial city, finely dressed denizens and arcades of old palms. Implicitly, it illustrates the vast wealth accruing from the island's plantation labour, and carefully omits those depicting sources of human capital (though Roussin and others did illustrate labourers and slaves).[62] There are others for whom little is known, including Eyckermans, Chambay, E. Bidache and Lamele. The engineer Adolphe Blondel photographed bridges, ports, railways; he and Désiré Charnay both made ethnographic images attempting to document Réunion's human diversity, their clearly resistant subjects identified from the African mainland, India, China and the Malay Peninsula.[63]

Meanwhile, privately commissioned portraits and *cartes-de-visite*
from the 1870s depicted local hierarchies established since slavery's end
(in 1848), commonly featured French colonial residents with Indian or
African servants.[64] The soldier Henri Matthieu, whose photographs were
later printed as a series of postcards, recorded interior scenes of colonial
life: families gathered in luxuriously appointed parlours where photographs rested on a table, and an African woman holding a tray gazed
directly at the camera.

Surprisingly, there is relatively little known about the early photographic era for Madagascar, the island nation closer to the coast of
Mozambique and Malawi. The region's flourishing photographic trade
suggests that many itinerant photographers must have worked there
before the appearance of the first-known local studio in 1889. That said,
Madagascar's earliest surviving photographic records are particularly
rich and well documented in the work of missionary William Ellis.[65] With
James Cameron, a fellow member of the London Missionary Society and
an artist, Ellis visited Madagascar in 1853. He hoped to secure the political
interest of Britain and those of his church in the midst of regional colonial
rivalry with France, which coincided with the tumultuous phase of the
Merina political expansion across the island.

While Cameron made daguerreotypes of the views, Ellis excelled in
producing portraits with the wet collodion process during an initial visit
in 1854. With hopes of gaining admittance to the capital, Ellis sent these
albumen portraits to the royal family, which would help him obtain
access to the Merina court at Antananarivo. (See chapter Four for further
discussion of Ellis's royal portraits in the capital city.) In one photograph,
On the Western Veranda . . . , Ellis dispensed with the studio conventions
of a painted backdrop and frame, and provided viewers – both familiar
and distant – a fuller vision of the surroundings. A group of his neighbours, including his landlady Rasoa and some of her children and servants,
are arranged carefully, and we can see the mission architecture of the
buildings on the ridge, and distant spectators. They coalesced in a way that
suggested further Ellis's interest in the intersection of domestic space and
urban neighbourhood. Yet some studio conceits help fix the frame such
as the bowls and baskets of fruit on the table. Ellis went on to produce a

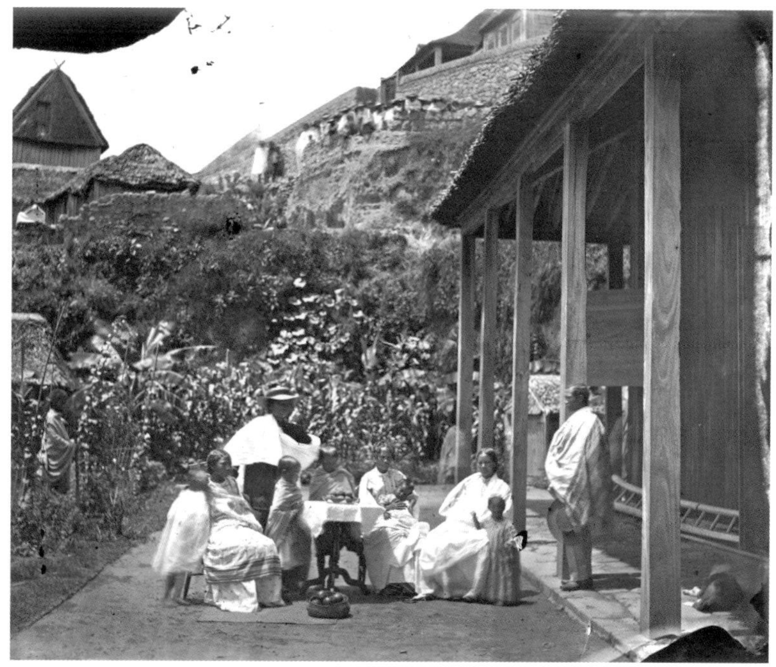

series of images of local people and grandly styled portrayals of Merina royalty, but he also documented significant events of the day. In doing so, he succeeded in presenting a selective, idealized and modernized view of the country for English audiences, by portraying individuals rather than anonymous natives subject to scientific or nostalgic depiction.[66]

The profusion of written records for Ellis's time there contrasts with the following decades, for which little is known until the opening of Razaka's (1871–1939) studio in Antananarivo in 1889. Razaka catered to the elite, producing portraits and photographing weddings, and his was among the first of a wave of studios that would appear across the island within a few years.[67]

Closer to the mainland, Indian entrepreneurs were among the first to bring their photographic expertise to east Africa's mainland port cities, and they dominated local commercial production for the latter half of the nineteenth century. A. C. Gomes came from Goa; he opened an offshoot of his studio in Zanzibar (off the Tanzanian coast) around 1868, and

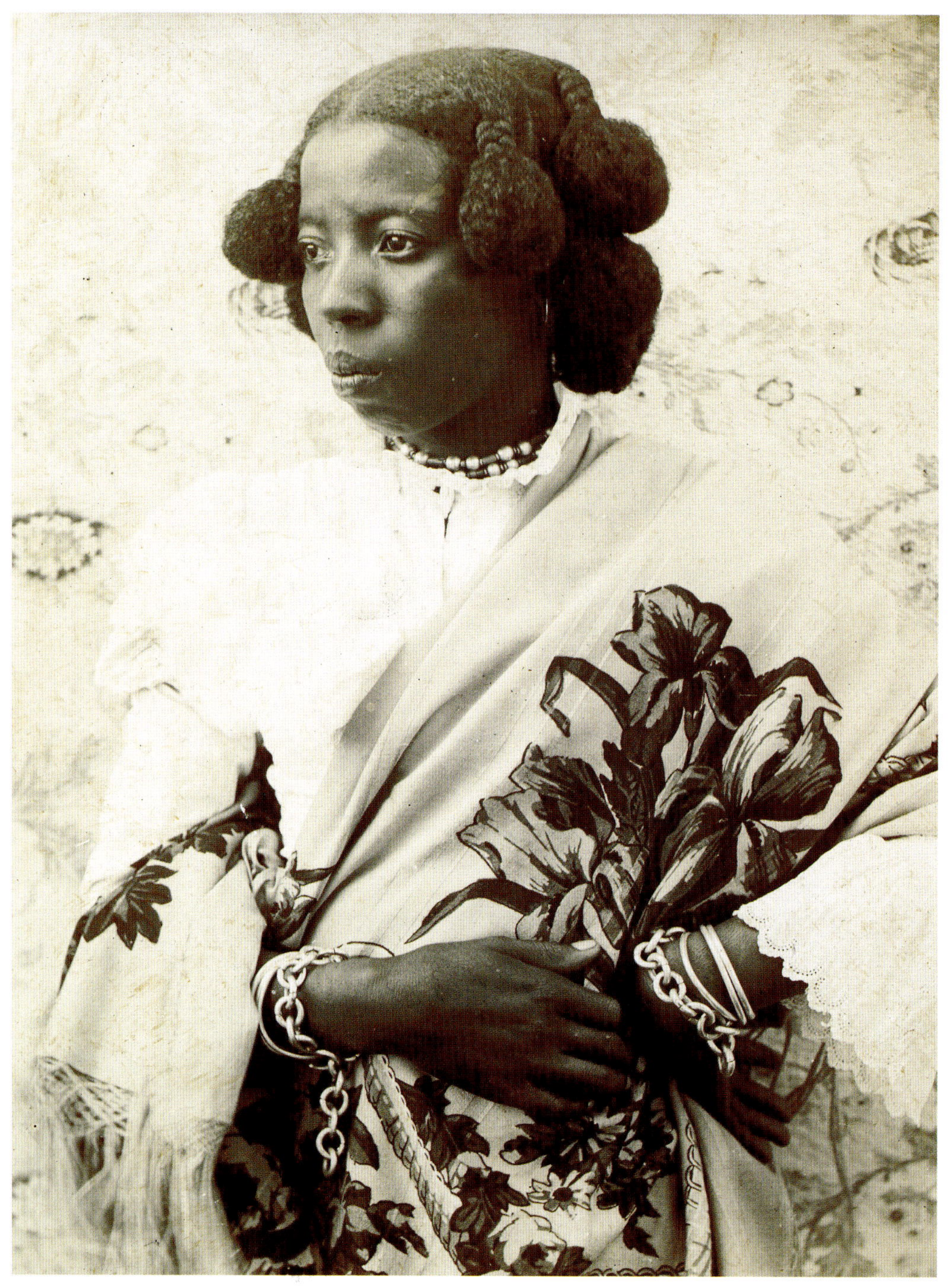

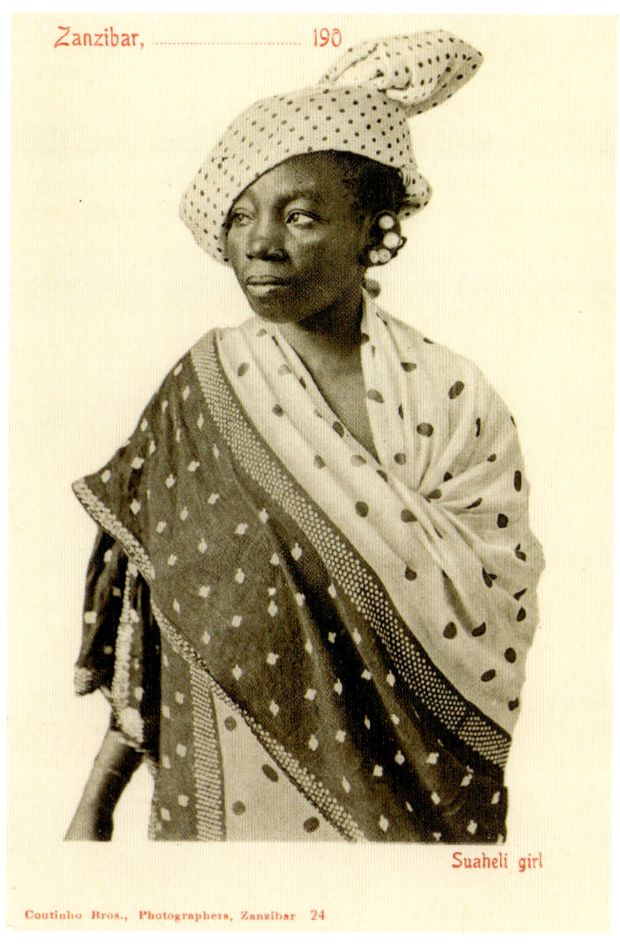

21 Felix Coutinho, '*Suaheli girl*' (Swahili girl), *c.* 1924, collotype postcard using a photograph from the 1890s.

22 Unknown photographer, *Portrait of an Unidentified Woman, c.* 1885–1910, silver gelatin print.

catered to the steamship tourism in the port town to produce and market postcards.[68] Others who came from from Goa to settle in Zanzibar were E. C. Dias, J. B. Coutinho and A.R.P. de Lord, who established studios in the 1890s, some of which had extension branches in Mombasa, the port town to the north. These photographers catered primarily to Europeans, the Indian merchant class and a tiny African elite. Many of them also produced postcards that featured African subjects, which circulated in Europe and around the world. Yet portraits such as the print by Felix Coutinho, titled *Suaheli girl* (1890s), are fairly opaque: it is uncertain whether this was a private commission, or instead part of a repertoire of staged images by the studio, which were very common.

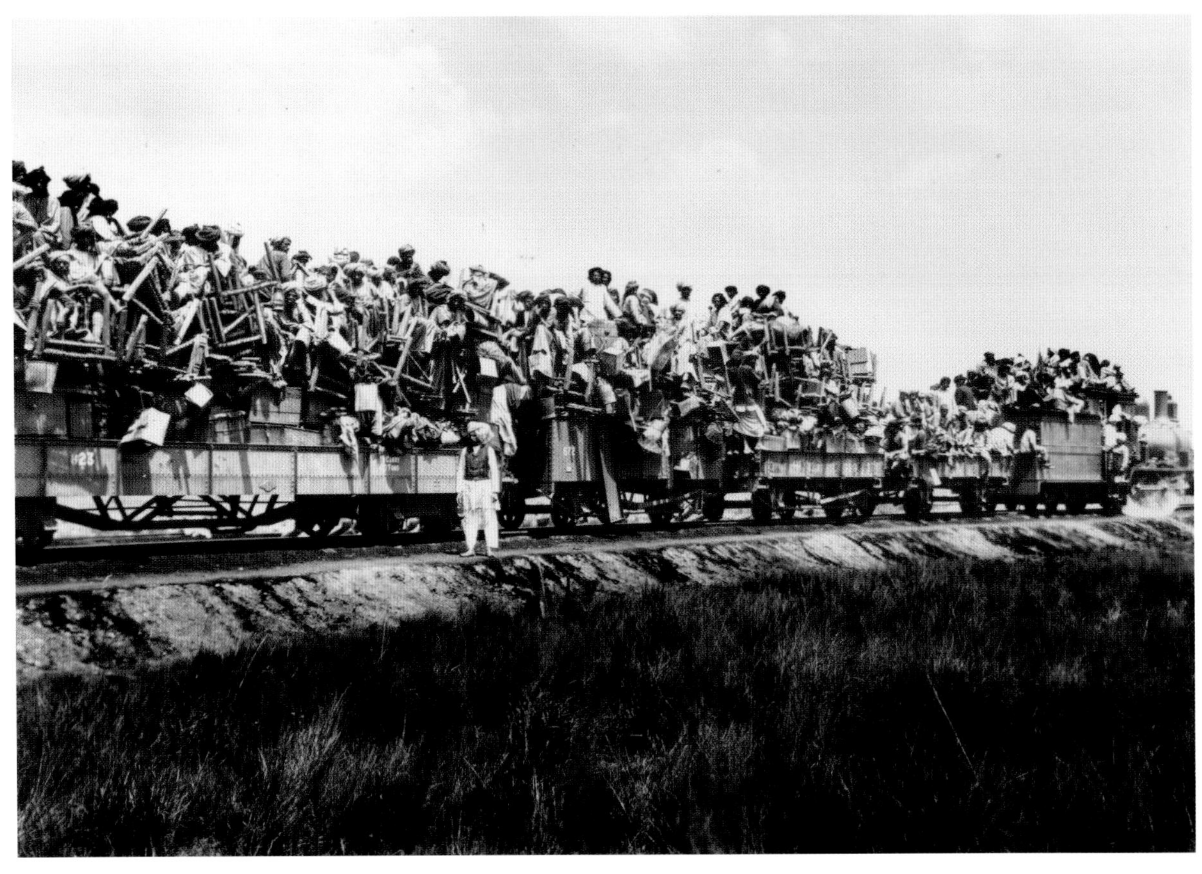

23 William D. Young, *Plate-laying Gangs Shifting Camp, Uganda Railway*, 1899–1901, silver print.

Further inland, European photographers followed the expansion of settlements, such as William D. Young (active 1890–1929), a British photographer who documented the construction of the Mombasa–Kampala rail line around the turn of the century. Young went on to found the Dempster Studio in Mombasa, and then another branch in the new upcountry town Nairobi in 1905.[69] Young's images of the railway persuasively convey the scale of the project and its labourers' efforts (opponents referred to it as the 'Lunatic Express'). Over a seven-year period, 32,000 Indians came to work on the railway, and many of them lost their lives. Meanwhile, other European photographers accompanied military campaigns, geographic expeditions and hunting excursions. In 1856

J. A. Grant documented part of Richard Francis Burton's and John Hanning Speke's expedition to look for the sources of the Nile. Around two decades later, the Austrian explorer Richard Buchta (1845–1894), who had settled in Cairo, published images of his excursions to northern Uganda in *Die Oberen Nil-Länder: Volkstypen und Landschaften* (1881), which are the earliest extant body of photographs from central Africa.[70]

To the northeast, significant early photographic efforts in Ethiopia were more closely aligned with royal prerogatives. But the first of these initial photographic forays appears to have been daguerreotype works by the missionary Henry Aaron Stern (1820–1885) in 1859, taken during his mission to convert the Falashas (Ethiopian Jews also known as 'Beta Israel').[71] Another series of images were produced by an expedition of the British Royal Engineers, who recorded the sights along the route of their invasion, later reproduced in albums by the expedition's officers. A historical footnote to this was the capture of the Ethiopian Emperor Tewodros's orphaned son Alemayehu, who was taken to Britain and later photographed by Julia Margaret Cameron in 1864.[72]

Sovereign interest in bringing photography and other new technologies to Ethiopia was a primary force underpinning its spread in the area. Under the reigns of Ethiopian Emperors Yohannes IV (1872–89) and Menelik II (1889–1913), photographers from abroad were welcomed. An unidentified Italian photographer took the earliest existing portrait of Emperor Yohannes IV with his son and heir Ras Araya Selassie, probably in the mid-1870s (illus. 24). In the 1880s, King Menelik I of Shawa invited three Swiss artisans to his court to help with its modernization, including the photographer Alfred Ilg.[73] His court was photographed by many foreign photographers during that period and his interest in photography's possibilities is evidenced in a number of commissions, such as his invitation of the Frenchman J. G. Vanderheym on a southern expedition, and his requests for portraits of Empress Taytu, the princesses and ladies of the court. The king used visiting photographers to document the first imported car into Ethiopia, and his inspections of Addis Ababa's new roads and the railway linking the town with Djibouti. So too were images describing the 1896 victory over the Italians at the Battle of Adwa rendered in portraits, depicting the victorious chiefs and their weapons.[74]

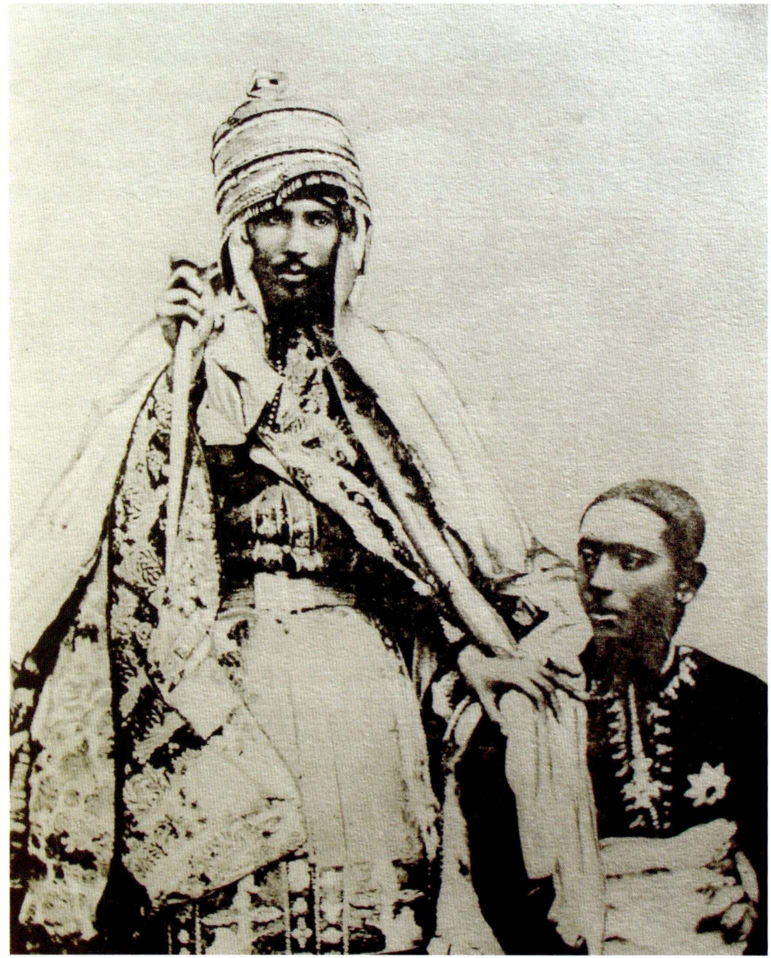

As elsewhere, the late nineteenth century saw the proliferation of royal photographic portraiture reproduced for the public, replicated on stamps and coins, displayed during funeral rites and composed for public monuments. These majestic portraits feature an attention to the regalia, ornamentation and entourage which echo earlier painted depictions of royalty. The first photographer employed exclusively by Ethiopian monarchy was the Armenian photographer Bedros Boyadjian, who arrived in 1904 and was naturalized as an Ethiopian; his work began a dynastic era of court photographers. More widespread studio attendance by Ethiopians would wait until the early years of the twentieth century.

As is true for much of the continent, the indigenous elite and settlers of east Africa were only a small minority of the population, those who could afford to patronize photographers. The material record of images to date takes in a range of views inflected by the imbalances, hierarchies and displacements brought on by the colonial era. This is particularly reflected in vast differences in the nature and condition of images from the nineteenth century, those found in archives and publications abroad versus those kept in private archives and collections on the continent. The democratization of photography would take a further step forward in the age of portrait studios around the turn of the century.

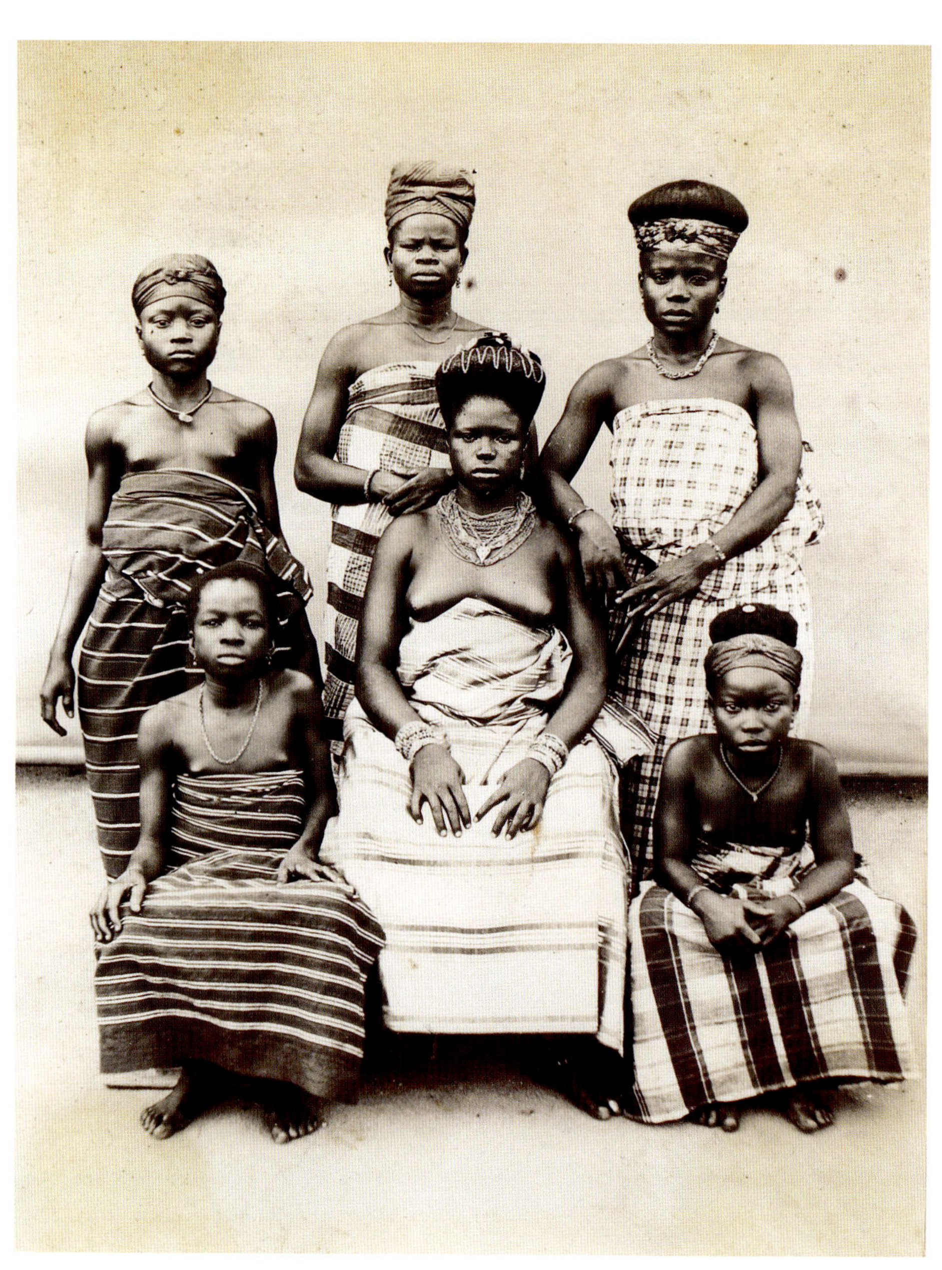

two

Portraits in the World

> There was a very large sprinkling of young females expensively got up in native attire. Although there were three or four professors of the art of photography on the spot . . . it is a pity that not one of them availed himself of such a favourable occasion to take a group of African fair ones, so that their likenesses might have been enclosed herewith, in order that you kind people in England might see how shamefully some of your would-be artists misrepresent African females in features, dress, and everything else.
>
> A spectator commenting on the occasion of a governor's visit to Anamaboe, Gold Coast, 1863[1]

From the second half of the nineteenth century, portraiture has comprised a fundamental form of photographic practice across the breadth of the continent, its variegations among the most expansive and richly varied of African creative practice. For early patrons, photography was inherently and intensely mobile: featherweight creations of startling immediacy, borne by restlessly migrating creative modernists. Photographers hopped mail steamers, moved across land according to rainy seasons,[2] attending festivals, sacred days and momentous events. A travelling photographer's 'specimens' were more than simply advertisements for potential patrons; they were also objects that could be bought and kept, reprinted as souvenir images, or published as postcards. They offered a glimpse of people and events from the next town over, or from across the continent. The allure of a great portrait – the arrangement of faces and position of bodies, their surfaces, the counterpoint of objects and

25 Unknown photographer, *'A lady, in centre, who desires to make known that she is of _marriageable_ age with her friends'*, c. 1890s, albumen print.

views within the frame – were seen by nearby and distant audiences, and then readily appropriated, adjusted and improved upon. The modernism of photographic portraiture on the continent entailed vivid collaborative intersections, and these were predicated on the movements of photographers, patrons and photographs within and beyond the continent's geographic borders.

Photographic portraits manoeuvred through space and time, and this continues. Yet there is something unsettling and disturbing in the disconnections, reiterations and imaginings that surround portraits of those once-known and privately remembered. Portraits – perhaps more emphatically than any other physical object – can provoke a sense of ethical and emotional loss. The circuits and movements portraits follow have intellectual, political and emotional forces for which it is sometimes difficult to account.[3] The spectator from Anamaboe mentioned in the opening quotation made it plain: 'likenesses' evoke not only personal and political subjectivities, but also transmit representations to viewers who did not know that something was amiss. With this, viewers' looking moves in any manner of unanticipated directions.

Photographic traditions in Africa took up the visual and interpretive aspects of local creative conventions, along with those imported from elsewhere, to create new modes of portraiture. Between those sitting before the camera and the many operators working beyond the frame, there was an enormous variety and many degrees of collaboration. While some portraits convey the momentous, there are others resolutely idealized, others improbable or uncanny, and some as flights of fancy. At the other end of the spectrum, mass-reproduction dislodged and created new aesthetic and social frames for viewing portraits, engendering completely different qualities and evocations. While this is true for all cultural production moving through the world, the consequences are worth observing discretely. With these portraits, our attention is compelled by their material and pictorial qualities, and by their momentum as objects moving through personal and public realms. We can discern the conjunctions of the initial social act of portrait-making and also the layers of instances of looking at them over time – each creating a new act and 'objecthood'.

> The Royal Photographic Gallery, Lutterodt & Son. Instaneous (sic)
> portraits, and Landscape Photographers, Accra, Freetown and West
> Coast of Africa. Established in the year 1876. Managers-Geo. Aug.
> Godfrey Lutterodt, Freetown, Sierra Leone; Albt Geo. Lutterodt,
> Ussher Town, Accra, Gold Coast . . . Portraits in cases as presents to
> Lovers . . . Enlargement of quarter and half plates to life size can be
> had from Two Guineas and upwards. Views and Types of the Gold
> Coast, Sierra Leone and Sherbro always on hand . . .[4]

West African photographers like the Lutterodts of Accra, as well as
hundreds of foreign and resident photographers, circulated along west
African maritime routes. They were among many modernists who collaborated with their subjects to produce distinctive and interrelated west
African photographic traditions in the nineteenth and early twentieth
centuries. Nowhere else is this more readily apparent than with the rise
of fashionable portraiture of young women's coming-of-age ceremonies.[5]

Such photographs are spectacles of feminine refinement in their own
right, which is fitting given they are distillations of lengthy and elaborate
initiation ceremonies that mark girls' ascendance to marriageable age.
The public and private processes during which girls were initiated into
womanhood were widespread, and there were resonances and similarities
among these rites along the coast of west and central Africa. Puberty
ceremonies variously entailed the seclusion of young women, special
fattening diets, applications of cosmetics, body marking and education
on topics related to marriage. Following these debuts, the young women
danced and sang, gave and received gifts, paraded in lavish clothes and
jewellery, and the general merriment was often tied in with official marriage proposals. As time passed, a photographer's visit became integral,
a means of commemoration and an enlargement of the spectacle itself.

These examples convey a glimpse of the emergence of this formidable
and wide-ranging modernist practice, its local threads and its larger
cosmopolitanisms. Debut portraits drew on the perambulations of
photographers and of the photographs themselves.[6] For instance, *A lady*

. . . who desires . . .' (illus. 25) betrays little sense of the surrounding ceremonies in the social space in which it is set. The photograph's composition is geometric, emphasizing the young woman seated; her breasts are exposed, indicating her unmarried status. A rope of gold festoons her new upswept coiffure, and lashings of chains and prestigious beads sparkle around her face. Her mother's gesture suggests protection and authority, and though she is surrounded by her attendants, the other initiates in her age-set are omitted from the scene. With the bright sunlight, it seems that this tableau was performed out in the open for the photographer, rather than in a shady courtyard of a family house. The choice to bracket out the urban social setting that was the backdrop for these performances was deliberate, negotiated between the photographer and the family, perhaps even the young woman herself.

This image's circulation and its audiences were perhaps even broader than her family had anticipated. This portrait was collected by a British colonial resident during his tenure on the Gold Coast, where it was kept and annotated in his private album. While some Gold Coast portraits in this particular album were labelled with names, indicating personal connections and the exchange of photos as gifts, others like this one appear to have been anonymous to the collector, who probably bought photos directly from the photographer's studio.

Similar private albums and photo collections of the era reveal how freely photographs moved around west African towns. They also evoke the variety of iconographic modes selected to encapsulate such celebrations. *'Cape Coast native girl . . .'* draws out this young woman's graceful demeanour, her potential as a mother and her familial wealth, artfully arranged. Gold ornaments emphasize her beautiful high forehead, her breasts are modestly covered (perhaps a nod to changing fashions) and she is turned to present her bustle to best advantage, a commonly worn embellishment which doubled as a support for babies carried on the back.

The commercial potential of such intimate and lovely portraits were apparently quickly realized, with visitors, residents and local customers buying, keeping and sending these portraits around in avenues quite distinct from those of migrating photographers. Debut portraits don't easily fit into the 'type' image. *Gold Coast, Young Woman with Attendant*

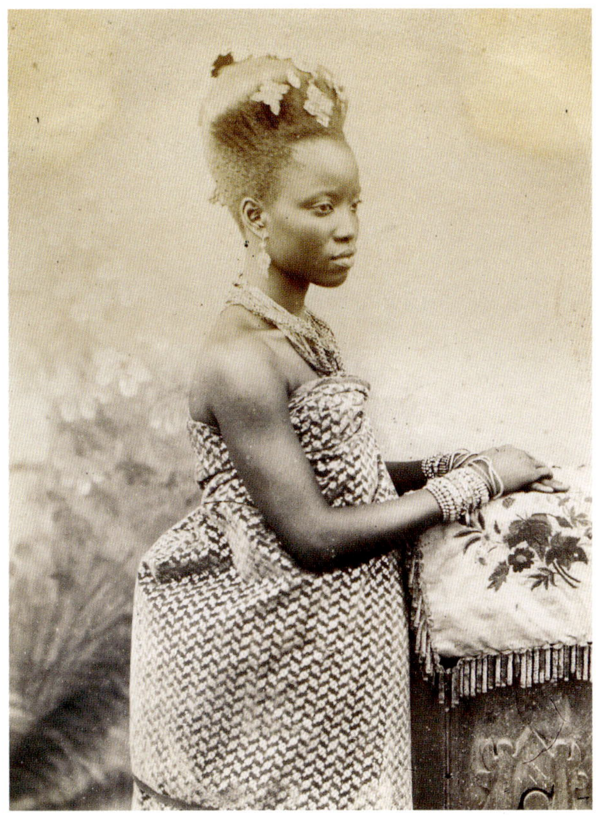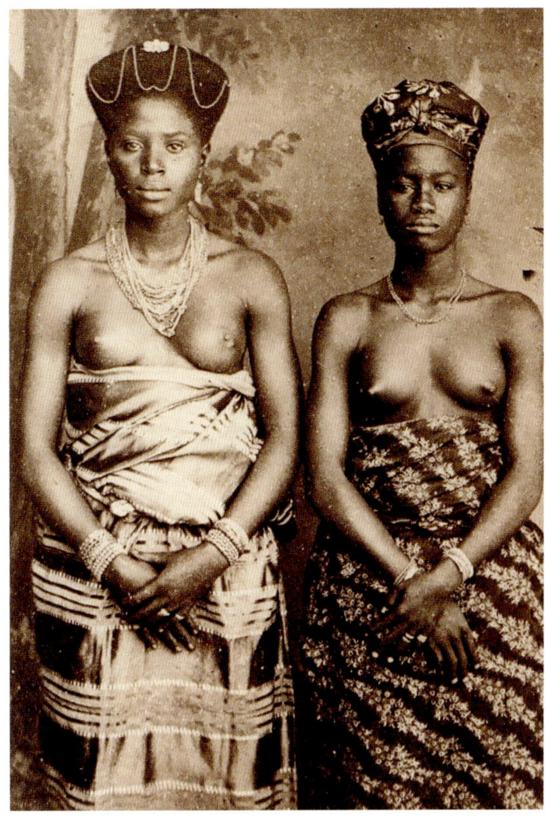

26 Unknown photographer, 'Cape Coast native girl decked with gold ornaments and desiring marriage', c. 1885–1910, albumen print.

27 Unknown photographer, *Gold Coast: Young Woman with Attendant*, c. 1890s, cabinet albumen print.

might be an initiation image, or even a formal wedding portrait, given the display of wedding rings. A Liberian traveller collected this portrait during a trip along the west African coast, and then sent it to Maryland, whereupon it entered the American Colonization Society's large collection of photographs detailing political and social life in west African towns as seen by its contemporaries in the late nineteenth century.

The portraits of Soussous celebrants, attributed to photographer and postcard printer A. James, are from Conakry, Guinea (*c.* 1900–1910), and the series features both individuals and groups of initiates. In one (illus. 28) young women signal the occasion by wearing or holding a white cloth, suggesting their passage through the coming of age ceremonies, including excision surgery.[7] Other images convey more of the process, suggesting a

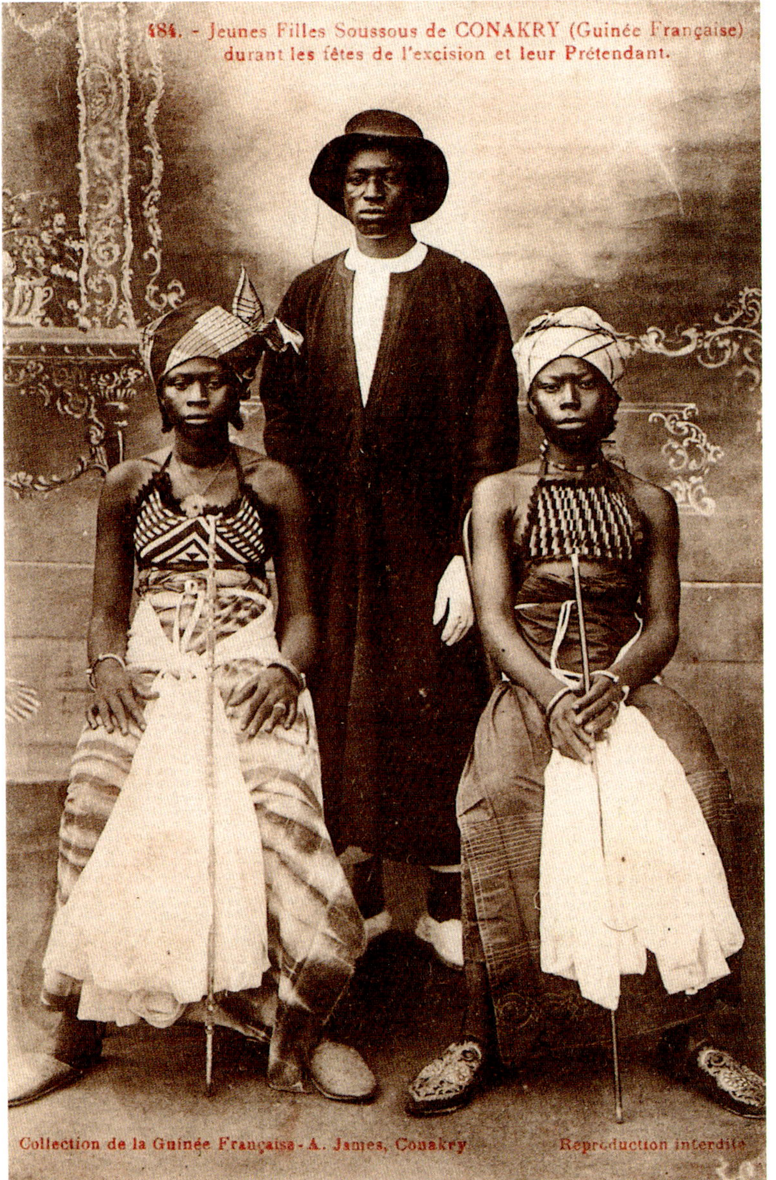

28 Attributed to A. James, '*Young Soussous women from Conakry, French Guinea, during their ceremonies of excision, with their attendant*', c. 1910, postcard.

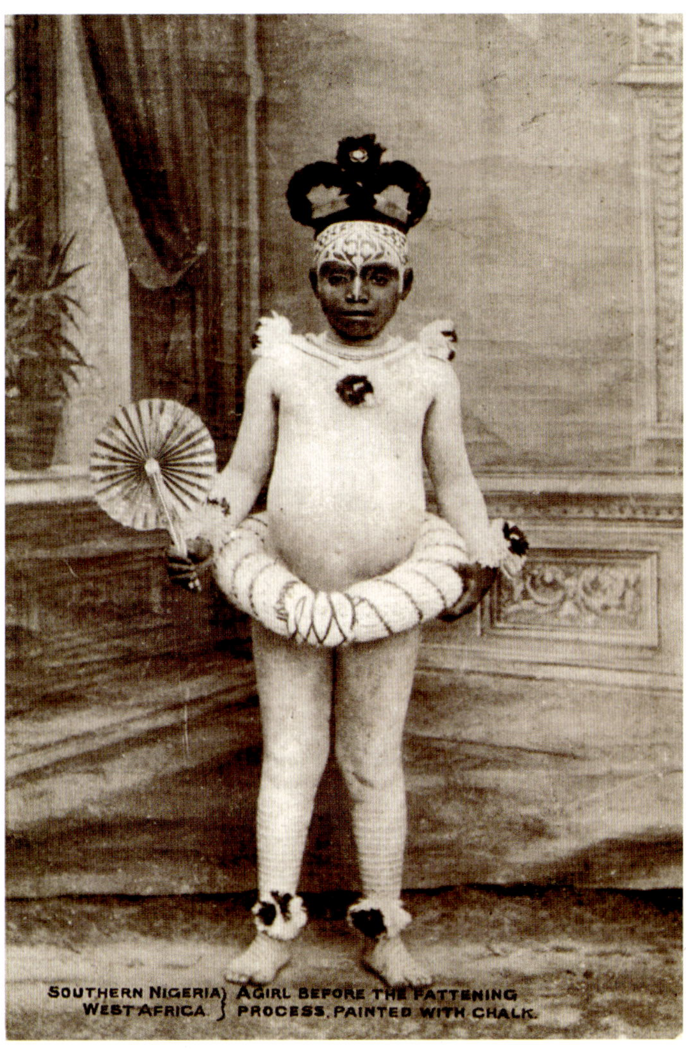

29 Unknown photographer, '*Southern
Nigeria West Africa: A girl before the
fattening process. Painted with chalk*',
c. 1906–8, halftone postcard.

number of elaborate stages of spectacle, as in
A girl before the fattening process. This postcard
suggests that moments of display were not
limited to the instant of a young woman's
debut. In all of these images, a long series
of events – the cumulative transformations,
visible rendered in fattened and carefully
altered bodies, proscribed dressing and
public displays – coalesce into one photographic moment. Photographers and patrons
together determined which of the modes and
moments befitted the production of an
elegant portrait, and while the debut portrait
appears to have grown to be a widespread
practice within emerging photographic
rubrics, the looks of such portraits were as
varied as they were lovely.

Most intriguingly, surviving evidence
to date suggests that these initiation images
from the nineteenth and early twentieth
centuries are almost unknown in today's
family collections.[8] Many have most likely
been lost, still others removed by descendants
who judged them according to changing
notions of decorum and suitable memory.
As prevailing ideas of displaying ideal feminine
beauty transformed, portrayals of ceremonial
dress were later interpreted by some as the
opposite, as nudity, or lack of dress. The
nature of editing one's photographic history resonates strongly, but
the precise interpretations of such editing are idiosyncratic and rarely
discussed. The apparent popularity of feminine portraits by the 1890s
appears not to have guaranteed their valorization for later audiences.
Photographic traditions from one place materialize as utterly different
legacies, and thus photographs are inseparable from their active audiences.

Curious Portraits

Tiny *cartes-de-visite* were portraits emblematic of the shrinking world of
the 1860s. Objects made for social exchange, they superseded national
and linguistic borders, and became another form of personal currency
for wealthy merchant classes, urban bourgeoisie and colonials around the
globe.[9] *Cartes-de-visite* were most often portraits printed with one's name
and a studio stamp. The *carte-de-visite* of Sierra Leonean Jacob C. Hazeley
is of particular interest here in how it resolutely marketed his status in this
cosmopolitan milieu. Hazeley, a merchant, lecturer and journalist, distilled
a tumultuous biography, dense with scholarship, travel, achievement and
cross-cultural disturbance, in tiny print on his *carte-de-visite*'s verso. It
appears to have been printed on the occasion of Hazeley's visit to the
1876 United States Centennial Exposition, at a time when exhibitions of
African curios set next to 'displays' of African people were increasingly
commonplace. Hazeley's portrait is bound with political and personal
force, anticipating and taking exception to less sophisticated depictions
he may have met along his way.

By contrast, the movement of postcards further highlights the
degree of distance (geographical and otherwise) that nineteenth- and
early twentieth-century portraiture might have traversed. Privately
commissioned portraits, selected by printers and circulated as anonymous images, were politically volatile in the way they were meant to
illustrate an imaginary Africa for faraway audiences. Postcards were so
widely disseminated that they appear to comprise the majority of nineteenth-century photographic representations of the continent. Engaging
and confounding viewers, postcard portraits defy their anonymity.

Portraits rely on visual nuances of dress and personal adornment,
social relations, respectability, body language and gesture. These critical
contexts were discarded when a portrait was transmitted to postcard form;
indeed, at times the point was precisely to make them into lovely and
mysterious ciphers. Some portraits were framed to surprise distant viewers
by illustrating someone's worldliness or refinement (usually signalled by
European dress). Others frame the surfaces of bodies and dress modes as
physical curiosities, suggesting subjectivities devoid of culture or history.

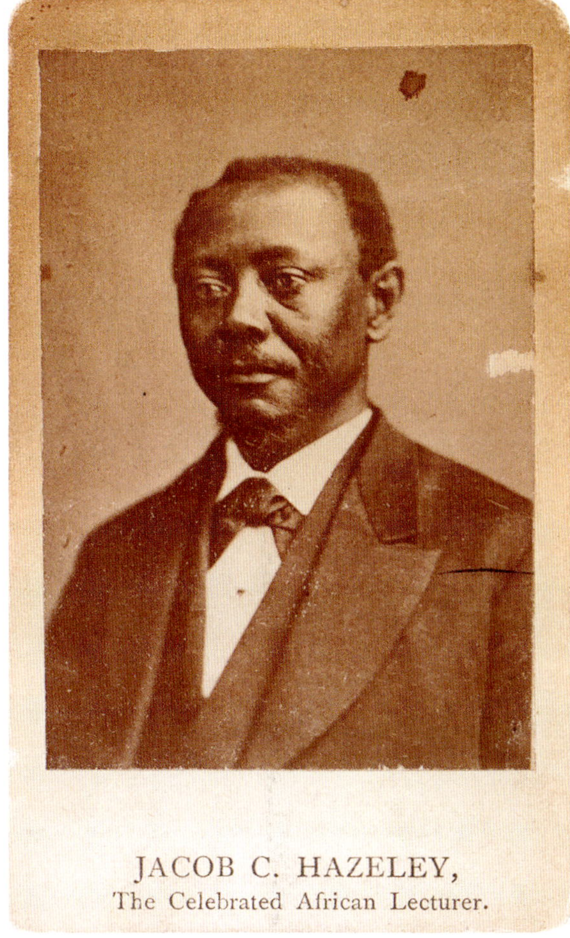

JACOB C. HAZELEY

was born at Freetown, Sierra Leone, West Africa, Sept. 17, 1835. He was the second son of Jacob Boston and Elizabeth Hazeley, His grandfather, Abraham Hazeley, emigrated from Novia Scotia in 1792, with eleven hundred others, in fifteen vessels, to the British settlement at Sierra Leone, in Africa. Educated at Zion Chapel Day School of the Countess of Huntingdon's Connexion. Visited Bathurst, Gambia, Sept. 1857, and ascended the Sene-Gambia River as far as McCarthy's Island; returned to Sierra Leone the same year. Visited London 1861. Was employed by the Queen's printers, Eyre and Spottiswoode, as a compositor for several months. Traveled through England partly with Rev. John Trotter, a missionary to Africa, Returned to Sierrra Leone, in 1862, as a merchant. Visited London again in 1865. Went to Cape Palmas, Liberia, in August, 1866. Visited Cape Coast Castle, Gold Coast, Sept. 1866. Returned to Cape Palmos, Liberia, the same year. Went to Cape Coast Castle, Gold Coast, again Nov. 1867. Visited the Gold Mines, seven days' journey into the interior, in the Wassaw Territory; returned to Cape Palmas, Liberia, in 1868. Went up Cavilla River in 1869. Was the intimate friend and companion of the worthy and celebrated Selim Aga, the Egyptian traveller, who was brutally murdered by the Grebos, Oct. 10, 1875, while unarmed and acting as a surgeon. He gave his Bible to his murderer, Bye-Weah, after reading a chapter. His head was afterwards cut off and his body thrown into a swamp, with the Bible on top of it.

Left Cape Palmas, in the Jasper, Dec., 29, 1875, and Monravia, Jan. 22, 1876. Reached New York, Mar. 6, 1876.

Present by complimentary ticket as special correspondent of " The African Times," of London, at the opening ceremonies of the United States Centennial Exposition, in Philadelphia, May 10, 1876.

30 Unknown photographer, *Jacob C. Hazeley, the Celebrated African Lecturer*, c. 1869, *carte-de-visite* albumen print, front and back.

Like many postcards, the *Malagasy Family* (illus. 31) almost certainly originated from a privately commissioned portrait, which was then reworked as a picturesque of local types. The family's dress, modest and beautifully embellished frocks and suits, might have suggested: (a) an acceptance of colonial customs or (b) their unenlightened mimicry, (c) the civility of elite Malagasy people, or (d) simple representative types of ethnic identity. Today we draw out even more narratives from this portrait-cum-illustration. Likewise, a postcard titled *'Accra – man and –*

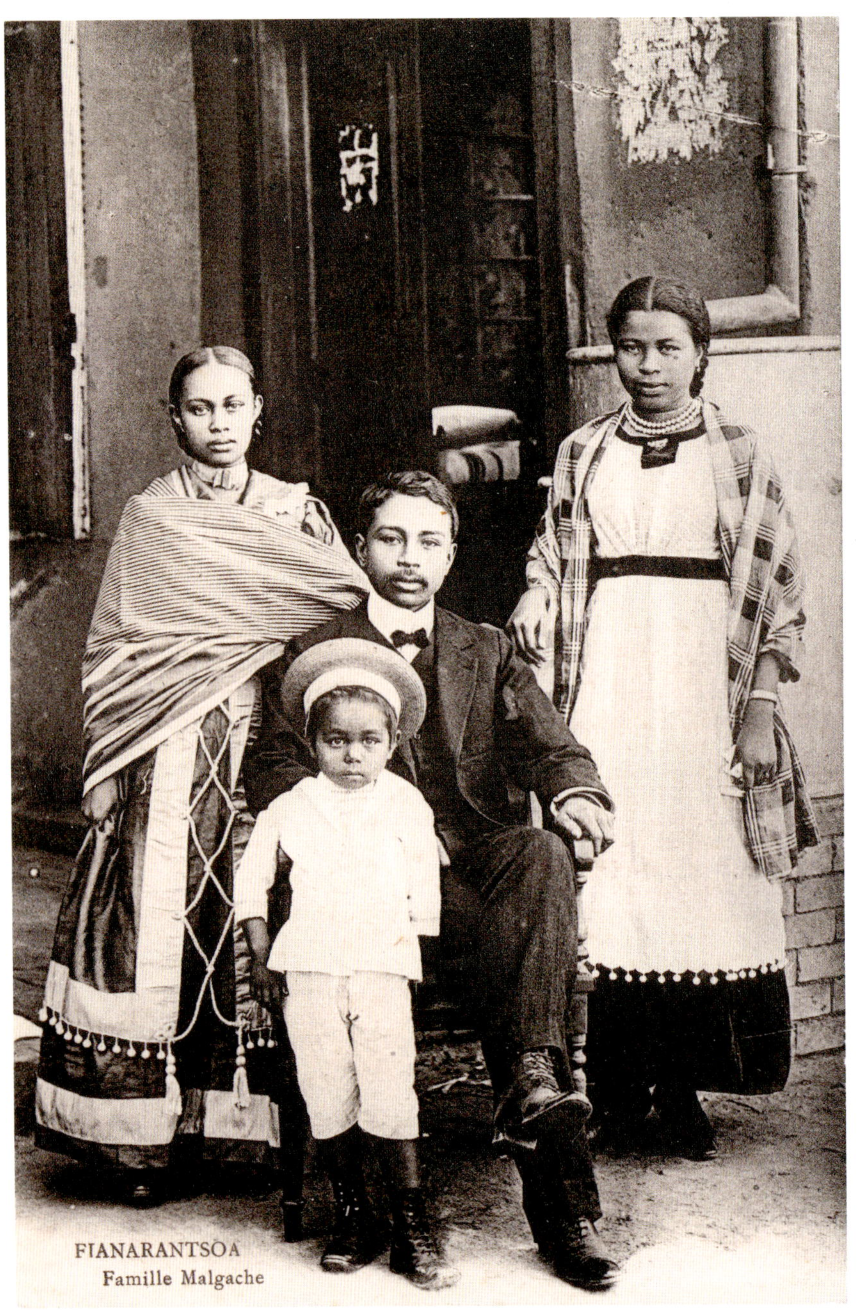

31 Unknown photographer,
A Malagasy Family, c. 1905,
collotype postcard.

32 Unknown photographer, 'Accra
– man and – woman in their native
costume Gold-Coast Westafrica',
c. 1906–8, hand-coloured
collotype postcard.

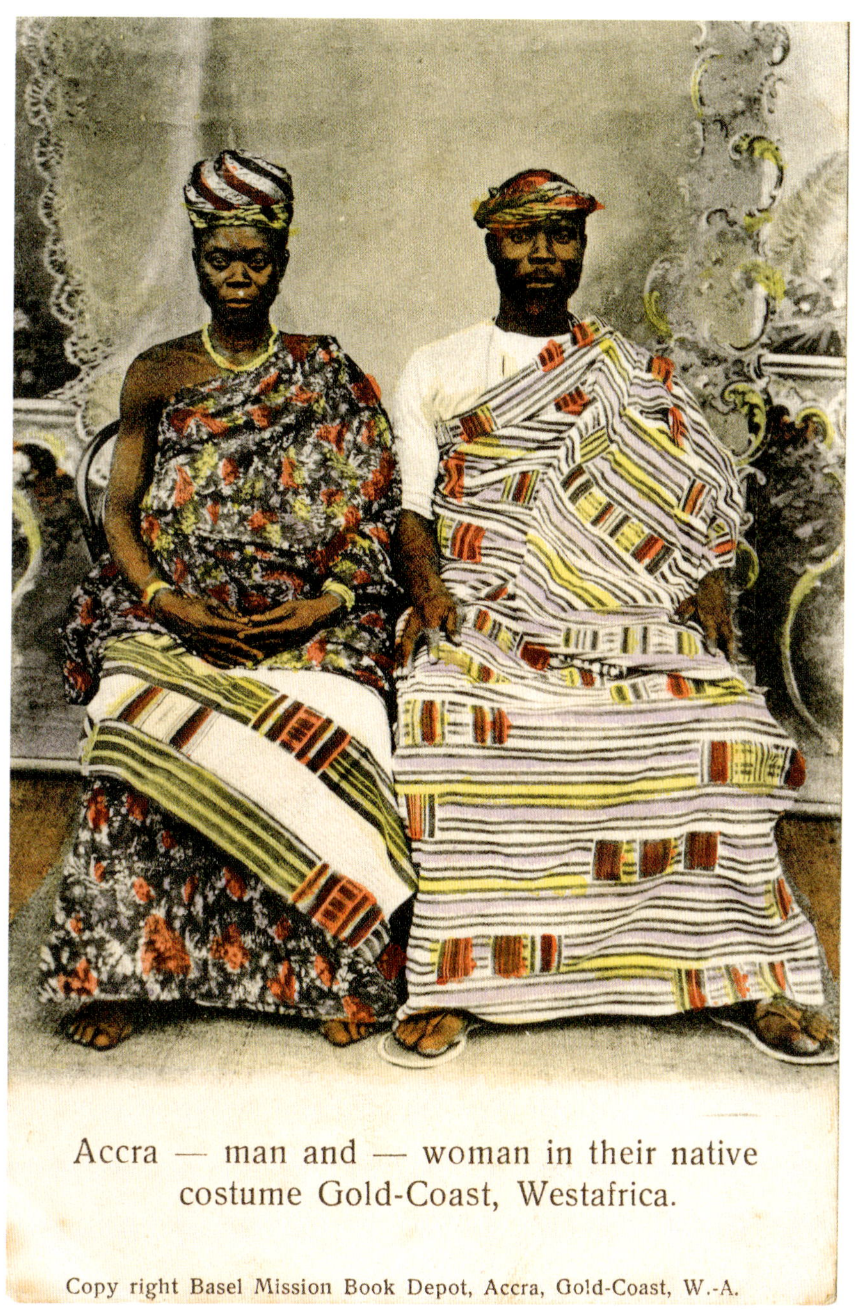
Accra — man and — woman in their native
costume Gold-Coast, Westafrica.

Copy right Basel Mission Book Depot, Accra, Gold-Coast, W.-A.

woman in their native costume Gold-Coast, Westafrica' (illus. 32) from the Gold Coast is distanced from the prevailing portrait modes of the day. It may be tempting to recuperate this image as a portrait of 'pride and confidence'[10] but it is more meaningfully read as emblematic of local photographic conventions, rather than the portrayed subject's deliberate rejection of 'colonial' representation. The leap of the portrait from a personal and political context to a published, erratically coloured, stiffened and flat-looking couple – circulated by the fairly culturally savvy Basel Mission publishers – is a much more interesting story within the frames of missionary postcard publishing than simplistic dualities of colonial vs local or European vs African. *'Arab Ladies, Zanzibar'* by the Kenyan photographer A. C. Gomes compels a careful look: two women and a girl gaze assuredly at the camera. As members of landowning classes dependent on mainland-born slave labour, the image suggests exotic prosperity. Fine shoes, head coverings, tailored dresses with flared trousers and shawls draped just so, all suggest a sophisticated display of wealth and elegance. While one wonders, and may reasonably doubt that the mass-circulation of this private image would have pleased its subjects, this remains for now one of the many questions posed for contemporary viewers to consider.[11] These merit attention beyond representing 'Africa',

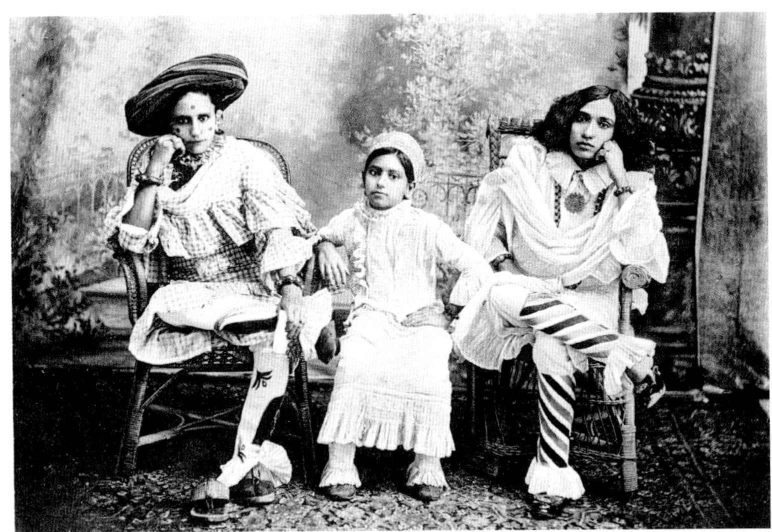

33 A. C. Gomes and Son, *'Arab Ladies, Zanzibar'*, c. 1870s, postcard.

because they evoke the faces and creative traditions of the past. They also confirm that the success of a portrait, remade into the postcard form, is but one glimpse into the circumstances of elite photographic patronage and subsequent image marketing.

Nowadays, the more obvious staged postcard photographs often rouse suspicion. A *'Missions d'Afrique'* card (below left) invites one to linger over the man's adornments, coiffure and beaded garments, visually suggesting a detachment from the cultural and political horizon of his contemporary embattled South Africa. Another common visual trope illustrates the physical (and moral) transformation that marked African conversion to Christianity. In *'Honest Martha and her sister'*, Martha's

34 Unknown photographer, *'Indigenous type distinguished by coiffure and beaded jewelry',* c. 1912, halftone letterpress postcard.

35 Unknown photographer, *'Honest Martha and her sister who has be[e]n civilised',* c. 1912, hand-coloured collotype postcard.

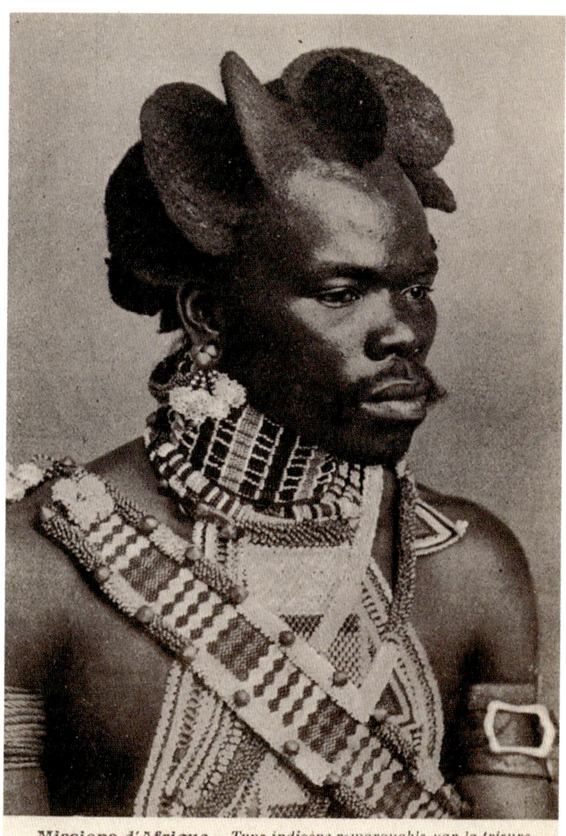

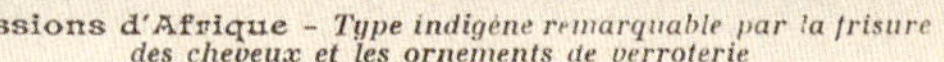

Missions d'Afrique – Type indigéne remarquable par la frisure des cheveux et les ornements de verroterie

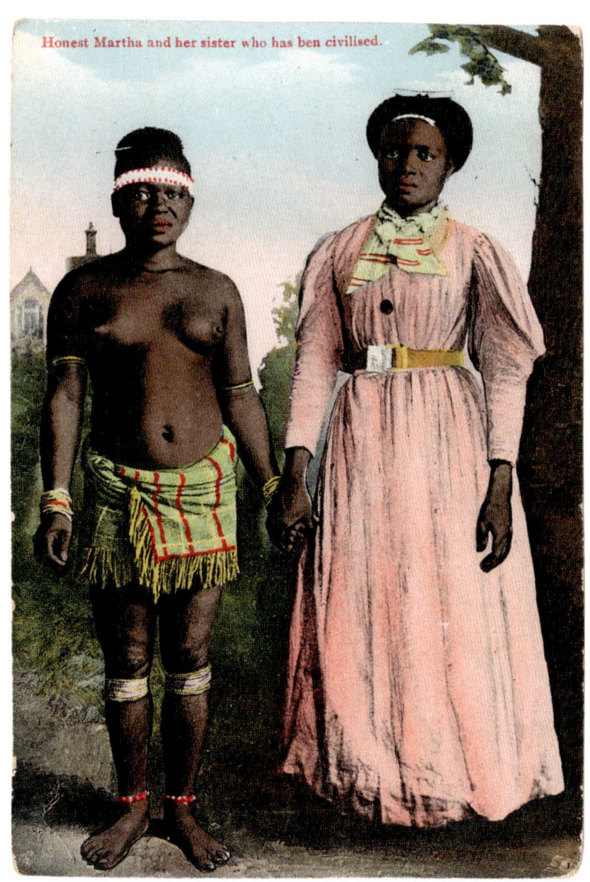

attire registers as immodest nudity, whereas the dress
and hairstyle of her 'sister' against a colonial architectural backdrop, sets out a seemingly inevitable Christian
progress. These South African images moreover suggest
overt power struggles between the subjects and the
photographer. What must have happened for their
staging? How did the depictions of 'heathen' and
'civilized' accumulate, and how were those frames
taken up or ignored or mitigated by other photographers on the continent? The same questions pertain
to the erotic images from studios in north Africa (there
was similar imagery popular in many parts of the continent).[12] The high theatricality of *'Dance of the scarf'*
was geared to satisfy longstanding Orientalist fantasies
of women lounging in harems. Few today would presume
that these images of sensual abandon, forbidden yet
accessible, were true collaborations. Nevertheless, erotic
and ethnographic imagery like these contain their own
force, and elaborate the politicized and aesthetic world
in ways distinct from the portraits of the Accra couple
and the Zanzibari women mentioned earlier.

Because local and resident photographers operated
in intensely complicated arenas, patronized by the local
elite, some occasionally staging more fictionalized studio
'portraits', some publishing these private images
broadly to supplement their studio work, today's audiences move
beyond those simple binary opposites of colonial/local production, or
the purview of a monolithic European gaze. One great reminder of this
are images that appeared in the first decade of the twentieth century
from photographers who published postcards of local political events
and personages, subjects that were obscure to audiences outside of the
colony and its environs. The diversity of these postcards suggests that
there were several interwoven strands of portraits produced for private
and public consumption. Slowly, the discourses of portraiture in Africa
moved beyond the simplistic outsider/insider inflections.[13]

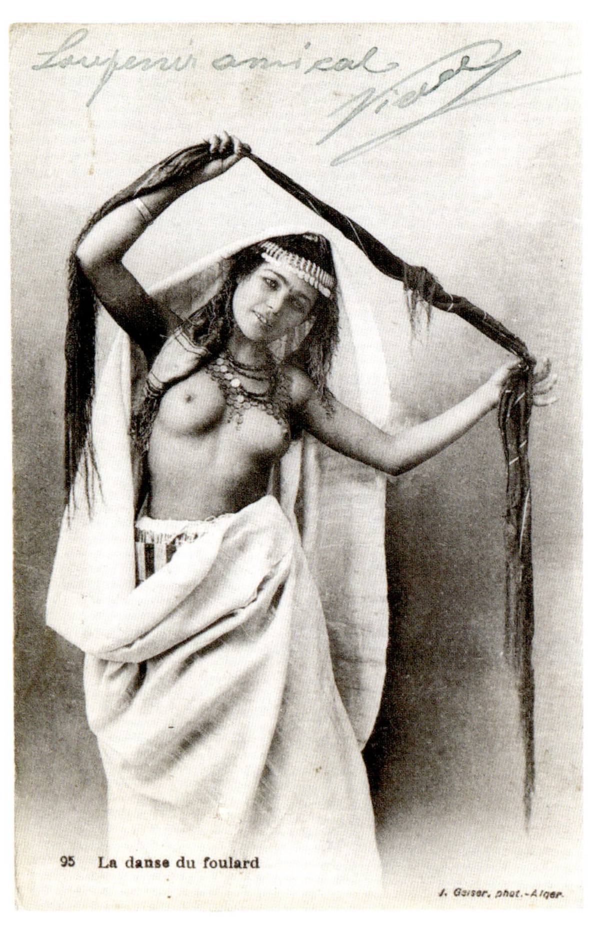

36 Unknown photographer, *'Dance of the
scarf'*, c. 1900–30, collotype postcard.

Not surprisingly, portraits of royalty, title-holders and elite comprise the earliest photographs from the continent. African rulers were sought out by pioneer photographers, and were among the first proponents and patrons of the medium. Elite portraits circulated in various formats amid local and overseas audiences. The negotiations between photographer and ruler suggest a large degree of control over staging and presentation, but this stands in contrast to the mass-reproduction and distribution of their images as souvenir prints and postcards.[14]

The king of Elmina, Kobena Gyan, who had been exiled to Sierra Leone in 1873 after he rejected British authority and refused to take a loyalty oath, returned to the Gold Coast in 1894. Gyan appears to have commissioned a variety of portraits, which consolidate a performative and photographic project on par with kingly reinstatement. A number of these appear to have been sold as souvenir prints by an Elmina studio. One of these shows Gyan surrounded by courtly entourage (illus. 38); collected by a visitor from Liberia, it was inscribed with his title and name. The effect of the portrait is altogether different when seen labelled in the album of a colonist resident on the coast. Thus, another of Gyan's portraits is effectively transformed by the labelling: 'A king of Elmina, exiled to Sierra Leone, and after a number of years, allowed by the Government to return, when he died' (illus. 37).[15] Gyan's triumphant portrait project was subverted by careful image selection and the juxtaposition of text, into an illustration of exile and futile return.

Other portraiture traditions entailed an extension of public commemoration. Funerals and commemorative ceremonies, for those who could afford them, were ostentatious celebrations once the exclusive preserve of royalty or successful traders. Towards the end of the nineteenth century, increasing numbers of elite and wealthy families also feted the 'transition' of its most important members, for example *'Burial costume in Lagos'*. A formal portrait of *Adamu-orisha* masqueraders on Lagos Island in the late nineteenth century shows them wearing wide-brimmed hats draped with lace and the expensive hand-woven cloth *aso-oke*. Commemorative events included a parade and other rites

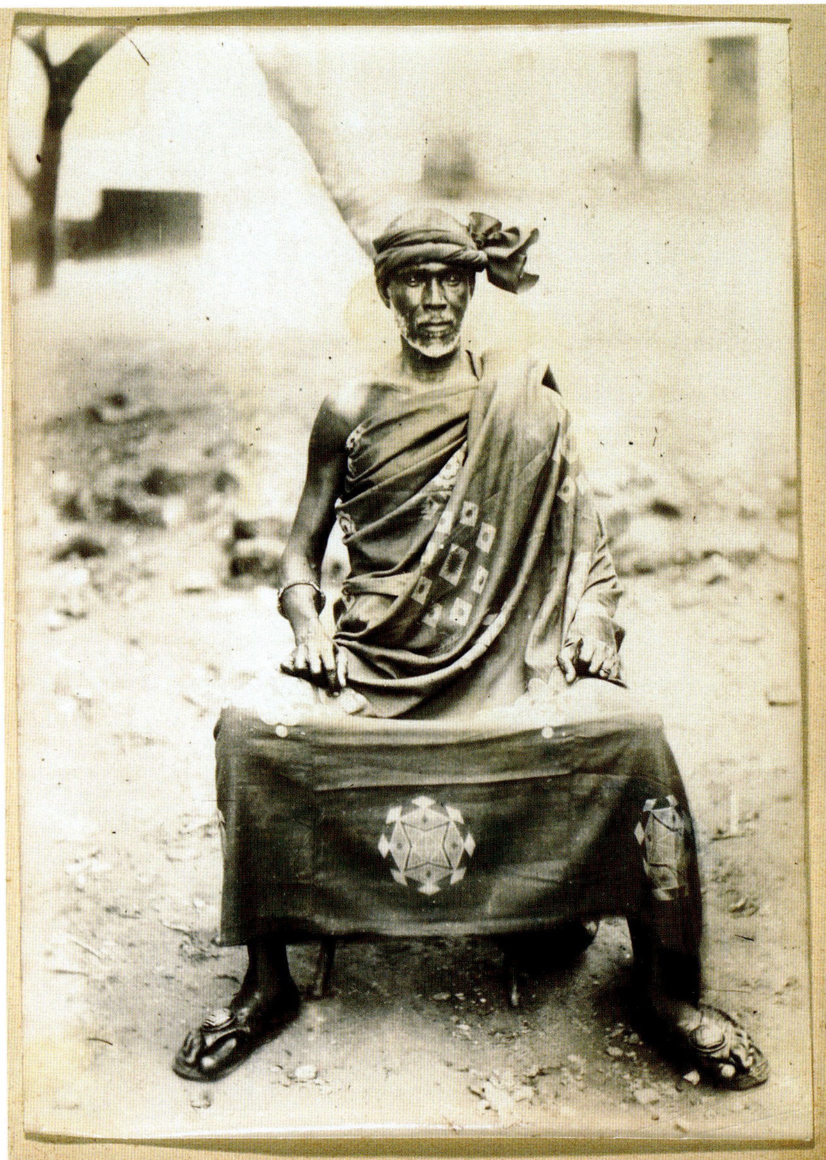

A king of Elmina, exiled to
Sierra Leone, and after a number of
years, allowed by the Government
to return, when he died.

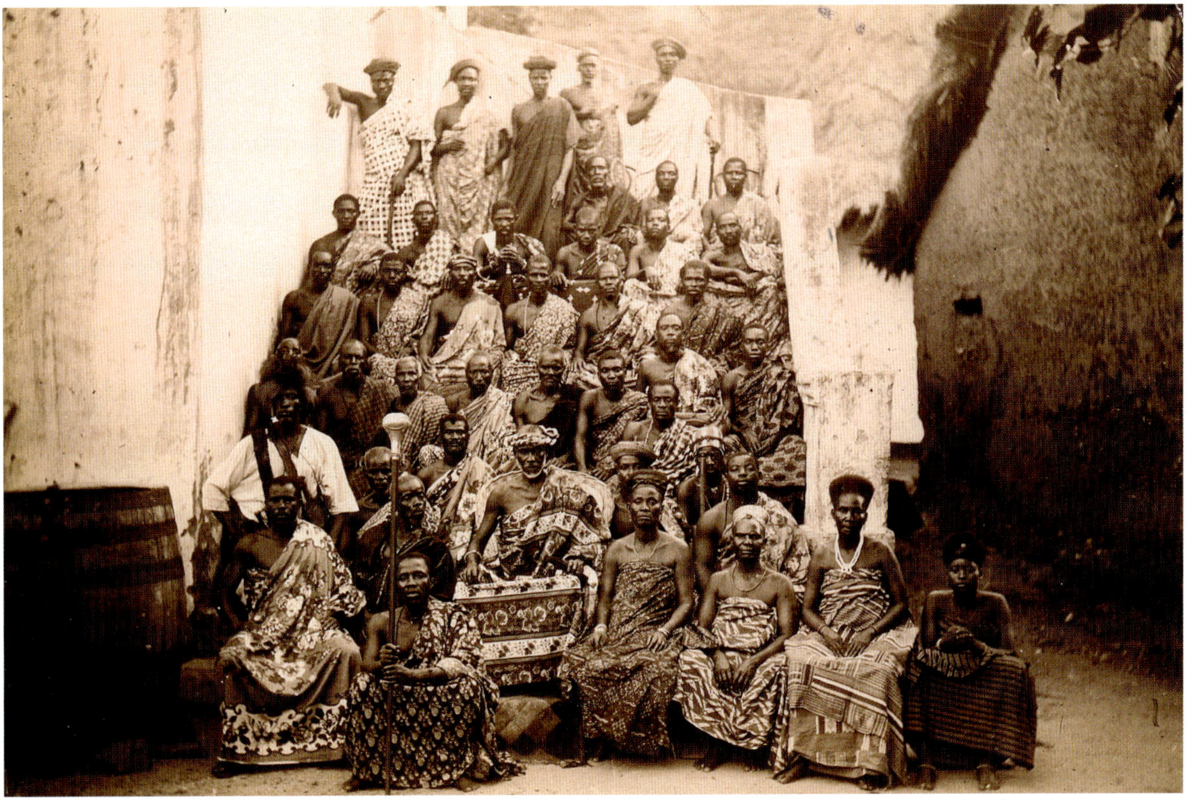

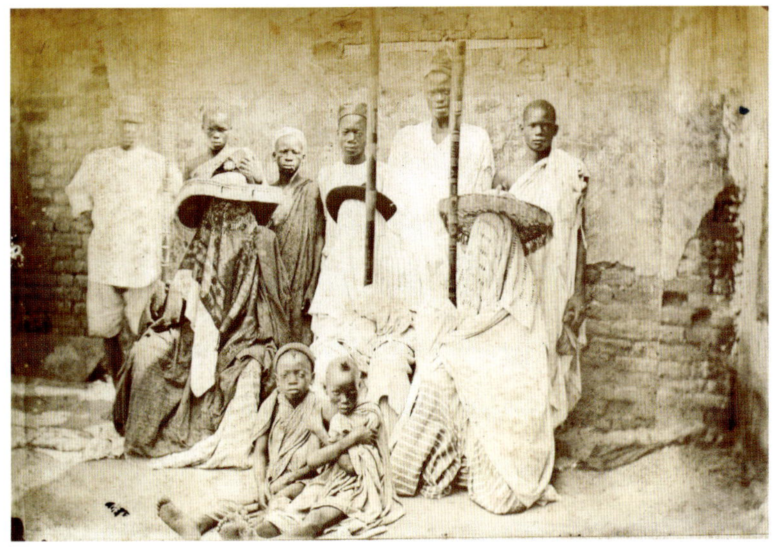

38 Unknown photographer, *Kobena Gyan with Entourage*, *c.* 1894, albumen print.

39 Unknown photographer, *'Burial costume in Lagos'* (Adamu-orisha masqueraders), *c.* 1877–95, albumen print.

opposite: 37 Unknown photographer, *Kobena Gyan*, inscribed 'A king of Elmina, exiled to Sierra Leone, and after a number of years, allowed by the Government to return, when he died', *c.* 1894, albumen print.

centring on an effigy of the deceased, with the larger festivities displaying the wealth and conspicuous consumption of the deceased's household after his burial.[16] Masqueraders posing for posterity makes perfect sense, since this portrayal was another means of recording the events honouring the dead. The image is recognizable as a portrait only for a fairly small audience: those who were familiar with the ritual know the masquerading figures in the context of this ceremony invoking individual and family prestige. As such, photos were reprinted and sold as anonymous souvenirs, and the requisite of verisimilitude in photographic portraiture slips further. In the case of the colonial album in which this image appears, the portrait is positioned adjacent to those of local and expatriate party-goers at a Lagos fancy dress ball.

From 1902, King Ibrahim Njoya of Bamum framed courtly displays for a number of visiting photographers, including colonial representatives, traders and missionaries.[17] Aware that these portrayals would be disseminated far beyond the kingdom's borders, Njoya cooperated with several European photographers to construct a range of visions to suit the political circumstances of the day. Njoya's efforts attended to the inclusion of regalia, court members and subjects. He donned Hausa robes or German military attire for portraits, as various political alliances held or faltered, and was photographed receiving diplomatic gifts from Europe. Each new photographic staging added to the complexity of the royal image archive, even if the accumulation of images circulated through the court and occasionally in German society. As foreign photographers and colonial writers described their fascination with the Bamum kingdom – its courtly arts, impressive architecture and urban spaces, and its charismatic king – the images created tended to support this romantic, if condescending, official opinion. Njoya's familiarity with photographers suggests his court was one of the earliest to articulate and overlap public persona as choreographed for photographers, and through them, audiences far away.

Sending African rulers into exile was a part of colonial expansion particularly well-suited to spectacle,

41 Jonathan Adagogo Green, ‘*King Ovonrami [Ovonramwen] of Benin responsible for the Benin Massacre prisoner on the Govt Yacht Ivy*’ (HRM Yacht *Ivy*), *c.* 1897, albumen print.

40 Helene Oldenburg, *King Njoya of Bamum with Entourage and trader Rudolph Oldenburg, taken in Foumban Bamum, Cameroon*, c. 1912, silver gelatin print.

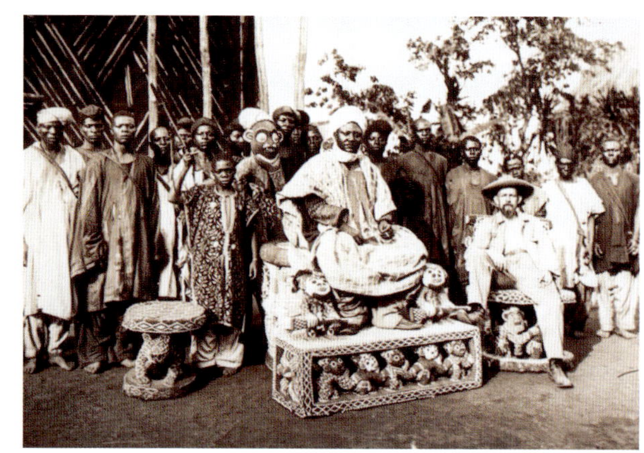

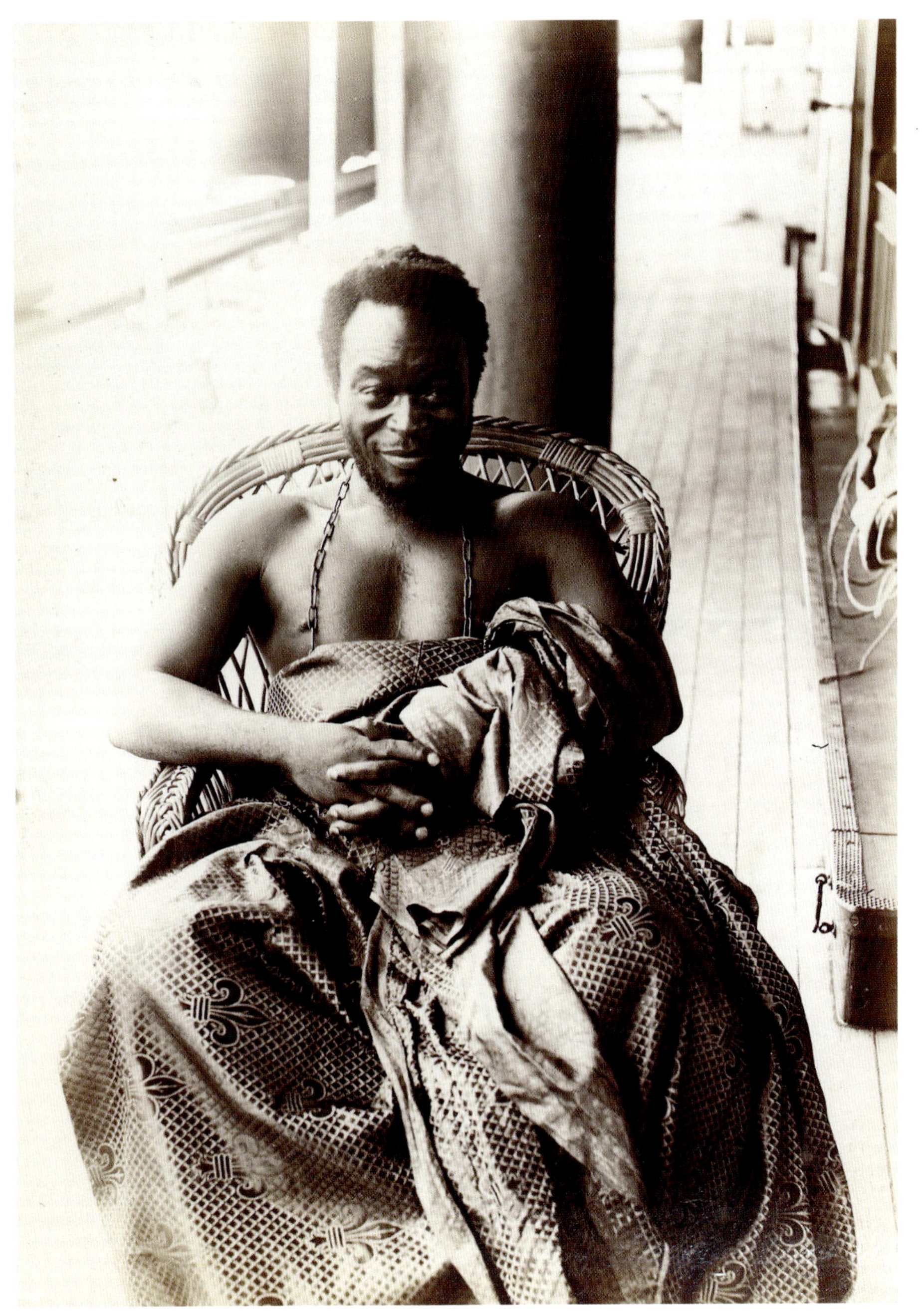

and these events were often ceremoniously photographed for posterity. Images taken before the detention and exile of kings who fought colonial forces, such as Samory Touré of the Mandé kingdom and Prempeh I of the Asante government, circulated in many forms. In Nigeria, the Bonny-Opobo-based photographer J. A. Green made several images of the defeated king (or Oba) of Benin, Oba Ovonramwen, after the British 1897 'Punitive Expedition' (illus. 41). Of course, the interpretation of these political portraits was in the hands of each viewer and the images enjoyed a massive circulation. A century later, the portrait of Ovonramwen was reclaimed by the court of Benin as a crucial representation of defiant royal authority, and a resounding symbol of the kingdom's endurance.[18]

Currently, in Benin City (present-day Nigeria) the Oba carefully controls not only the occasions of his public display for photographic portraiture, but also ownership and dispersal of his official royal depictions. Because of this, any image of present or former kings is implicitly a mark of exclusive prestige for its owners. Court photographers, beginning with S. O. Alonge in the 1920s, have documented public events at the palace on commission from court visitors, which are displayed as markers of their special status and access to royal authority.[19] Photographing in parts of the palace which are out-of-bounds are met with the stringent ritual sanction by palace officials, and even important shrines accessible to the public are off-limits to all photography. Images of the Oba are released only by permission of the palace at certain public events and ritual occasions, and the strict control of any royal portrait heightens their value.[20]

Latter-Day Modernists

Photographic portraits from mid-century Senegal and Mali still remain among the most recognizable of African photographs for western museum-going audiences. This is because of the flurry of exhibitions, publications, collection and marketing of photograph archives of Seydou Keïta, Malick Sidibé and others.[21] Keïta's (1921–2001) lush images were masterfully presented to appeal to European and American audiences: their recirculation has rendered them monumental. Keïta's well-preserved large glass-plate

42 Seydou Keïta, Untitled portrait, 1952–5, gelatin silver print.

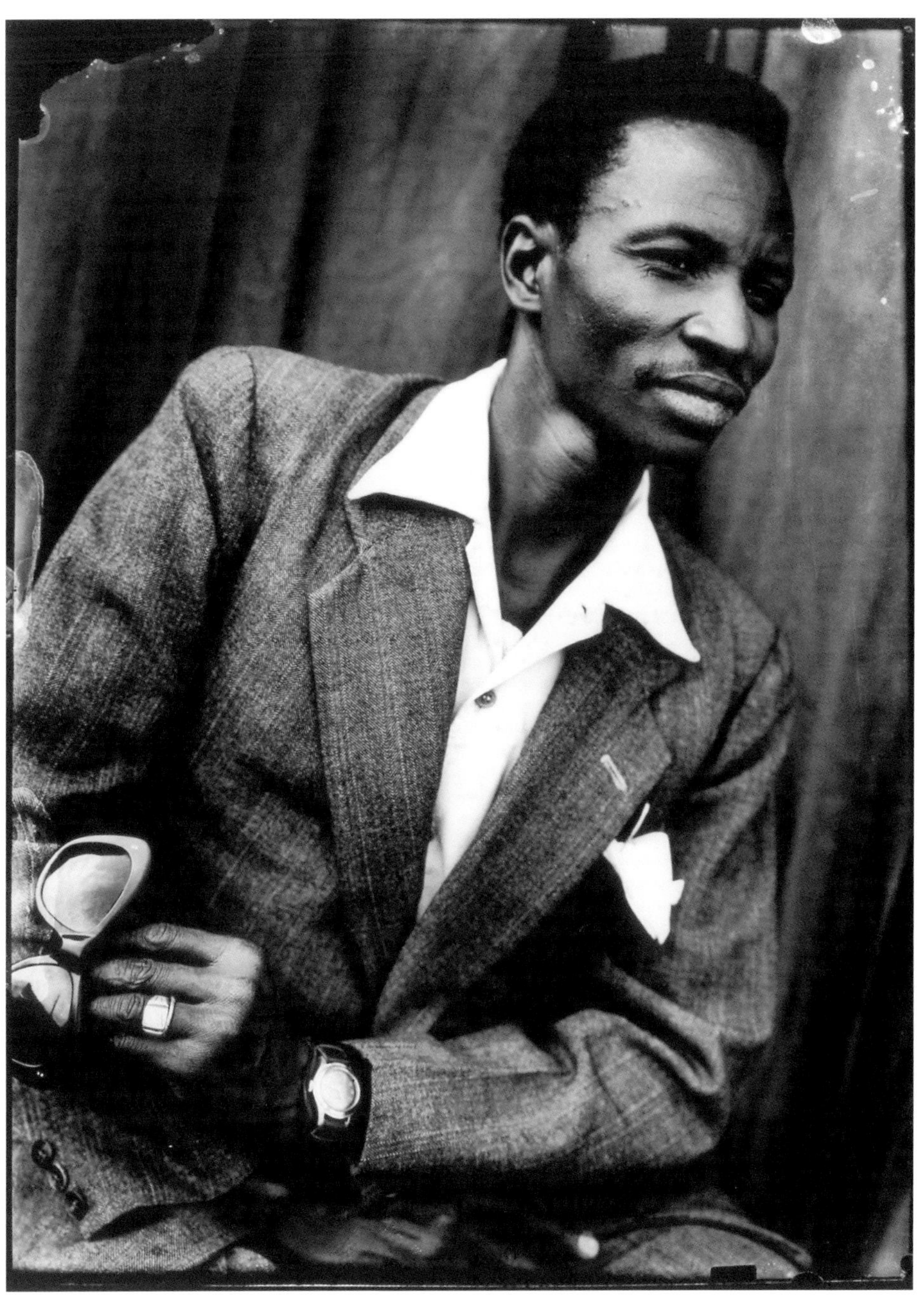

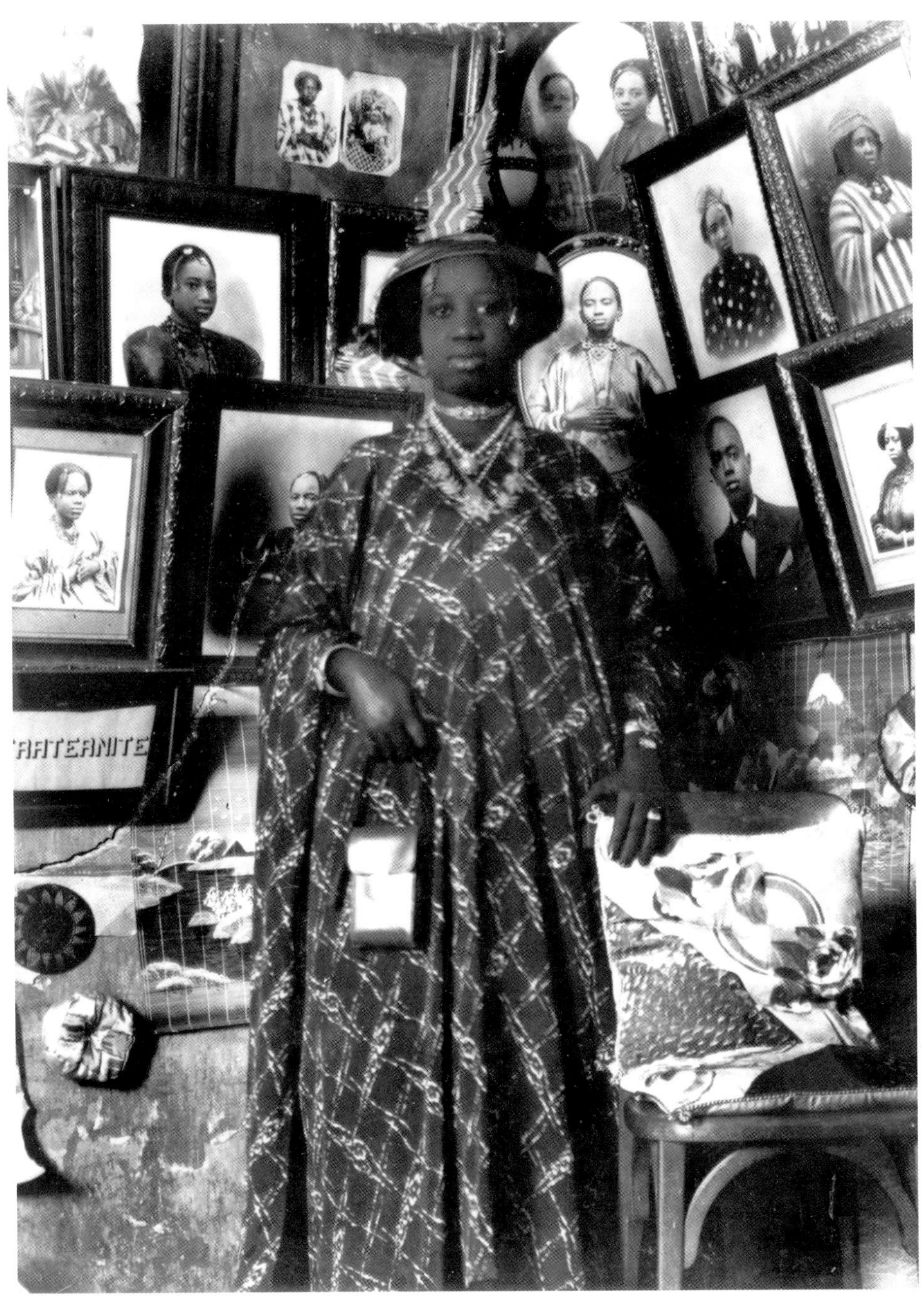
FRATERNITE

negatives allow for intensely rendered detail, with patterns of cloth, backdrops and geometric gestures of pulsating vividness. This effect is magnified when enlarged many times beyond their originally printed scale and heavily filtered, as was the case for their 1994 exhibition. Critics feasted on what was for them startling conjunctions of heavy amber beads with thick spectacles, plastic flowers and radios, and hand-woven cloth; other commentators rummaged through anthropological texts or personal memory, creating narratives of modernity to fit the illustrations. Keïta, in interviews, remembered providing props for his subjects' choices, and considered his methods as 'an artist' expert in arranging his patrons to their best, most distinct and idealized effect.[22] The photographer was highly esteemed in his city, the international rail hub of Bamako in Mali, and also in surrounding countries. With many portraits considered here, the more we look at Keïta's portraits, the more we wonder and the less we can be sure we know.

Compelling in other ways is the portrait opposite by an unidentified Saint-Louis, Senegal, photographer. Dating from the 1930s, it positions an unidentified woman surrounded by a panoply of portraits, most of which were probably taken in the 1910s.[23] She is framed in such a way that one's eye ranges between her rounded figure and the expanse of delicate images, which seem almost flat and painterly by contrast. These photographs, some in turn adorned with smaller images, intensify the significance of the portrait-moment. There are many subjects; the effect projects forward in time, linking the woman, these other performances of beauty, and future audiences in a way that emphasizes a tremendous photographic legacy.

Van-Leo (Levon Boyadjian, 1921–2002) came to Cairo from Turkey in the 1920s, and with his brother set up a studio in 1940. His portraits of mid-century personages at the height of cosmopolitan pre-revolutionary Cairo reflect the artistic fervour of the city, and the vision of his remarkable studio. The city drew the adventurers, soldiers-of-fortune, entertainers and international stars fleeing the blackouts and restricted consumption of wartime Europe; their glamour drawn out in his Cairo studio was redefined in Van-Leo's subjects. His approach echoed the dramatic play of light and shadow, refined tinting and lush close-ups of the day's Hollywood

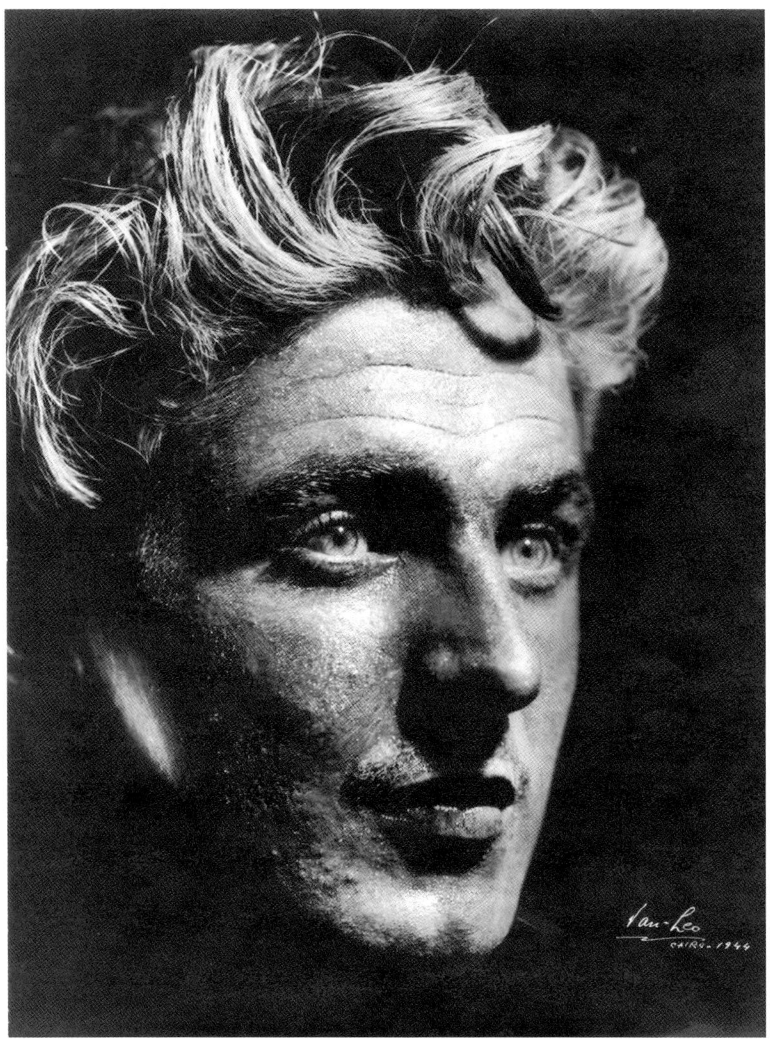

44 Van-Leo, *Teddy Lane*, 1944, silver gelatin print.

film photography. He portrayed many of Cairo's literary and artistic figures, inspired by this international clientele. For his portrait of South African performer Teddy Lane, Van-Leo coated his subject's face in grease, then sand, rendering dimensions of shadow; this exemplifies Van-Leo's fascination with the face as a mask and an icon.[24] His studio created an immediately recognizable aesthetic, a vivid reaction to the pictorialist

45 Samuel Fosso, *Self-portrait with Friend*, 1970s, black and white print.

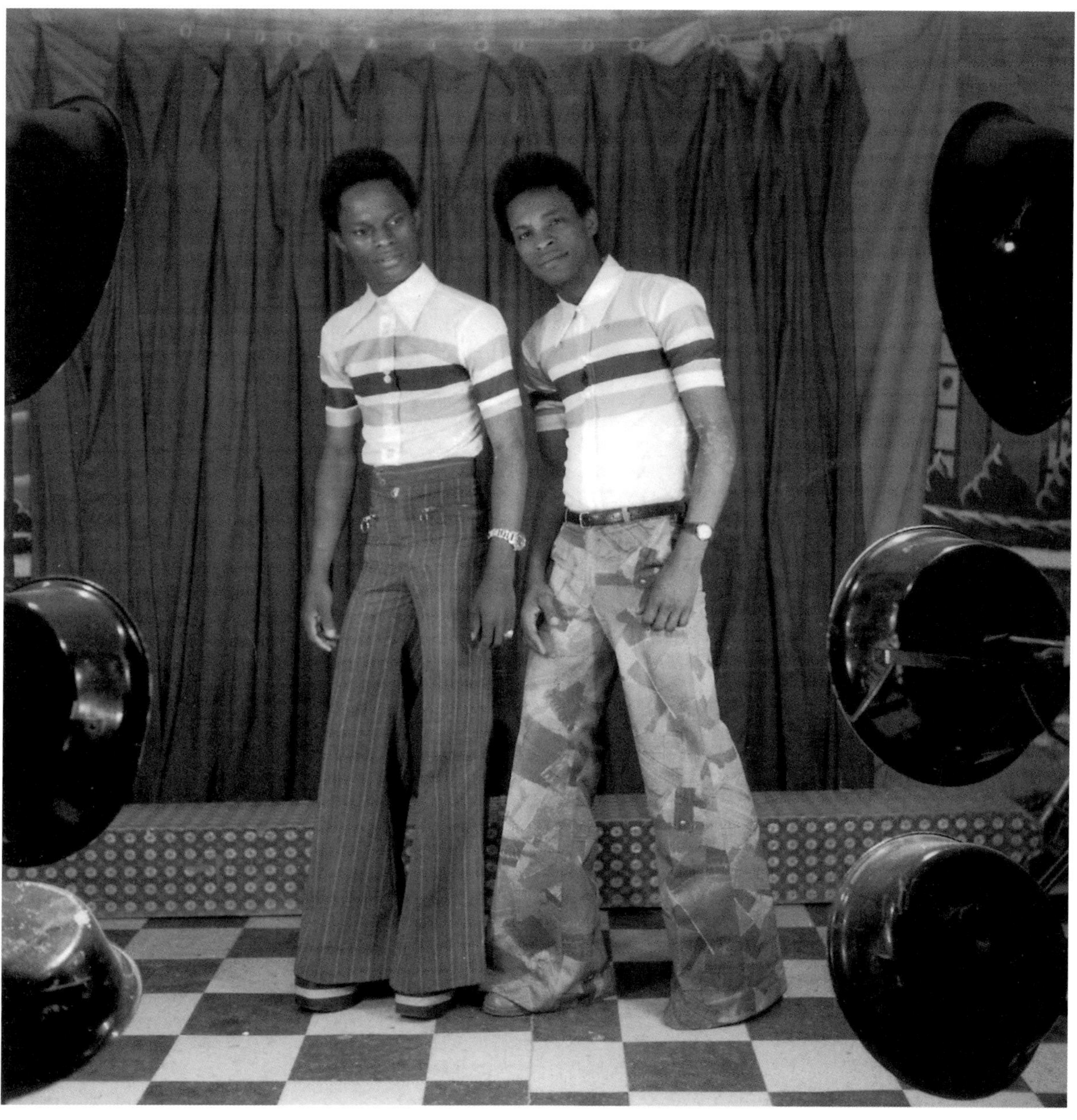

approach of earlier Armenian photographers in Egypt. His work's pains-taking and deliberate creations included a significant collection of self-portraits, an autobiography-as-chameleon effect that both projected and obscured the photographer.

Samuel Fosso (b. 1962) was the owner and photographer of Studio Photo Gentil from 1975, a fairly modest operation in Bangui, Central African Republic. His early portraits reveal his exceedingly good eye for framing his patrons' movement and gestures in choreographic space (illus. 45). Using the ends of film rolls, his first self-portraits as a youth were startling experiments in theatricality, the sense of performance heightened by the inclusion of studio apparatus, curtains, studio lights, edges of linoleum. After Fosso's work drew international attention at Bamako's 1994 photography exhibition, he deepened his exploration of the photographic studio as a personal and performative space.[25] Complex imaginaries emerged, such as the chief laden with gold and faux leopard skin, surrounded by printed textiles of gigantic hand-mirrors, alluding to all the 'village chiefs, African kings . . . [who] sold the lives of their people . . . to other Africans, to Westerners, to Arabs.'[26] For his recent project 'African Spirits', Fosso transforms himself into iconic black legends, from Patrice Lumumba to Angela Davis. Fosso's drama attends to the face, gesture and the possibility of portraiture that downplays distinctions of gender, nationality and time, invoking instead the multiple layers people present socially.

Contesting the Surface

Most of these portrait traditions are linked by the tangible record of collaboration between photographer and subjects. Beyond this, many other things impinge on portraits: they are kept, lost, renewed, altered, left to decay, destroyed. Photographs are also the raw materials for new extraordinary creations. Such objects craft hopeful, resilient, even admonitory narratives afresh, reliant on the possibilities of the photo-graphic universe, and pushed beyond this realm with astonishing varieties of techniques. This pervasive phenomenon, little recognized, points out the supreme value inherent in a photo's changeability and mutability, which is especially riveting in this select and unevenly globalizing digital age.

People change photographs to alter conceptual aspects of an image, as well as to improve its formal qualities. When Frederick G. C. Lutterodt (part of the noted lineage of Accra photographers) died in 1973, it was distinctly unsettling that not a single portrait was deemed suitable for his memorial photograph. His relations then took a full-length formal portrait, clearly depicting Mr Lutterodt's face (crucial since his face should be recognizable to viewers when printed on obituary posters); the fact that it was a wedding portrait from a very short-lived marriage was easily fixed. The resulting image was re-photographed and the bride cropped from the new portrait, though a trace of her hand is just visible on his shoulder.[27]

Routinely, portraits are radically decontextualized in order to compose an appropriately singular kind of memorial image. A memorial portrait of Maku Quaynor of Accra derives from a similar process, where a much older portrait was reprinted to exclude the nature and subject matter of the original image. In this case, she was photographed with a large entourage on the occasion of her return home as a shrine initiate. Mrs Quaynor wore the white cloth and adornments, and carried a small pot and broom, all of which signalled the occasion of her changed status. For an appropriately lasting memorial image, her family took this older photo and pared from it all references to this initiation debut, rendering it more generalized but still recognizable. It may also indicate that portraits convey controversial circumstances (such as belonging to a shrine that not everyone might have supported), and even then, the controversy may not be acknowledged by the family at the time. Portraits are commissioned to record important realities, but family members determine which of these are worth remembering later on. And their remaking of photographs enacts a distancing, an idealization, and a remaking of personal and social and familial memory.[28]

Conjoining photographs suits other real-life limitations. Liam Buckley has noted that photographers in the Gambia – a place long immersed in the fallout of civil wars of neighbouring Liberia and Sierra Leone – reunite distant lovers in photographs, or bring together a son and his long-deceased

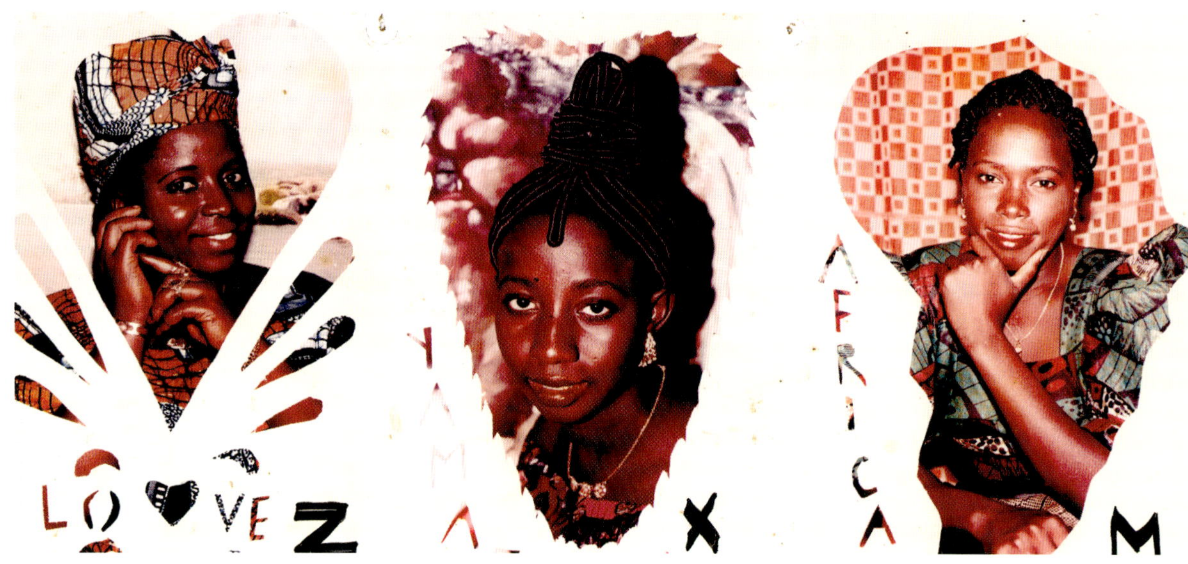

father. Photographs are sliced, intermixed with older photographs, made to illustrate people's longed-for impossibilities. Other studios rely on the fine 'tailoring' and 'cutting' skills of artists employed by photographers, to make intricate 'Love Signs' portraits (above). Intricate cut-outs frame faces of loved ones with hearts, flowers or keys, with even finer blade-work spelling out captions in English and Wolof (a language spoken in Senegal, the Gambia and Mauritania), such as lines from popular songs: 'isn't it pleasing?', 'amour', 'my heart'. The aesthetics of tailoring, longing, polishing and improving the surface of a photograph, reflect people's interest in appearance rather than any effort to distil personal or individual essence.[29]

Some photographers have specialized in the creation of fantastic narratives and spaces to satisfy their patrons' imaginations. Photo-collages by Ugandan photographers Ronnie Okocha Kauma (b. 1976) and Afanaduula Sadala (b. 1968) allow subjects to stand at the door of an airplane, while away the day with women on exclusive hotel beaches, or peek out from the interior of a cashpoint machine. One Kauma portrait shows a man larger than life, surrounded by airplanes, bodyguards and in the company of no less than the king of Buganda and President

46 Portraits (names unknown), colour photography and cut paper by Doudou Jen, New Millennium Image Hunters Love Signs, 2000.

47 Ronnie Okocha Kauma, *Portrait of a Man with President Museveni and Bodyguard*, 1999, photo-collage.

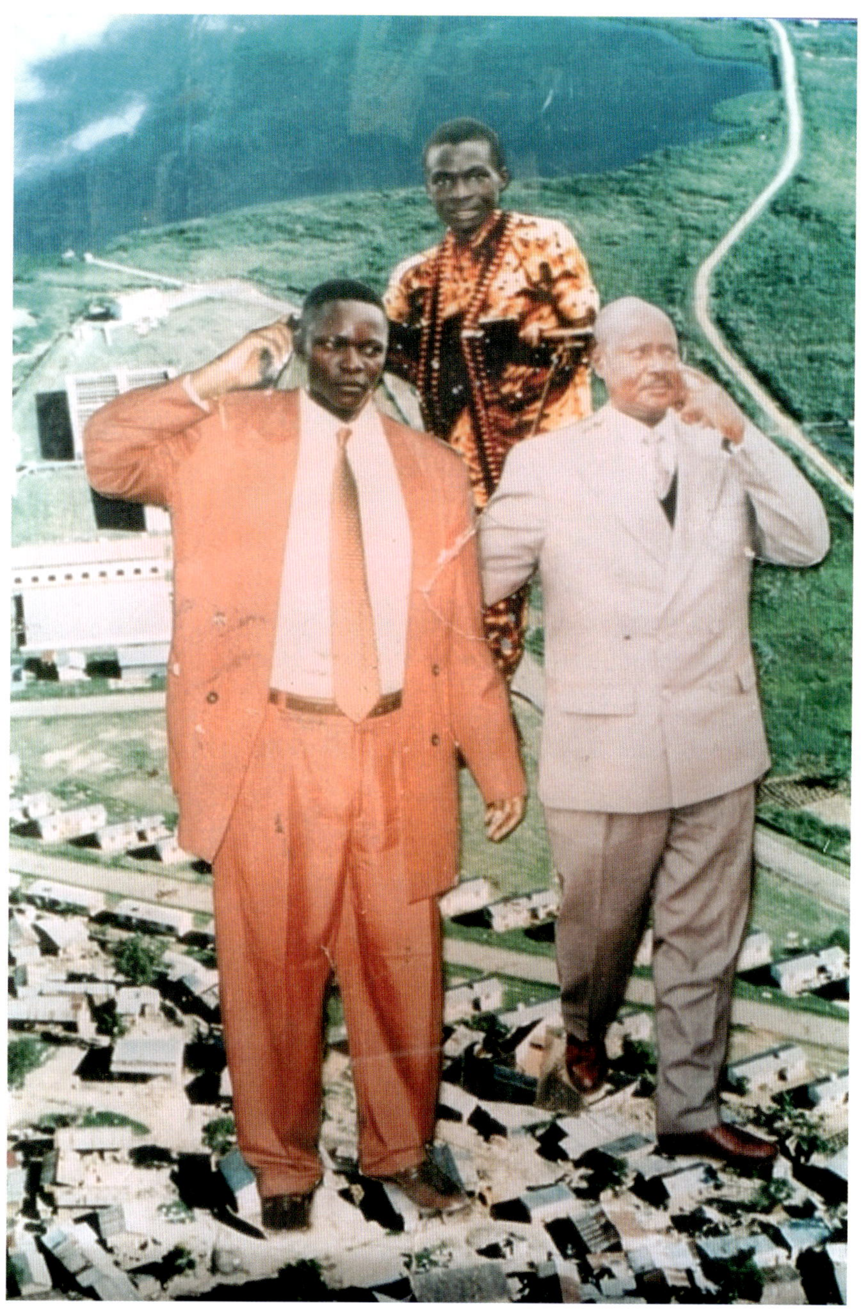

Museveni (1999). Another of Kauma's portraits combine his client's face with the body and accoutrements of a Catholic bishop, but as the artist worried his creativity may put his client beyond the pale, he situated a disguise of dark sunglasses on his 'bishop's' head.[30]

A very different approach to cutting photographs is seen in the more abstracted and geometric effects of Omar Said Bakor's studio in Lamu, Kenya (active *c.* 1960s–1980s). Faces are arranged on cut-outs of flower-pots, nestled within a bird's breast, or the painted faces of radiant girls beam from the hearts of smiling photographed men.[31] There are endless possibilities for aesthetic play on the photographic surface as an end unto itself, such as those seen in the photomontages of Photo Dieudonné of Zinder, Niger. The portrait opposite transforms the delicate features of a woman's face into a study of graceful comportment. The effect of its multiple exposures, with its interplay of light and detailed surface, evokes the calm rhythmic dynamism of a printed cloth's oversize patterning.

Colourful and fanciful painted backdrops, such as those used by Ghanaian photographer Philip Kwame Apagya (see illus. 49), are common-place means used by photographers to create another layer in the creative arsenal of portrait-making. Patrons of Apagya (b. 1958) are framed enjoying a soda in a well-appointed living room, or coming down the gangway at Kotoka International Airport.[32] The fantastic backdrops emphasize the sense of effort, artifice and artistry as a collaborative endeavour – one contributed to by backdrop painters, photographers and the subjects themselves. Apagya's description of how he works bears out this sense. The fundamental qualities of his successful portraits are comprised of painted surfaces, the performance of subjects in appropriate poses, their appearance within public spaces and according to the calendar of religious observation:

> At the end of Ramadan, I hang my Kaaba background on the side of the mosque, and they get snapped in many various places, as if they were in Mecca. There [are] a lot of styles to pose to *become a Muslim*.[33] (emphasis added)

The extent of how convincing the objects are pictorially is often beside the point, and notions of what is a satisfactory depiction reside in different

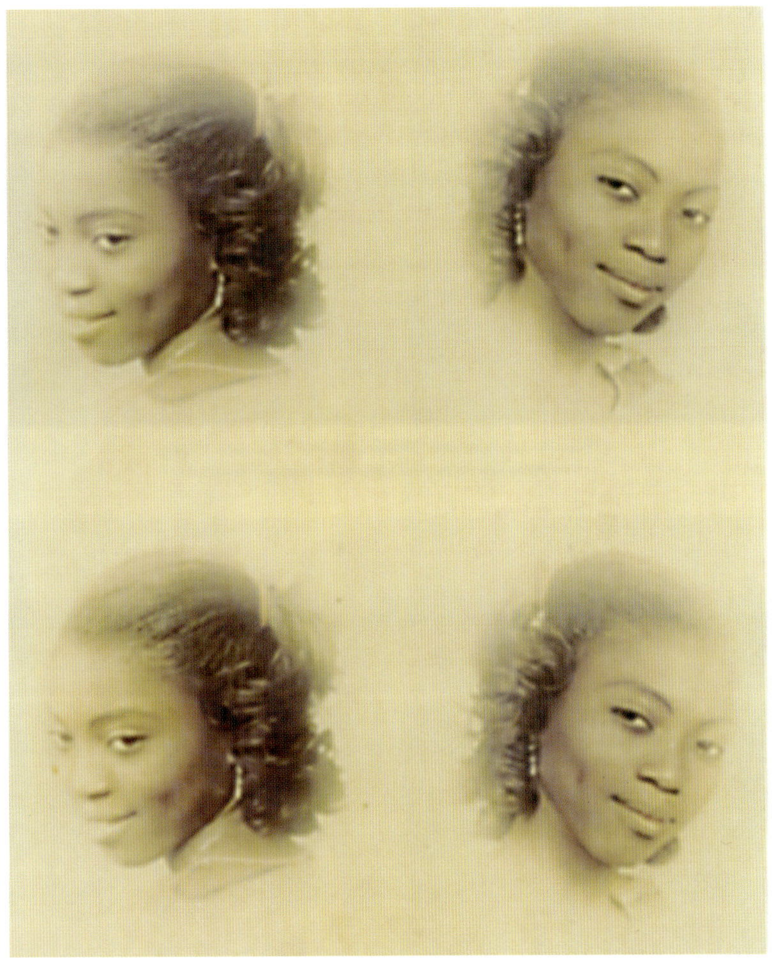

48 Dieudonné Agaounga (Photo Dieudonné, Zinder, Niger), *Portrait of a Woman*, 1990s, multiple exposure colour print.

qualities. For example, Kauma's logic of the integrity of the photograph is in the process of cutting and then re-photographing: a new negative effectively polishes the edges and smoothes the surface, and so becomes another index.[34] A photographer's skill in reprinting from a positive photograph is of less concern than individual choices made about the editing of its conceptual content.

Portraiture has long been the richest and most widespread of photographic practices on the continent. Its very diversity and richly

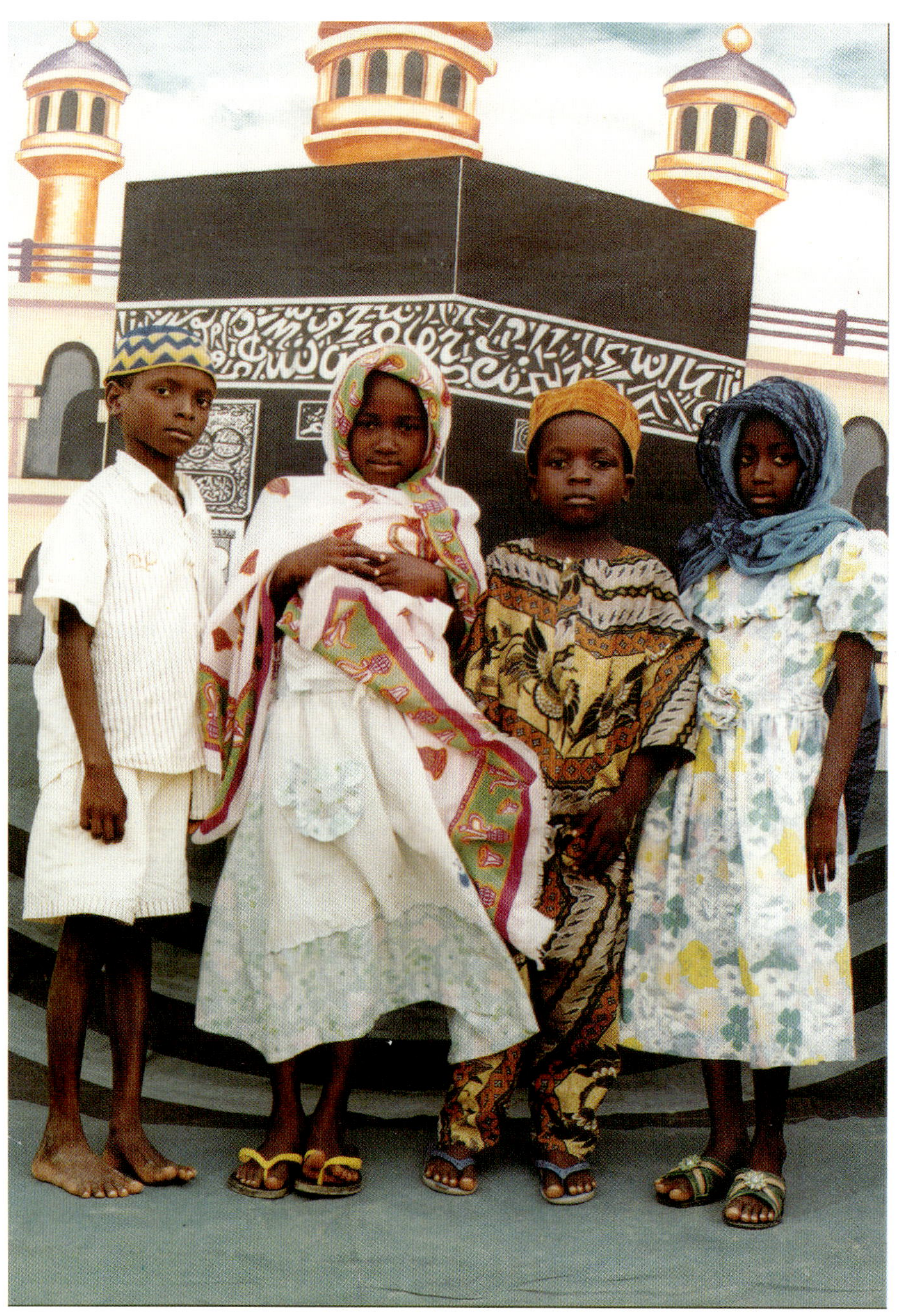

articulated conceptions of personhood, identity and memory which it entails, are not always made obvious or apparent by looking at the image's surface. It is folly to reduce these varied practices down to displays of identity, naïve experimental self-fashioning or contestations against 'colonial' depictions. Portraits spring from some of the earliest of photographic traditions on the continent. As we come to terms with the depth and history of these artistic movements, we are better poised to consider and appreciate their prominence as collaborative and open-ended creative acts of photographers, patrons, subjects and audiences across space and time.

49 Phillip Kwame Apagya, *Children in Front of Kaaba Backdrop*, 1996, colour print.

three

'Observers are worried . . .'

> With photographs, we have concrete proof that we have not been
> hallucinating . . .[1]

Even while ambiguous and multivalent, the photographs in this chapter are
potent records of some of colonialism's worst deeds in Africa. For parts of
the continent, much of what we know of early photography is bound in the
visualizations of colonial archives. This imagery extends from postcards
to anthropometric studies, and was compiled by travellers, scientists, commercial photographers and employees operating within the new colonial
spaces of Africa. These photos linger in private collections, museums and
archives today. Their larger effect points not only to photography as a
means of creating taxonomies of Africans, but also as a way to consolidate
visions of imperial order. Colonial photography in the Congo Free State
ranks among some of the more heavy-handed of propagandistic imagery,
and this must be understood within the political context of its creation[2]
(although there are almost certainly many more photographs which will
come to light and complicate this story further). Conjoining pro-colonial
ideology, images and texts, and intermingled with the imagery of force
and atrocities, such depictions of the Congo were made for audiences
abroad and formed their own genre of bad deeds. In contrast to these
narratives that framed Congolese labouring bodies, there were a few
incendiary images created by activists, which eventually emerged as a
sharp jolt to audiences in Europe and the USA. But in larger terms, these
were inadequate in the face of the Congo Free State's vast social disruption,
systematic slavery and widespread extermination unparalleled elsewhere

in early colonial Africa. While these photographs helped rouse the attention of an international audience, photography would not emerge locally as a relevant means of resisting political oppression for some time.[3] However, the roots of this activist photography spawned new forums for colonial photography in Europe, particularly in anti-slavery campaigns and journalism.[4]

The situation in South Africa offers an utterly different paradigm. Here photographers worked actively to subvert, document and upend the state's propaganda from the 1950s, in an attempt to record the colonial government's worst offences. Documentary photography became a declarative force to combat the visual agitprop of the apartheid government, and was in itself a means of fighting the larger system by exerting political pressure from within and outside of South Africa's borders. With its tradition spanning five decades, photographers changed tactics and approaches, constantly updating what 'resistance' meant throughout the struggle against apartheid. Their images were conceived as participatory objects, forms of agency capable of penetrating barriers erected within South African society itself and communicating the need for international intervention beyond the country's borders. These extensive political projects entailed their own kaleidoscopic set of narratives.

Far from being singular examples, the cases of South Africa and the Congo fostered activist documentary photography which relied on reaching audiences abroad, particularly Europe and the USA, as well as breaking down local barriers to accessing information via photographs. They suggest that photography's documentary function in relation to colonial oppression was less ambiguous in the face of such extreme political coercion and widespread propaganda.

Congo Free State

For European and American audiences, nineteenth-century travellers to the Congo spun an evocative myth of darkness to be reconnoitred, mapped and pictured.[5] The newspaper impresario and explorer Henry Morton Stanley began criss-crossing central Africa in 1871. With his expeditions composed of European officers and African bearers and guides, Stanley led searches to find the missing missionary explorer David Livingstone and rescue Emin Pasha, and also sought and mapped the source of the Congo River. He later set up treaties with African leaders to take over lands and oversaw construction to access the interior of what would become King Leopold II's private colony, the Congo Free State. Newspaper accounts and his four volumes recorded facets of these encounters, though Stanley was to a lesser extent known for the destruction left in his wake: communities terrorized, injured and killed, including a heavy toll of sickness and exhaustion of his own entourage.[6] The newspaperman published prolifically, and his journal accounts and books brimmed with photographic and printed illustrations, maps, charts and various depictions of the expedition, as well as images borrowed from earlier authors. These were widely reproduced abroad, selling a tantalizing and mythic image of 'darkest Africa' to a receptive public.[7]

The Belgian King Leopold II asked Stanley to map and secure Congo territory for his own private entrepreneurial ventures.[8] Stanley's account of this journey was released contemporaneous with the Berlin African Conference (1884–5), at which European imperial powers claimed shares of African territory. Initially, King Leopold's claims to the Congo Free State were based on the use of what it decreed were 'empty' lands, and that this was also an effort to eradicate the Swahili-Arab trade in slaves. For Leopold to manage and justify taking over holdings the size of western Europe as a personal fiefdom required an extensive information campaign that was multi-pronged and constantly shifting.[9]

This robust propaganda campaign generated spin for years, employing an international legion of book authors, journalists, newspaper editors, scholars and lobbyists. At the height of the imperial age, this political rhetoric was a backdrop to all manner of photographs and mass-produced imagery. Ethnographically labelled postcards embellished the myth of primitive people in need of moral guidance and modernization; meanwhile depictions of local conscripted labourers building roads and bridges were meant to evoke narratives of beneficent European technologies and supervision. Illustrated papers, souvenir albums, postcards and stereographic slides conveyed the massive scope of colonial projects,

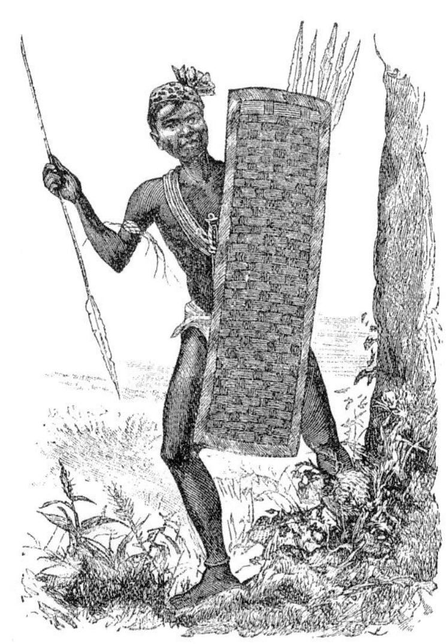

50 Artist unknown, 'Native departing for war', c. 1884, engraving.

51 Unknown photographer, *Young Mayumbe Girls*, c. 1910, collotype postcard.

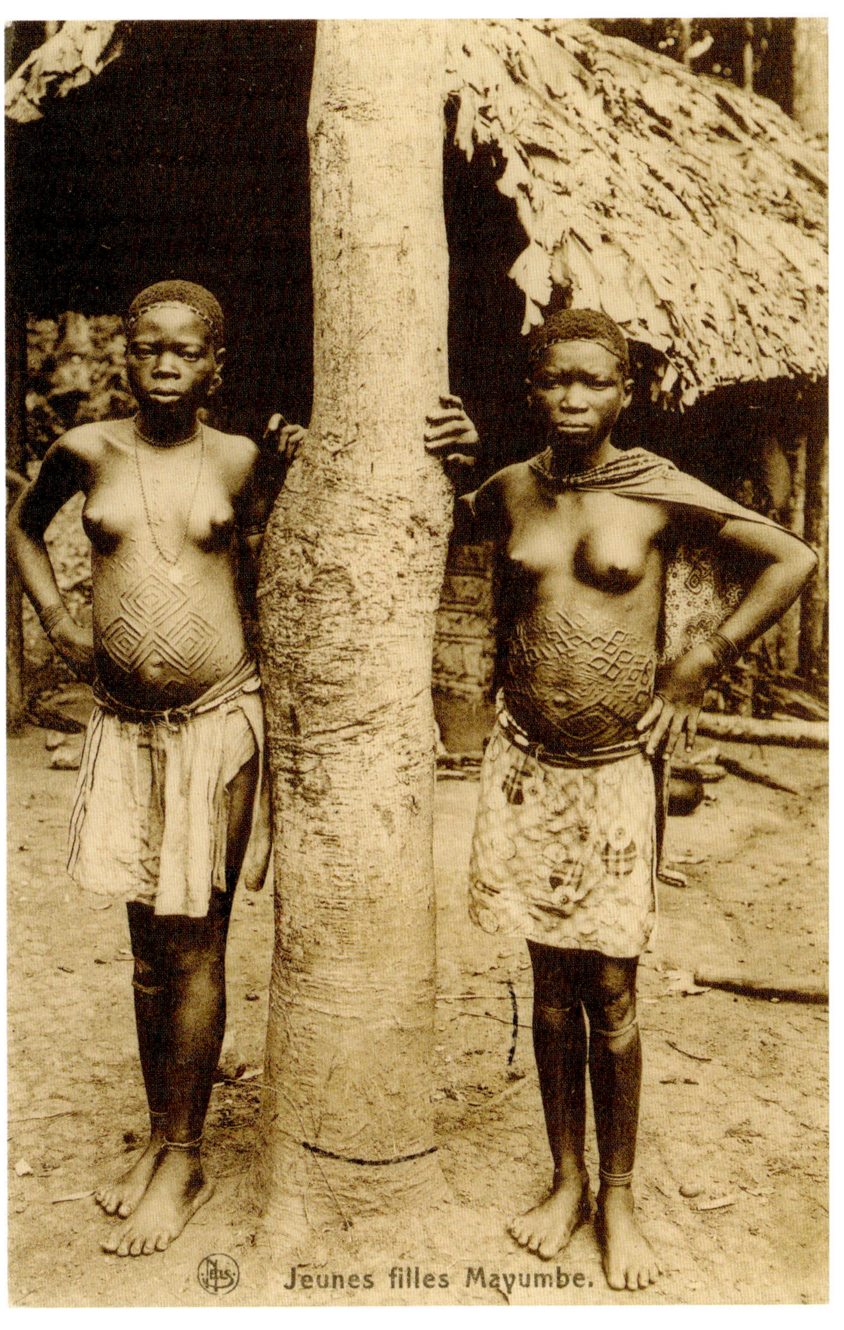

Jeunes filles Mayumbe.

wherein central Africa was rendered as a place to be explored, exploited, improved upon and civilized.[10] Leopold was initially interested in the Congo for its ivory and minerals, but as the worldwide rubber boom took off in 1895, his wealth accumulated from a vast military-driven slave-holding enterprise put in place to gather raw rubber sap. The resulting European fortunes, and the practices that garnered them, drew increasing attention from companies and governments in Europe and the USA.

Visual Force

Apart from these, there were smaller outfits who contrived entrepreneurial and 'civilizing' storylines on a smaller scale; there were professional and amateur photographers and postcard printers, many of whom had ties to military and mercantile establishments. Their images were often recycled for years after their creation: postcards and illustrated commercial magazines like *Le Congo illustré* (1892–5) formulated depictions of central Africa's wealth as a place brimming with potential riches. Jean Audema, a colonial administrator in the French Congo during 1894–1905, issued large quantities of his photographs in postcard editions from 1900 to 1910.[11] Emile Gorlia was a passionate and prolific amateur who travelled widely in the

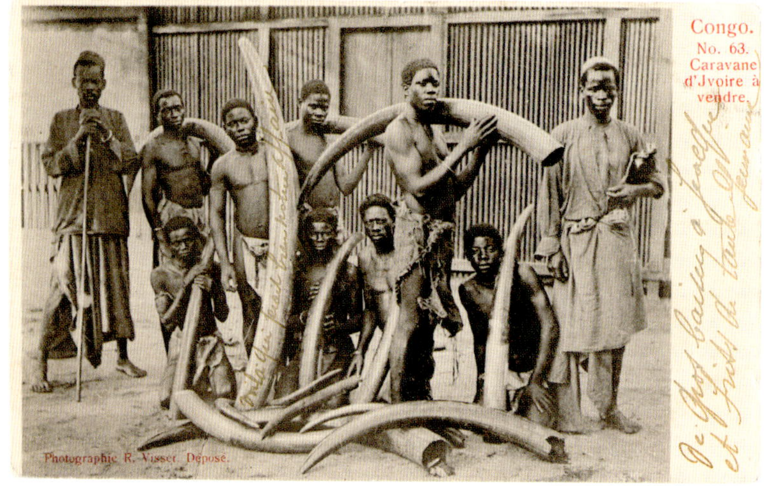

52 Robert Visser, '*A caravan of ivory for sale*' (French Congo), c. 1890–1900, collotype postcard.

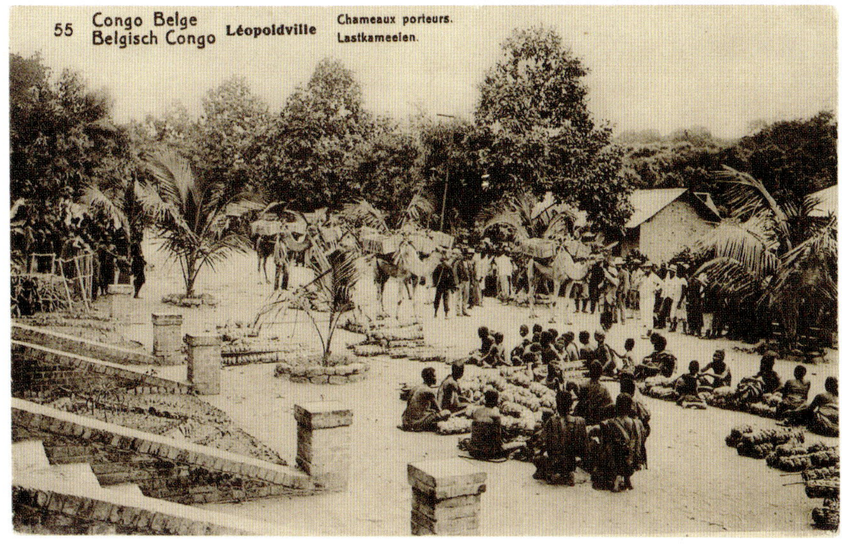

Belgian Congo as a colonial judge beginning in 1909, and whose photographic records are an interesting counterpoint to dogmatically labelled postcard imagery.[12] Robert Visser, a German plantation director working for a Dutch trading company in different parts of the French Congo, Congo Free State and Portuguese Congo during 1882–1904, produced imagery which tended towards the dramatic.[13] In one image, he gathers a group of men proffering elephant tusks, and suggests the conflation of the photographer and dealmaker, a merchant's eye attuned to commercial possibilities. Ivory was among the first commodities to be exploited in the area, with great quantities forcibly bought for a pittance.[14] The caption 'Caravan d'Ivoire à vendre' takes the positive spin effected by the staging one step further. The artfully-arranged composition opposite decorously presents objects of tremendous wealth to distant audiences, amenable elephant hunters and their better-clad overseers offering visual and material gifts. The caption takes up that fiction of exchange.

Yet it was not always necessary to stage depictions of the forces that drove Congo labour. *Camel Bearers* above presents a commonplace scene, the delivery of rubber to a colonial administration station. Facing the entrance to a colonial building in Léopoldville, women, men and children

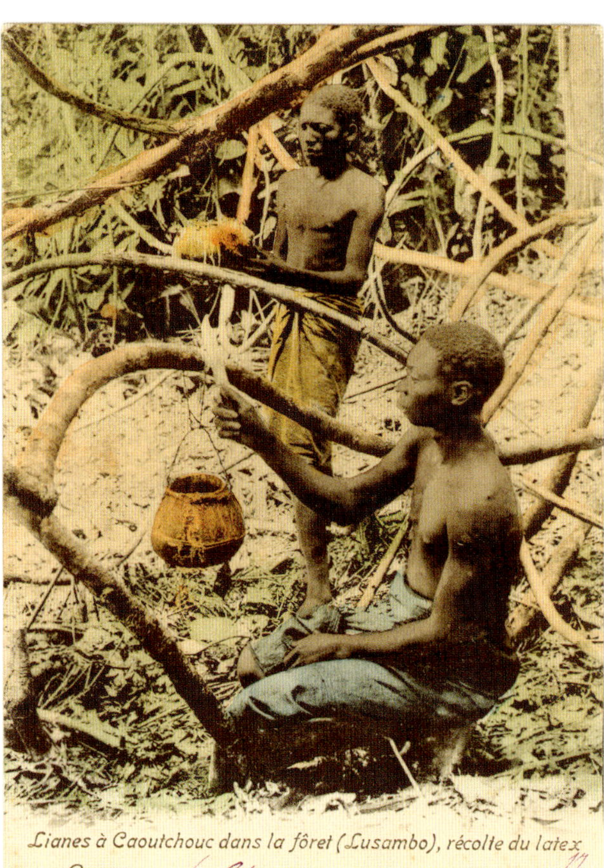

54 Unknown photographer, '*Harvesting rubber in the forest (Lusambo)*' (Congo Free State), c. 1895, hand-tinted postcard.

sit in rows in the foreground, surrounded by their bundles of gathered rubber sap. Behind them, more bundles have been neatly bound with basketry and rods. Camels, imported from northern Africa, wait with their burdens, ready to set out for the coast. African and European staff of the post, Hausa traders brought from the Sahel and soldiers of the Force Publique (FP) complete the tableau. It would appear to be a straightforward harvesting and shipping enterprise, except it is not immediately apparent that the rubber collectors were likely conscripts

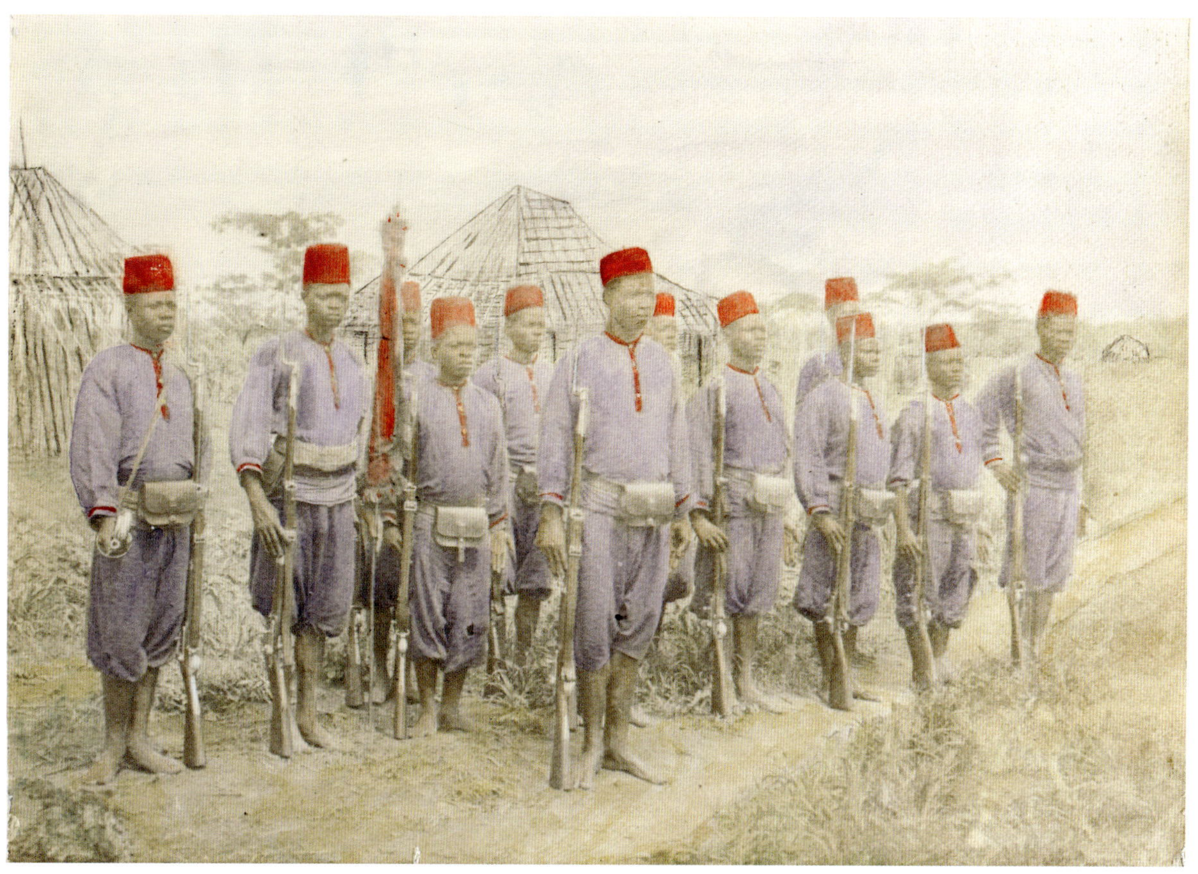

or slaves. Rubber harvesting was intensely difficult and painful, requiring gatherers to smear their bodies with the sap from rubber vines, let it dry, then rip it from their skin. This process was so onerous that people 'must be forced to do it', as it was put by one Belgian officer.[15]

An unknown photographer conceived a particularly peaceful scene of such work (illus. 54). Two men attend to their pots hanging from vines, their knives poised to renew the cuts. Nothing in the images suggests the physical demands of rubber sap on flesh, nor indicates the means by which people were compelled to this harvest. The photographer's choice amounts to a staggering elision: the pervasive violence required to produce this quiet picture of subdued men at a simple task. In 1899 a

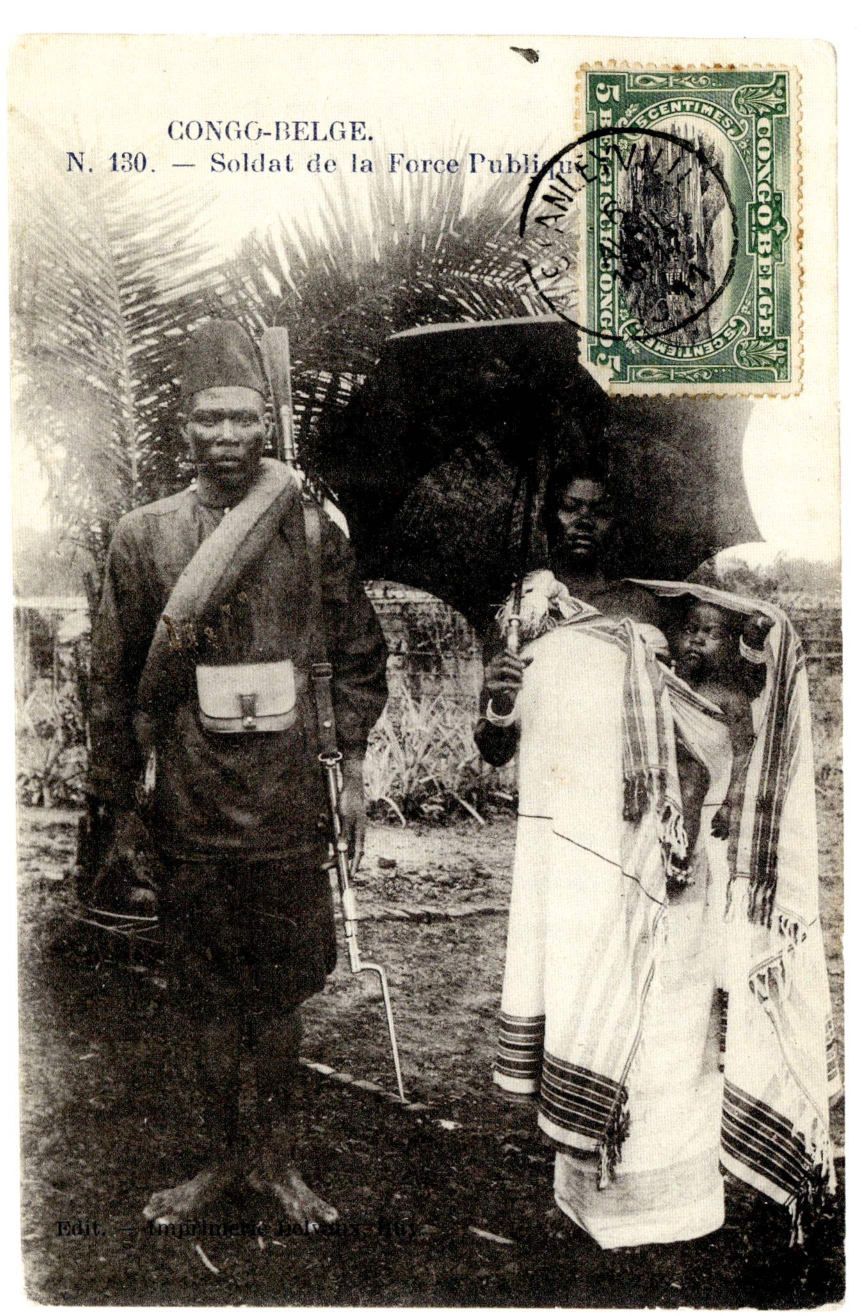

CONGO-BELGE.
N. 130. — Soldat de la Force Publique
Edit. — Imprimerie Delvaux, Huy

British Vice-Consul, investigating increasingly alarmed reports in Europe of the abuses, noted:

> An example of what is done was told [by an officer] . . . To arrive in canoes at a village, the inhabitants of which invariably bolted on their arrival; the soldiers were then landed, and commenced looting, taking all the chickens, grain etc, out of the houses; after this they attacked the natives until able to seize their women; these women were kept as hostages until the chief of the district brought in the required number of kilograms of rubber. The rubber having been brought, the women were sold back to their owners for a couple of goats apiece, and so he continued from village to village until the requisite amount of rubber had been collected.[16]

Leopold's stratospheric profits from the rubber boom came at a terrible human cost: enslaved and conscripted labourers who built the infra-structure to transport the rubber and other goods were coerced by a multinational European militia and a much larger army of African soldiers, the Force Publique. Portrayals of these soldiers, in blue uniforms and red fezes, became photographic emblems of the order of the Congo regime (illus. 55). The Force Publique originally comprised west and central Africans, and were promised good wages; they were later replaced by forced conscripts from Congo districts. Integral to the early Congo photographic record are photographs of soldiers, military music bands and the inspection of forces at their camps. The portrait opposite of an unnamed soldier, poised as the fierce enforcer ready with rifle and bayonet, marks a bizarre contrast with his beautifully clothed and jewelled wife and child, composed under a showy umbrella. Portraits of soldiers stand in for palatable depictions of a colonial regime's discipline; at the same time they portray working men, enforcers and enforced. Their unidentified portraits circulated in the same visual world with another ubiquitous visualization of progress-and-order: ranks of prisoners in chains.

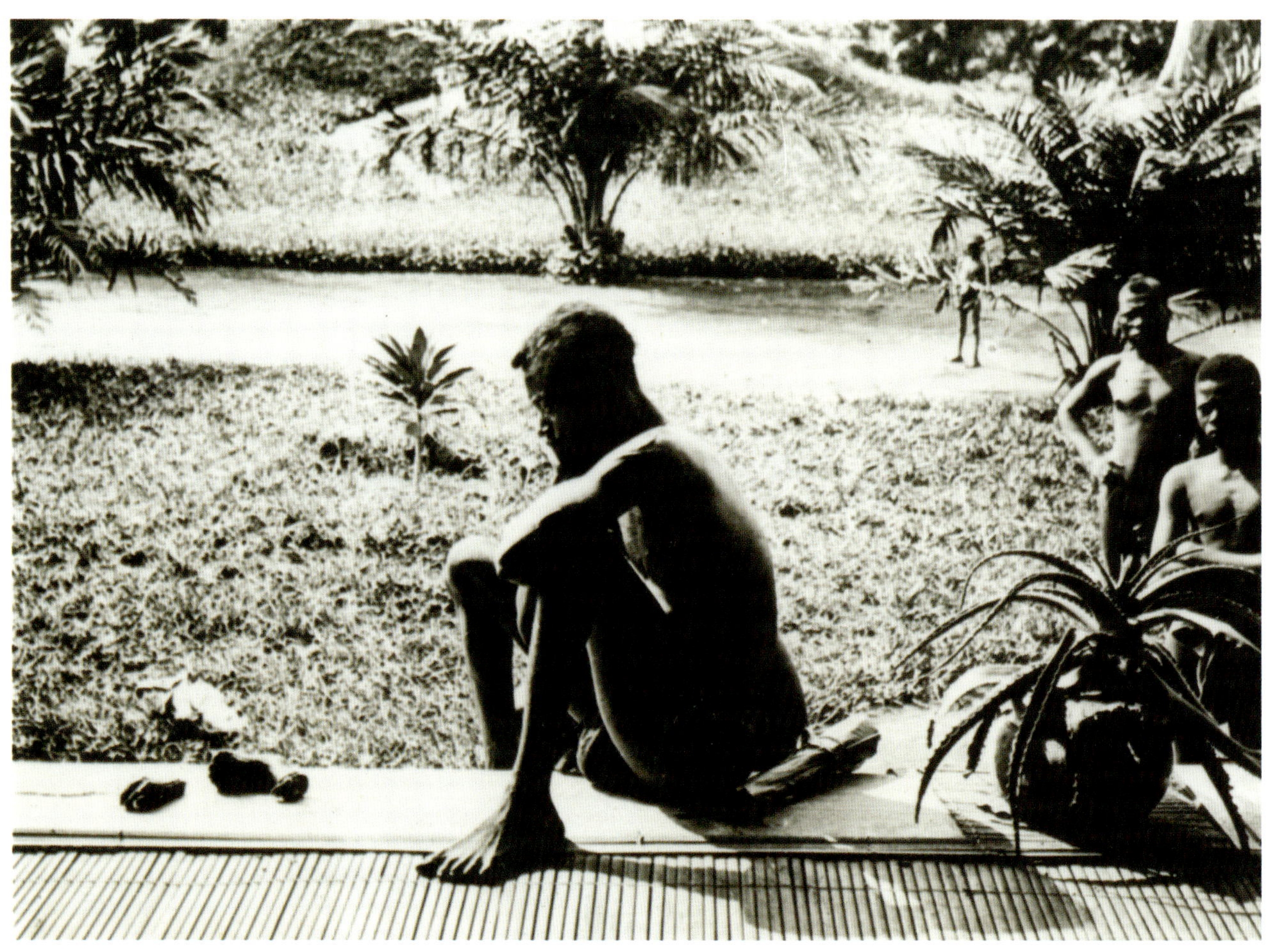

57 Alice Harris, 'Nsala of Wala with severed hand and foot of his five year old daughter murdered by ABIR militia', 1904, print from lantern slide.

Eventually, broader public attention was drawn to abuses in the Congo Free State by trading company employees, various dissidents within the colonial ranks, nosy visitors and resident missionaries. Early public charges of 'crimes against humanity' were levelled at Leopold by African-American George Washington Williams during the 1890s, notably the collecting of human hands as a gruesome means of tallying soldiers' use of bullets during village raids.[17] Critical journalists were banned from entering the colony, and correspondence from European dissidents and others within the commercial and government enterprises was monitored by the censorship office in Boma. Still, documents attesting to the institutionalization of hostage taking, kidnapping and mass killing trickled in, finding their way to a most methodical and well-informed critic of the Congo system, Edmund Dene Morel (1873–1924). Morel had been a trading company employee and outraged at the slave economy fundamental to Congo trade, became its most vocal critic and published extensive documentary evidence in his newspaper, *The West African Mail* (1903–5). Morel and British Consul Roger Casement founded the Congo Reform Association in 1904. Morel's publications, meetings and lantern slide lectures included testimonials from other witnesses, particularly British, American and Swedish missionaries.[18]

These reports and photographic records formed a core of an international protest against Leopold's atrocities. In Morel's lectures, 60 lantern slides framed subjects wholly absent from the voluminous postcard imagery. Many of these were taken by the British missionaries Alice Seeley Harris and John Harris, who lived in Congo from 1898 to 1905, and photographed adults and children whose hands or feet had been cut off. Energized by Morel's association, the Harrises also published illustrated leaflets, and delivered lectures with lantern slides to bring attention of these atrocities to the UK and other European audiences. Their photographs shocked audiences in a way that scenes of hostages in chains, burnt and cleared villages, and depopulated swathes of land could not. The concentrated efforts of people such as Williams, Morel, the Harrises and other missionaries, as well as Roger Casement and untold numbers of Congolese who rebelled, fought and died, all eventually brought enormous pressure to bear on Belgium. In 1908, Leopold sold his Congo Free State to the government of Belgium for over 200 million francs, at which point it became the Belgian Congo. During his regime and its aftermath, roughly 1880–1920, the area's losses of about half of its population to murder, starvation, exhaustion, exposure and disease, and the next generation because of the precipitous drop in birth rates, amounted to about ten million people.[19]

Apologists used photography to repackage and purvey imagery of peaceful conditions and untouched natives,[20] and these visual tropes persisted in photographs and films made under the direction of the Fonds Colonial de Propagande Economique et Social (The Colonial Fund of Economic and Social Propaganda) created in 1937.[21] Film production was geared towards emphasizing the cooperative relationships between Belgian colonials and Congolese during the years when African independence movements were gathering force. After independence, the information agency Congopresse was its successor, and it employed European and Congolese photographers.

The imagery of Congolese workers under Leopold's regime trace a visualization of the larger forces ordering the public spaces and the moments in which they were photographed. While photographers, postcard printers and newspaper editors were not unified under Leopold's powerful arm, they tended to pair images and words from disparate places in careful ways: these led present-day audiences to wonder about what lay beyond the frame. In the face of indigenous societies' devastation and propaganda, activist missionaries and journalists used photography's perceived standing as an 'incorruptible witness' to counter the massive rhetoric campaign.[22] These photographs' distribution made them effective parts of a larger political response, but they offered no allusion to the larger web of personal networks of how people in the Congo survived or experienced the calamity of Leopold's regime and the years that followed. Furthermore, while this activist approach led to new uses of colonial photography for journalists and in anti-slavery campaigns, it also cultivated old notions of dark savagery on the continent.[23]

The archival record, or the fraction of it that has been studied, so far appears to reinforce the one-sidedness of the historical pictorial record, but there are yet masses of images to be collected, currently housed in the Royal Museum for Central Africa at Tervuren, Belgium – the museum built to display the treasures of Leopold's voracious collecting. Congolese collections of imagery, from studio archives to private family collections, have been disrupted by significant political chaos. The possibilities for rewriting or at least elaborating on photographic legacies beyond the colonial framework in central Africa are more pressing than ever.[24]

South Africa

In contrast to central Africa, the photographic landscape in the Republic of South Africa, as has been suggested in earlier chapters, was denser and more varied, and it is against this backdrop that a formidable tradition of activist photography would emerge. Grand 'documentary' efforts in anthropological and exploration veins made their marks, as well as the ubiquitous scenes, views and types, but there was also the quotidian imagery from small studios. Art photography of the European salon tradition emerged early in the twentieth century, and the exhibition circuit, as well as the spread of amateur clubs, and the growing infra-structure of illustrated print journalism, each influenced the emergence of photography as a medium for activism. Thus photographic practice from the late nineteenth century was among the most varied and docu-mented on any part of the continent.[25]

This discussion is a necessarily limited treatment of the ways in which photographers in South Africa created a thoroughly political creative practice as part of a much larger political movement. Their work docu-mented now-iconic resistance fighters as well as those whose names went unrecorded; and illustrated a timeline of important moments in political struggle, such as the Defiance Campaign of 1952, the 1958 Treason Trial and the 1976 Soweto riots.[26] Photographers also turned their attention to daily life away from the frontlines, views that brought into focus the effects of the apartheid system for distant audiences in South Africa and beyond. Photographers themselves worked – alone, for institutions, publications and group efforts – in concert with other artists, writers, politicians and organisers. Documentary 'struggle' photography was not a cohesive movement, but a broad set of practices working against a particularly confined and propagandized society. At the same time, photographers questioned the results and reception of their images once they were distributed and dispersed in the world.

Activist Pioneers

Depictions of the majority of South Africa's population were circumscribed by colonial and white photographers for much of the nineteenth and early twentieth century. Resident photojournalists worked in south African cities from the 1890s, such as H. C. Shelley who photographed the Anglo-Boer war (1899–1902). Black 'subjecthood' – as framed by European and white South African photographers, particularly from the 1920s – tended to operate within a narrow ideological agenda, such as Alfred Martin Duggan-Cronin's (*c.* 1874–1954) efforts to catalogue 'types' of indigenous southern Africans,[27] or the work of Constance Stuart Larrabee (1914–2000) whose quite different approach was also marked by a preservationist intent.[28] Quite apart from these, a South African pictorialist school emerged, beginning with the first Cape Town exhibition in 1906.[29] It would herald a fundamentally conservative salon approach that greatly influenced the trajectory of white South African photography.[30] A small number of black-owned photography studios (and those probably owned by Indian and 'coloured' photographers as well) were an exception to this elite practice. Much of the record of these small studios has been damaged or lost in the forced removals of the twentieth century.

Alongside the expansion of white amateur camera clubs, and in spite of unequal education, there eventually emerged an opening for wider photographic practice. This included the Progressive Photographic Society, established in the late 1950s, as the only venue for black photographers. That documentary photography might register the concern for

58 Jürgen Schadeberg, *Drum magazine Office*, 1954, black-and-white print.

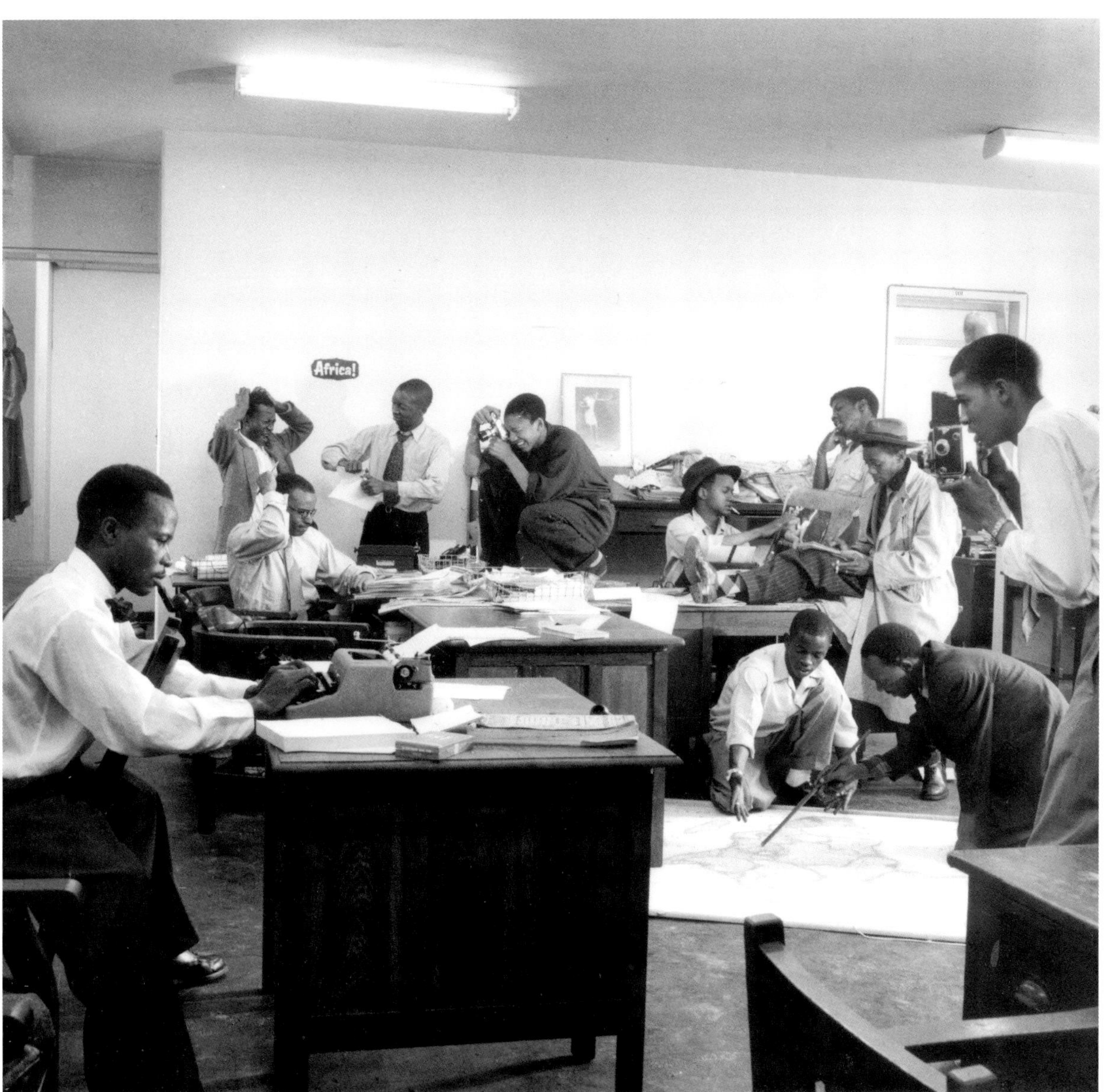
Africa!

a more democratic political representation was part of the zeitgeist.
Documentary photo-essays appeared in European and American maga-
zines including *Vu*, *Illustrated*, *Picture Post* and *Life*, and their liberal bent
was echoed in projects such as 'straight' photography of the American
school. Coinciding with a moment when South Africa's urban centres
were flush, there was a wartime exodus of sophisticated picture editors,
designers and photographers from Germany, bringing new notions,
editorial skills and styles with them.

Drum magazine, directed towards a local sophisticated black urban
readership, was a product of these international influences. Under the
direction of the photographer Jürgen Schadeberg (b. 1931) who emigrated
from Berlin in 1950, a wave of the first black photographers established
themselves professionally (within the confines of state strictures).[31] The
magazine became an unprecedented venue for the work of black South
African photographers in the 1950s, as well as numerous pioneer writers
and activists. The investigative reportage spotlighted black beauty queens,
boxers, jazz musicians, *tsotsis* (gangsters) and other personalities of South
Africa's urban life. A post-war optimism, coinciding with a period of
relative affluence, created the congenial atmosphere for *Drum*'s forward-
looking inclusiveness, geared towards a new audience of black townships.[32]

Hardening apartheid policies, instigated by the Afrikaner National
Party's 1948 electoral victory, grew more oppressive throughout the
1950s,[33] and Schadeberg noted the threat photographers and journalists
posed to the state:

> During the early 1950s there were virtually no photographers report-
> ing or recording events in the so-called non-white world . . . [and]
> people accepted and welcomed without suspicion the lone photogra-
> pher. Even the authorities . . . were puzzled as to why this crazy man
> bothered to photograph blacks. Only later, in the mid-1950s, did it
> become more difficult to record political events. When police were
> present . . . black photographers were often beaten up and arrested.[34]

A number of significant photographers and writers came through *Drum*'s
ranks, photographers including Schadeberg, Peter Magubane (b. 1932),

Bob Gosani (1934–1972), Alf Khumalo (b. 1930), G. R. Naidoo, Ian Berry (b. 1934) and Ernest Cole (1940–1990).[35] Apart from documenting political meetings, they illustrated the commonplace: nightlife in township shebeens (underground drinking clubs which flourished as the right to associate freely was curtailed), and the glamour embodied in a burgeoning entertainment scene rising in the country.[36] In writings and photojournalism, *Drum* took on as much as was possible, showing people protesting the structures and restrictions of hardening apartheid policies: boycotts, trials, church sit-ins, demonstrations concerning Sophiatown resettlements. Yet the more troubling, investigative images of *Drum* photographers were published only with difficulty, including portrayals of pervasive township violence, the absurdist transportation system, the brutality of the prison labour system, the working conditions on farms, and the pass system. Bob Gosani's images of a naked prisoner doing a *tausa* 'monkey' dance (a method of body searches at Johannesburg's 'Number Four' prison for black men) assault standards of decency, but were particularly searing in tandem with journalist Henry Nxumalo's reportage of his five days in prison, describing larger systems of prisoner abuse. *Tsotsis* were emblems of rising crime resulting from displacement, lack of school and underemployment, and they were illustrated as stylized well-dressed gangsters partying in *shebeens*, ambiguous models of modern audacity and ruthlessness. Reportage sometimes resulted in changes, as with 'Number Four' prison's improvement for a time. It also inspired its audiences: amongst the magazine's erudite black audience were African National Congress (ANC) members who created the Freedom Charter (before the contributing parties were banned), and those who rallied at the 1952 Defiance Campaign. Yet *Drum* reportage could only be subtly critical in the face of the new policies, and could not condemn the government or advocate for political parties. Further, its photographers could relay their images to larger and international audiences only with great difficulty, a frustration that plagued photographers for decades to come.[37]

Leon Levson (1883–1968) toiled in near-anonymity for most of his life, but now is recognized as one of the first committed to document black urban working life.[38] Eli Weinberg (Latvia, 1908–1981), a trade

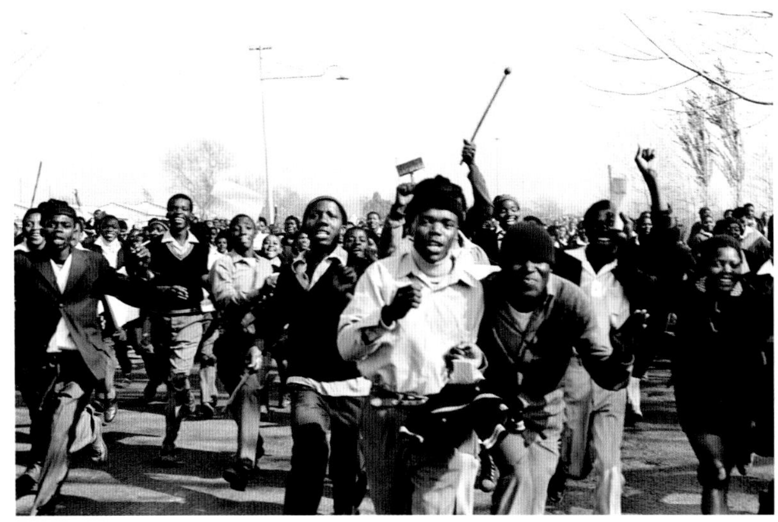

unionist with ties to the ANC, was an equally unrecognized photographer during his day, spending much of his time under house arrest and whose work was banned.[39] Weinberg documented political events such as the work of the Congress Movement until its ban in 1960, the Defiance Campaign, the Treason Trial, and portrayed everyday life under mounting political oppression, as well as making portraits of leaders such as Nelson Mandela and Walter Sisulu. Two banned books were published just before his death in exile: *Portrait of a People* (1981) and *Unity in Action* (1982). *Portrait* was contraband in the country, and it comprised a hallmark of documentary photography that inspired a generation of activist photographers.[40]

Peter Magubane, like many notable photographers of this era, periodically dropped from view as a result of harassment, banning and imprisonment. He had apprenticed at *Drum*, and later worked for newspapers documenting events of historic importance: the 1960 Sharpeville Massacre, the 1965 Women's March on Pretoria and the Treason Trial (1958). Magubane also rendered the political in quotidian life, documenting the living and working conditions of urban blacks making do under the shade of apartheid. In 1963, a Johannesburg gallery exhibited his work, and although the government prevented him from showing

previously published news photographs, he achieved some measure of
fame as the first black photographer to exhibit his work in the country.[41]
In 1969 Magubane was banned and arrested, spent nearly two years in
prison, and was then banned for another five years from taking photographs.[42] Among his most formidable depictions are those of domestic
life in the huge township of Soweto and the 1976 riots there, photographs
for which he was again imprisoned. He commented on the perilous
reality of black photojournalists at the time:

> By the 1970s nearly all the adult black politicians had been detained
> or jailed and their parties outlawed. This may explain why the riots
> that broke out in Soweto in June [1976] involved mostly children . . .
> I photographed such things as policemen firing at students carrying
> signs protesting the fact that they had to learn Afrikaans in school,
> students burning cars . . . This went on for several days. It was diffi-
> cult to work as a photographer in the township. The police do not
> like to see people taking pictures when they are shooting . . . The
> students too, at least at first, used to resent being photographed.
> I and my black colleagues were beaten . . . by both sides.[43]

Around the same time, a young Ernest Cole also saw the necessity of documenting apartheid's realities for a broader audience, but he eventually
concluded that the medium was futile to convey subversive ideas within
the systems of his native state. Cole tirelessly worked to depict the field
of vision particular to South Africa, divided into restricted white cities
and native Bantustans (territory set aside for black people) that effectively rendered non-white South Africans illegal in their own country.
Children cared for babies as absent parents travelled great distances to
work in cities; labelled park benches relegated blacks to the kerbs; the
ill curled under beds and on the steps of overcrowded hospitals. Cole's
images turn unblinkingly to the public surfaces of social separation:
its restrictive signs, segregated park benches, the long queues of people
waiting to renew their passbooks. Cole also worked subversively, taking in
the more shocking sights hidden from the ruling public. He hid cameras,
used decoys and managed to fade into the background like one of his

models, Henri Cartier-Bresson, waiting to capture those tellingly decisive moments in unprecedented breadth.[44]

Like a few of his generation, Cole illustrated the conditions of the forced migrant labour systems that the establishment of 'homelands' necessitated, and put faces on the victims of township crime burgeoning with the displacement, forced removals, and broad insecurity of police harassment and violence. His work was so troubling that he began to think of his photography as part of an effort to end South Africa's ever-tightening oppression, and with that, sought to distribute his pictures to international audiences. One point of inspiration was the Civil Rights struggle (1955–68) in the United States, and he worked on getting to the USA in order to publish his book.

> It was [when I started working for *Drum* in 1958] that I became aware of the existence of the UN and the Afro-Asia block, which was strongly attacking South Africa . . . So I decided I could help the outside world by photographing . . . what life was really like [there]. I was of course aware that after finishing it, it wouldn't be possible to remain . . . but didn't care, because this is a chance that . . . all of us have taken if you don't want to live under those miserable conditions . . .
>
> When I started out, I was so far away and South Africa being so isolated [I was convinced] that all the noise [from] the UN was heading somewhere, that they were going to step in and bring about some change. But in coming away I found that it was just one of the topics on the UN's agenda, that it was up to us there to bring about change . . . I think [my photographs can] be useful, even if it's not for the UN, but for our children, it's evidence. It's of course not possible for them to see it now . . .[45]

With police in pursuit, Cole fled the country with his archive of negatives, and eventually made his way to New York. His book *House of Bondage* (1967) was the result of his mammoth undertaking. It was the first published photographic account by a black South African. It contains hundreds of images of people, jarringly anchored in situations that are by turns slightly and appallingly shocking. Cole's commentary makes

each portrait and scene inextricably linked to the next: teachers overwhelmed by sweating pupils; one of a crowd of street boys in the night,
hands out, stunned by a passerby's slap; a stand of patient and uncertain
recruits waiting processing in mining camps. Cole's portraits of middle-
class educated blacks, women in hats and shades speaking up at meetings
and political conferences belie the photographer's pessimism: he noted
that their efforts to prepare for a multiracial democratic society further
alienated Afrikaners, and as peacemakers or leaders 'leading the blacks
out of bondage . . . the river is wide and there is no bridge to cross'.[46] Yet
his portrait of the larger-than-life ANC president Albert Luthuli and his
wife, en route to Oslo to receive the Nobel Peace Prize in 1960, is very
much one of these images. The serious man, gazing directly at the camera
as he glanced from his paper, brow furrowed, is far from monumental,
yet its weight is forceful for viewers who recognize Luthuli's role internationally, and his isolation and banishment at home. *Bondage* ends
with his most austere images, those of people who have been banished,
a form of political punishment. They are whisked away to live in remote
areas of the veldt, and left. Brutally lit skies and barren lands overwhelm
Cole's subjects, utterly isolated, haunted with worry about families left
behind, cut off from the world.

House of Bondage was banned in his country, as Cole predicted it would
be. Cole remained isolated and lonely in the USA, and the *New York Times*
executive editor, Joseph Lelyveld, noted:

> Exile meant the surrender of his creative obsession. Perhaps in ten
> or twenty or thirty years he would be able to go back to it. But now
> he was through on his own . . . he was free and that was something,
> but he was also stranded.[47]

Cole died in New York in 1990 on the day Nelson Mandela was released
from prison.

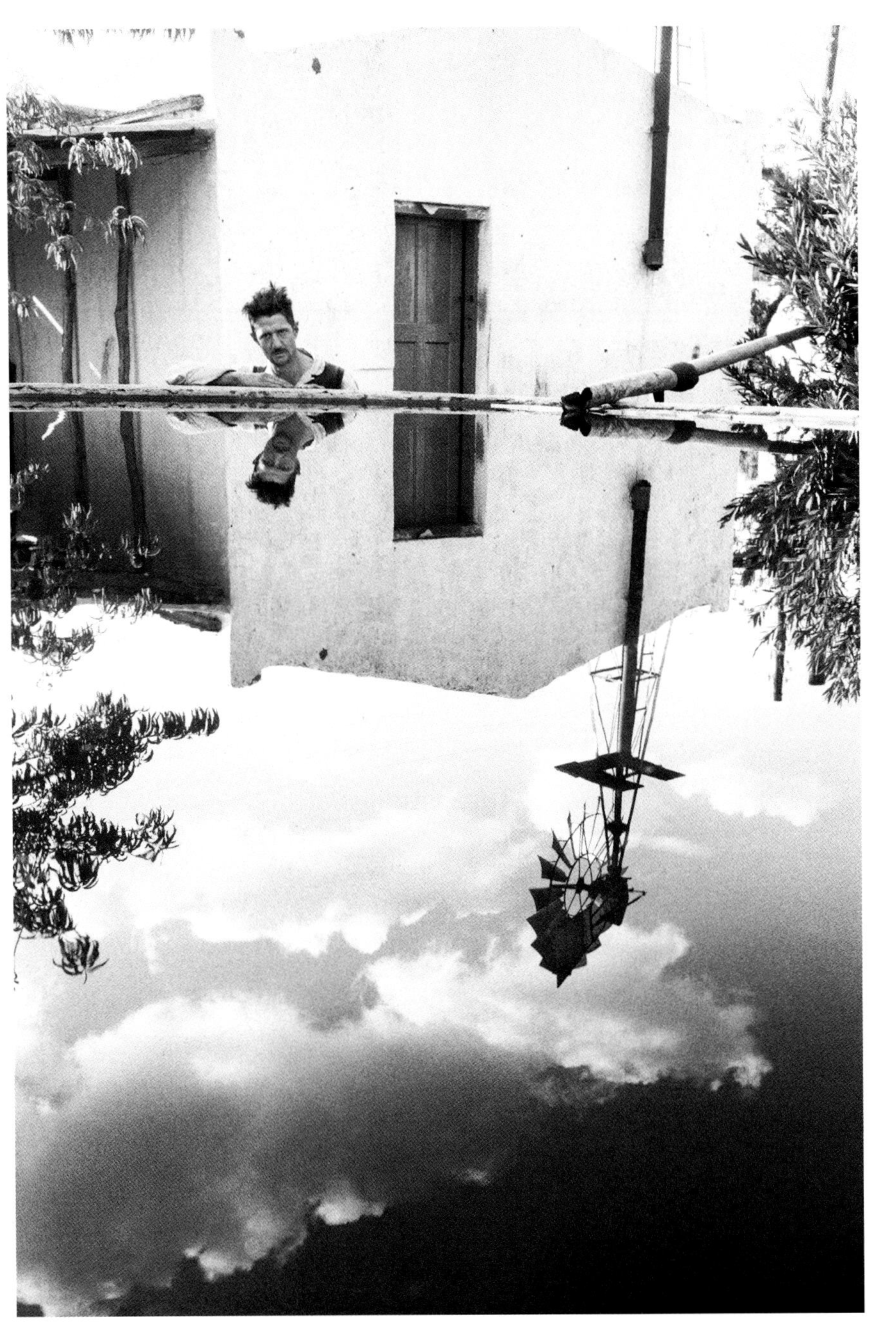

Shifting Approaches

Some white photographers who were contemporaries of Gosani, Magubane and Cole had more room to manoeuvre as photographers within the country, and had greater access to international markets. Ian Berry (b. England, 1934) was eighteen when he arrived from the UK, and later was working for *Drum* when he captured the height of police violence during the 1960 Sharpeville Massacre. These images were landmarks, the only ones to capture the massacre as it unfolded, and these were used later in a trial to prove the innocence of those slain. Shortly after, he left South Africa, moving alongside a large exodus of liberal whites moving to the UK, and there he joined the Magnum photo agency.[48]

These early documentary photographers were aware that a corpus of documentation, more so than a few potent images, was more able to convey the breadth and character of this political oppression, and to allude to, if not directly illustrate, its underlying ideologies. They recorded situations that in essence became publicly-owned facts, which under ideal circumstances were seen and distributed widely enough that they were considered to embody a fundamental social problem.[49] That many images could not get distributed or seen until well after they were taken, along with the reality of South Africa's international isolation, meant that photographs as social facts were considered tangible-enough evidence of a threat by photographers, their subjects, and the government intent on controlling imagery. Yet as we see, the act of making pictures was not enough, nor was it clear that hurling these images over the walls, into the range of vision of distanced and blinkered white South Africans, would produce significant change either. It was necessary to get images transmitted abroad, but even then, foreign news editors usually referenced the country's situation in terms of single, sensationalistic images.

One South African photographer whose documentary work was initially supported by international clients was David Goldblatt (b. 1930). He worked from the 1960s as a full-time photographer, and his first monograph, *Some Afrikaners Photographed* (1975) featured portraits of those implicated in apartheid's ruling structures. In doing so, he drew attention to precarious notions of the race and class of those in power; this was the

60 David Goldblatt, 'A railway shunter who dreamed of a garden watered by this dam, Koksoord, Randfontein, Transvaal', from the series *Some Afrikaners Photographed*, 1962, black-and-white print.

flip-side to the overtly dramatic imagery of black struggle. Goldblatt's subjects, in image and word, are full of stubborn contradictions:

> I wanted to understand the character of the people who could pro-
> duce a policeman who would sjambok (bullwhip) a black child one
> day, only to dive into a raging stream to save his life the next.[50]

Goldblatt maintains that his curiosity extends to the choices that people make for themselves within this system, and he uses his camera both as a means to explore his world and as the occasion for such explorations.[51] His work attends to everyday actions and views; his titles and framing mark their particularities to ensure they do not stand for any kind of whole. Mentioning his connection to writers such as Nadine Gordimer, Goldblatt's work encompasses the particular and the detailed, gestures and landscapes and events which register as images and scenes within a particular context.[52] Nevertheless, the political pervades his formidable expanse of projects: relentless and careful cataloguing of South Africa's regions and cityscapes, mine shafts and billboards. The photo-essay *The Night Riders of KwaNdebele* (1983–4) documented the five- and six-hour commutes that removed people working in Pretoria forcibly endured under the Bantustan separationist policy.[53] Goldblatt has also documented the wretched living conditions of migrant mine workers, and more recently, the built environment and landscapes after the fall of apartheid.[54] With Magubane and Schadeberg, Goldblatt has been an instrumental mentor for a younger generation of photographers; he has worked alongside this younger generation of photographers who began to organize themselves along very different lines.

If the early generation of activist photographers worked in relative isolation, the most violent years of apartheid following the 1976 Soweto riots also produced an efflorescence of creative political expression, wherein artists of all stripes, as 'cultural workers', committed in new ways to the struggle. In June 1982, the Botswana National Museum hosted the first collective exhibition of photographers, displayed at the 'Culture and Resistance Festival' who ranged from the formidable Goldblatt to many younger photographers. As a result of this meeting, some younger participants formed the Afrapix Collective in Johannesburg in 1980, with early members including Omar Badsha, Lesley Lawson, Jimi Matthews, Peter MacKenzie, Mxolise Moyo, Cedric Nunn, Biddy Partridge and Paul Weinberg. Two objectives articulated within the group were the decision to consider documentary photographers as agents of political change, and to serve as an agency and photo library that would encourage new photographers.[55] The catalogue for the 1983 exhibition at the Market Photo Gallery, Johannesburg, *South Africa through the Lens*, included a kind of manifesto on documentary photography in the face of such extreme political conditions:

> The camera doesn't lie. This is a myth about photography in South Africa in the Eighties that we will not swallow. In our country the camera lies all the time – on our TV screens, in our newspapers and on our billboards that proliferate in our townships. Photography can't be divorced from the political, social and the economic issues that surround us daily. As photographers we are inextricably caught up in those processes – we are not objective instruments but play a part in the way we choose to make those statements. [We] show a South Africa in conflict, in suffering, in happiness and in resistance. They examine the present and beckon the viewer to an alternative future . . . Social Documentary Photography is not, in our view, neutral. In South Africa the neutral option does not exist – you stand with the oppressors or against them. The question we pose is how do photographers hit back with their cameras?[56]

One fundamental shift from Afrapix's creation was their work organizing projects and movements that would allow their work and ideas to reach a much broader audience, within the country and outside. Most middle-class whites had access to cameras as a matter of course, but the collective began to create grassroots educational programmes to teaching photography to blacks across the country. With more crackdowns on journalists and photographers, and access to townships increasingly blocked, the thinking was that local community group participants could most effectively document political events and atrocities and find

ways of disseminating the images, becoming a new kind of witness.
Cedric Nunn, one of the young self-taught photographers who came
out of this movement, remembers the project as teaching a visual literacy,
a means to critically assess and analyse the imagery produced by the
state, and then create photographs that undermined and rejected the
state propaganda's visual logic.[57] Santu Mofokeng, Humphrey Phakade
'Pax' Magwaza, Judas Ngwenya and Rashid Lombard were other black
photographers who began with Afrapix's 'Each One Teach One' educational initiative.[58]

Activist photographers' clarion call, that the medium could never
be innocent or neutral, led to some increasingly militant approaches.
The apartheid regime feared any image that suggested revolt and heavily
censored the papers, radio and its television station, creating legislation to
even more thoroughly suppress freedom of expression, most profoundly
during the states of emergency in 1985, 1986 and 1988. Photographers
responded by focusing on the most troubling of images, which they
called 'morally honest propaganda'.[59] Subject trumped approach, and
an anti-aesthetic came into play: 'With all respect due to technical
competence, militant photography should be free from all aesthetic
bonds and concern itself only with the force of its social impact.'[60]
Despite their efforts, for much of the turbulent 1980s such disturbing
images of brutality only occasionally were seen abroad, and almost
never within the country.[61]

Getting images disseminated outside the country was increasingly
urgent. London became a political and cultural centre of resistance
after liberal white South Africans began to migrate there in the 1970s.
Craig Matthews and Cliff Bestall filmed what was later referred to as
the Trojan Horse incident on 15 October 1985, where police hid themselves in crates on the back of a police truck, waited for kids to throw
stones at the truck, then shot some children who were around the
scene. Matthews and Bestall, as with other photographers, tended
to take films and videos directly from an incident to the airport for
posting abroad.[62]

Twenty photographers who received a grant in 1983 to document the
effects of poverty on the country, later exhibited and published in *The*

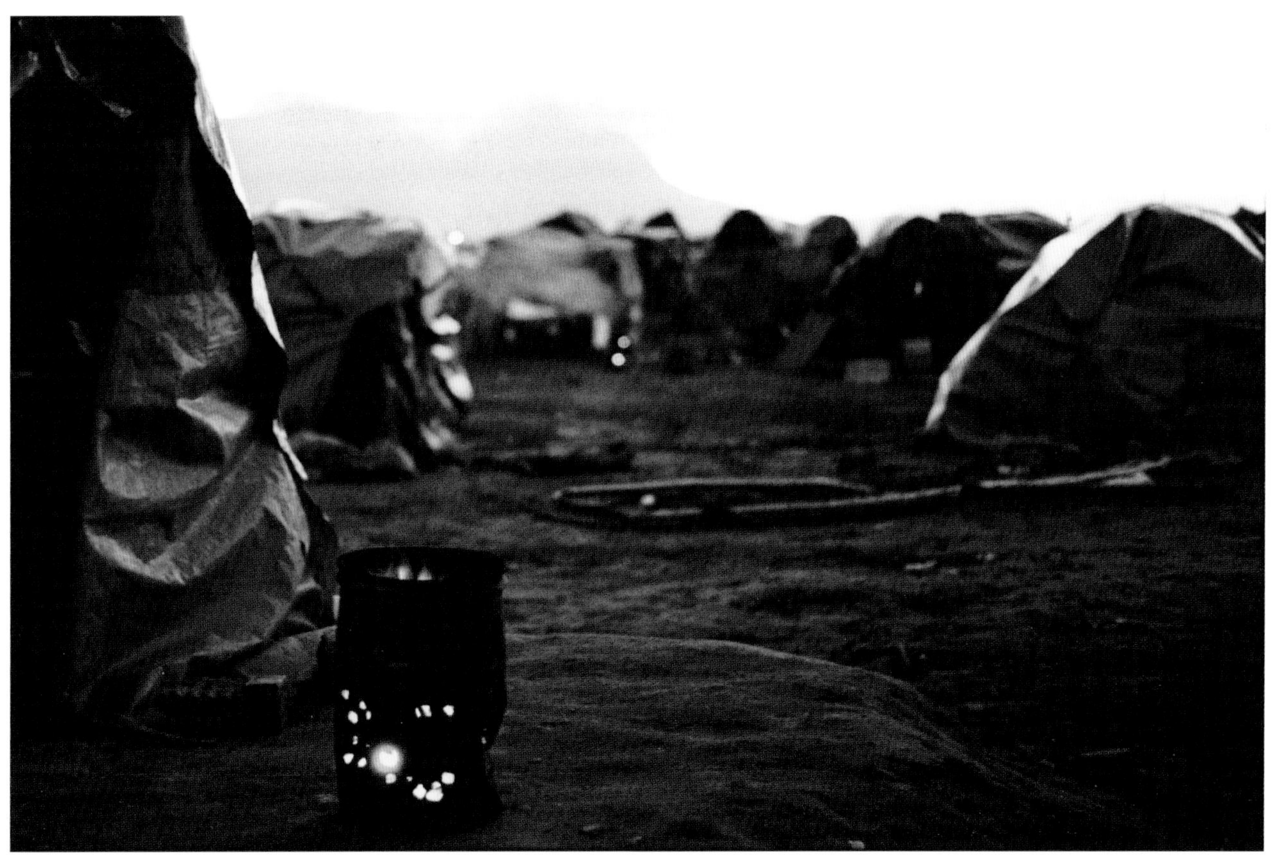

61 Chris Ledochowski, *Plastic Shelters, Memani's Camp, KTC Squatter Camp, Guguletu, Cape Town*, 1983, black and white photograph.

Cordoned Heart (1986), edited by Omar Badsha.[63] These images revealed the extent of rural and urban impoverishment, and indicted the political and social systems in much the same way the photographs of the Farm Security Administration (FSA) project documented systemic poverty in America in the 1930s. Essays were integral to each set of images. The exhibition showed at the University of Cape Town, and toured to London and extensively within the USA.

Cordoned Heart photographers scrutinized the steady deterioration of workers' conditions since Cole's day. Chris Ledochowski's *Plastic Shelters* (above) make the conditions recorded in the 1950s look robust by comparison. The Western Cape and Cape Town had long been claimed

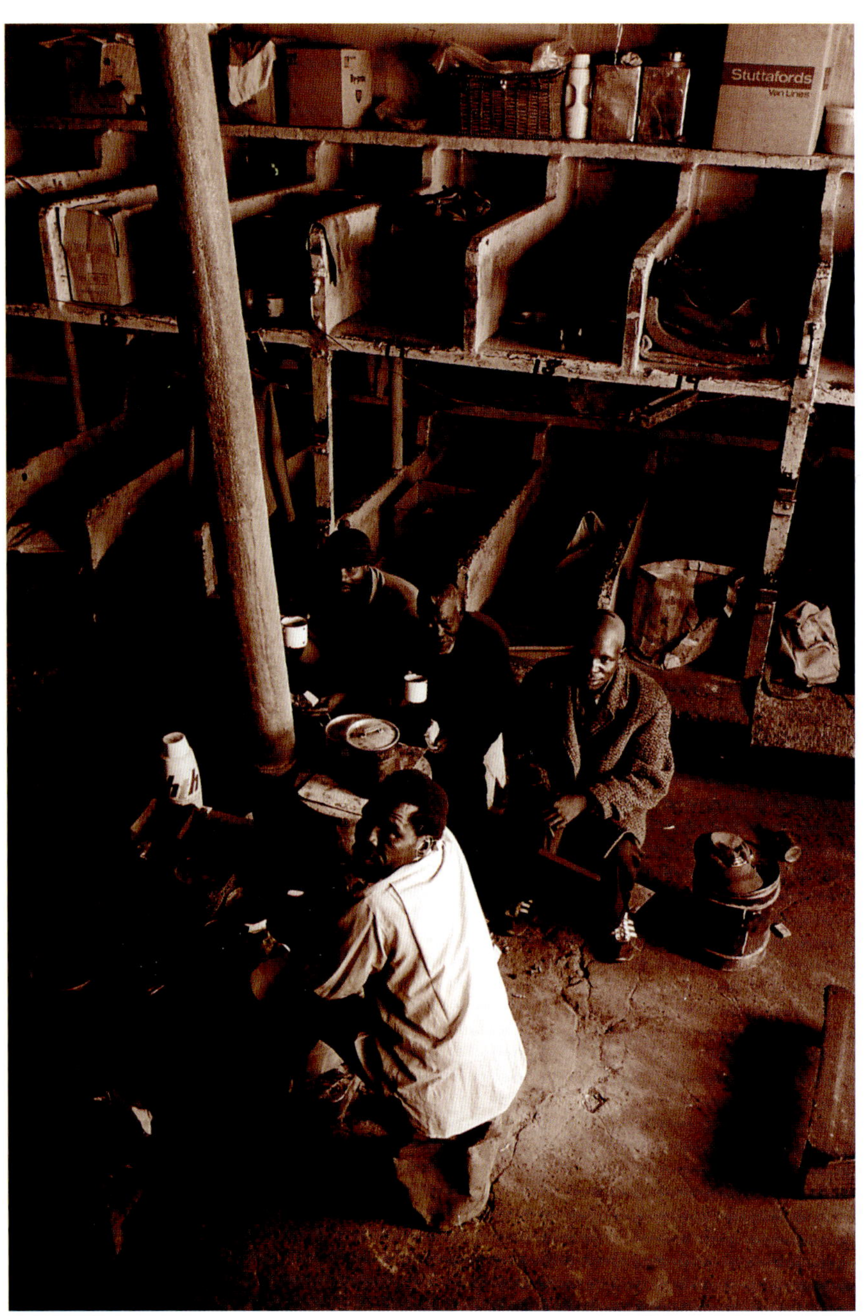

as exclusively white districts, and efforts to keep Africans out of the area were renewed with the Afrikaner National Party's ascendancy in 1948. As the population of Cape Town swelled, so did the demand for labour, and township population exploded. Long-established black and coloured Cape families built houses in a township named Crossroads, but eventually squatter camps grew alongside it, as people refused to suffer massive migration, life in labour barracks or reserves, and the division of their families. Although the government threatened for years to bulldoze the area – as they had other towns nearby – the settlement proved enduring. After years of organizing, the government finally relented and let the community build. Ledochowski's *Crossroads* (1984) attends to the makeshift fragility of these temporary structures, engineered for quick dismantling each morning before the day's police raids.[64]

The contents of one's house suggest, at some level, the extent to which its inhabitants have reprieve from struggling to survive, and so Ben Maclennan's 1980 image opposite of a labourers' compound provides another affront to a system based on exploitation. Four miners in Johannesburg draw together around a stove, interrupted by the photographer. Rows of 60 x 180 cm concrete slot beds are the spaces leased to miners, on contracts of several months. The constant stream of desperate cheap male labour meant there was no incentive for the company to improve the conditions of its barracks. The scene profoundly captures the pervasive phenomenon of workers' social estrangement; in the case of miners, they were prevented by law from living with their families. But mining was a major source for employment, such that two out of five urban men were forced by economic necessity to live away from home.[65]

The approach of *Cordoned Heart* did more than draw attention to the scope and the costs of the country's immense inequalities. Many photographers were coming to terms with the visual and ethical problems of presenting an unrelenting stream of images of poverty. Even though others before them had documented organized political resistance, *Cordoned Heart* presented people organizing in localized political spheres in the effort to combat larger systematic poverty. In doing so, it highlighted the activist imperative of photographers working in tandem with democratic movements.

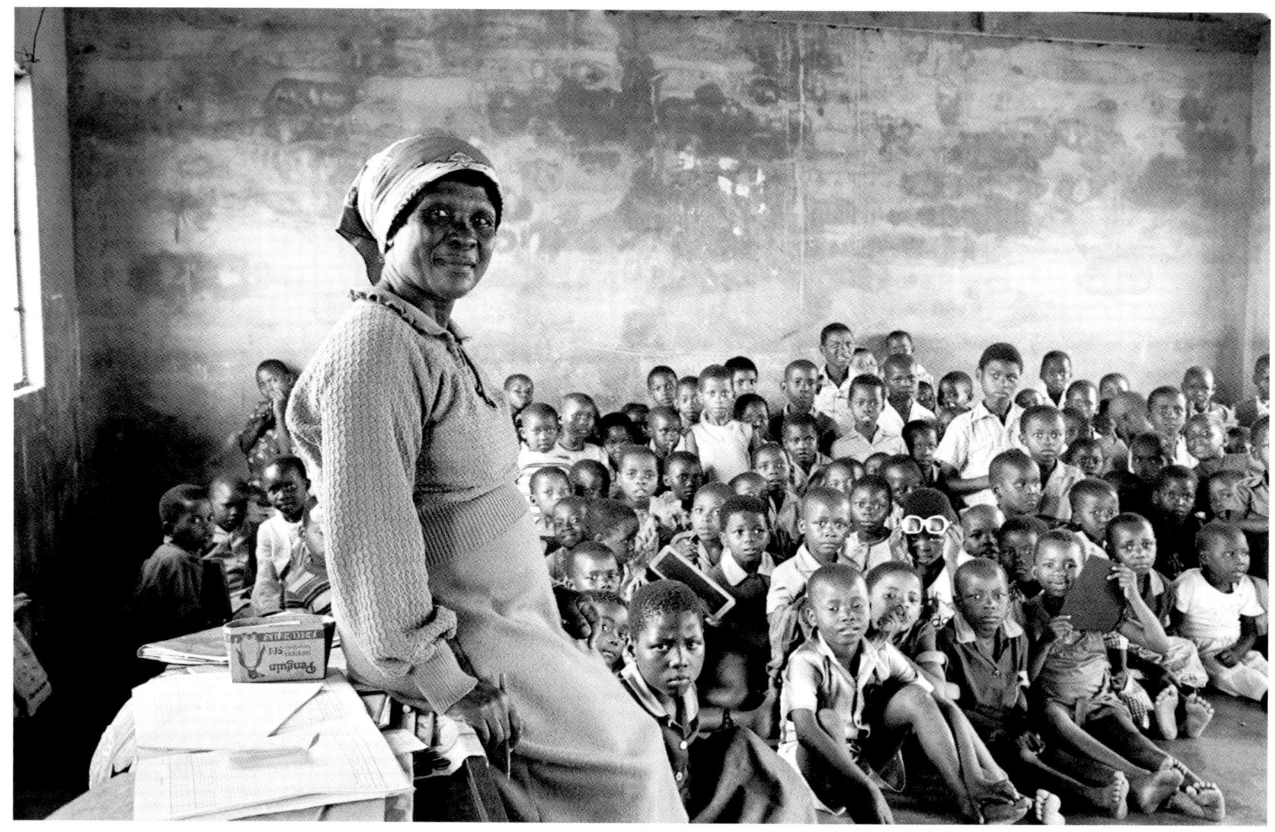

Such is the case with Omar Badsha's work depicting people in the settlements of Inanda, a township of 300,000 outside of Durban. His subjects are subdued; there are mundane views of speakers addressing crowds at resident meetings, juxtaposed with women reinforcing the walls of their houses with another layer of earth. Badsha brought views of poverty into close range, unspectacularly. One foregrounds a persevering teacher, crowded by pupils who overfill the frame, while highlighting a classroom bereft of supplies or furniture. Educational poverty, like other institutionalized deprivation, hid in plain sight. Physical, geographical separation meant that the majority of white South Africans had little sense of the human costs of apartheid's logic, the systematic creation of second-class citizens deprived of infrastructure, with education as ideological programming.[66]

63 Omar Badsha, *Teacher with a Class of Eighty Children, Inanda, KwaZulu, Natal*, 1983, black-and-white photograph.

Next came Afrapix's large-scale project *Beyond the Barricades: Popular Resistance in South Africa in the 1980s* (1989). Photographers including Paul Weinberg, Chris Ledochowski, Lesley Lawson, Rashid Lombard, Rafik Mayet, Jeeya Rajgopaul, Paul Alberts, Santu Mofokeng, Gideon Mendel, Gille de Vlieg, Anna Zieminski and many others documented the long and particularly bloody period of resistance during the states of emergency. Theirs is a catalogue of violent and peaceful demonstrations, military and police action, mourners and funerals. They encapsulate the potential of the photographs as 'part of collective memory that stands against the government's efforts to blot out our history [of resistance]'. They constituted evidence: 'irrefutable documentation of popular resistance and state brutality . . . instrumental in bringing the South African struggle to the international arena.'[67]

The threat photographers presented to the establishment was such that photographers were branded as instigators of insurrection and terrorism.[68] During the states of emergency, (roughly 1985–90) government crackdowns became increasingly severe as Pieter Willem Botha's government (1978–89) tried to eliminate all opposition; photographers were particular targets for government oppression, and new laws attempted to control every journalist's movements and production.[69] *Beyond the Barricades* was the war photography of undeclared battles, and the title makes it clear that people were beginning to see the endgame, trying to envision a post-apartheid South Africa. In 1987, the largest anti-apartheid festival was held in Amsterdam with the exhibition *The Hidden Camera: South African Photography Escaped from Censorship (De Verborgen Camera)*. It included the work of 32 photographers and also circulated smaller shows for younger photographers, making galleries of South African community halls, churches, worker conferences and the like. By this time, an anti-aesthetic of raised fists of resistance, dramatically angled lines of coffins and mourners, smoke-filled skies, barbed wire and attack dogs, and the dignified faces of protestors formulated a dependable visual refrain. The goal of the political camera was again reformulated, hoping to encourage a community workshop tradition that 'demystifies the technological aura surrounding photography; decentralises the control of photography; empowers people to record and document their own experiences, lives and histories'.[70]

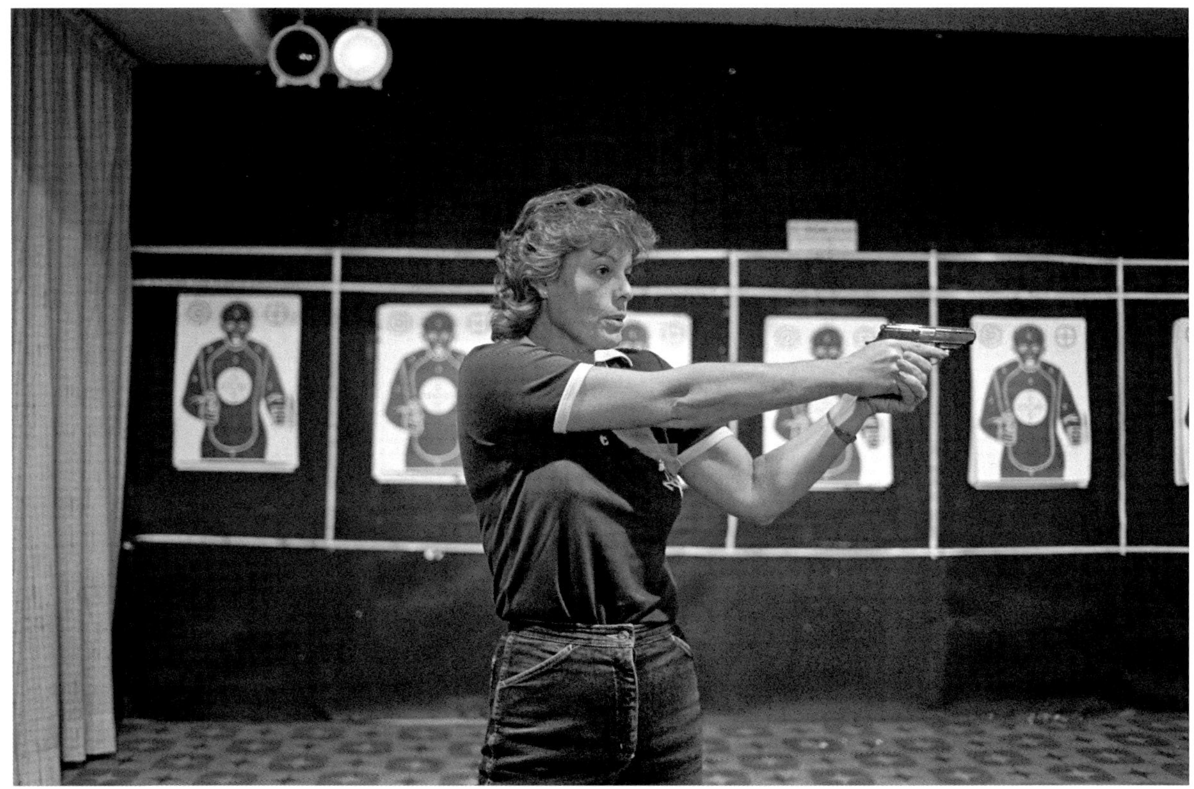

Established photographers' work was shown with new frontline activists, and images revealed an attention to a broader base, and the subtler envisioning of the struggle. Lesley Lawson trained her lens on circles of white South Africa less commonly seen, as in *Shooting Range, Johannesburg.* As with her other images, she examines violence and the shows of force that were required to maintain the status quo in South Africa.

Like Lawson's image, several works by Paul Weinberg renew familiar vision in the arena of white domesticity. His portraits are often contemplatively constructed, for example *'Priscilla Biyana . . .'* (opposite). Mrs Biyana looks up from her dishwashing, framed by a view of her white employer's immaculate sun-soaked garden grounds; a thick wall separates the view of her employer lingering over breakfast and a paper,

64 Lesley Lawson, *Shooting Range, Johannesburg*, 1987, black-and-white print.

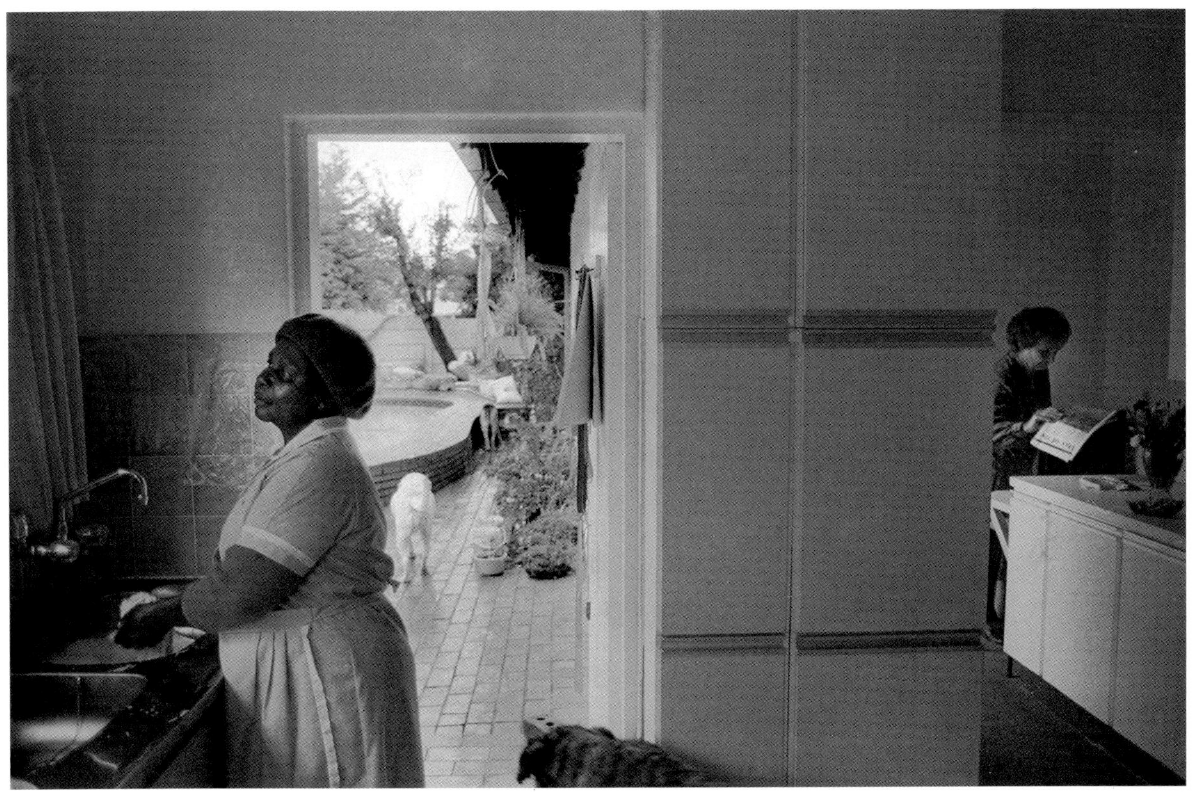

oblivious to the photographer. Even when broaching these oppositions in intimate social scale, Weinberg's attentive composition draws us into an interior moment, reinforcing the sense of politicized time and place.

Gille de Vlieg's *We Starve in Rural Areas* (illus. 66) is one moment in the steady stream of civic peaceful protest, in this case for South African Women's Day. This demonstrator, surrounded by abundant stacks of rice and boxes of soap, delivers her message and commemorates the day three decades earlier, when women marched to Pretoria to protest against carrying passbooks, the law that would prevent them from coming to cities to look for work. The woman's statement, her straightforward moment of confrontation and the day within a timeline of political protest, are all of a piece. Campaigns against the government were widespread by that point, with international pressure building steam;

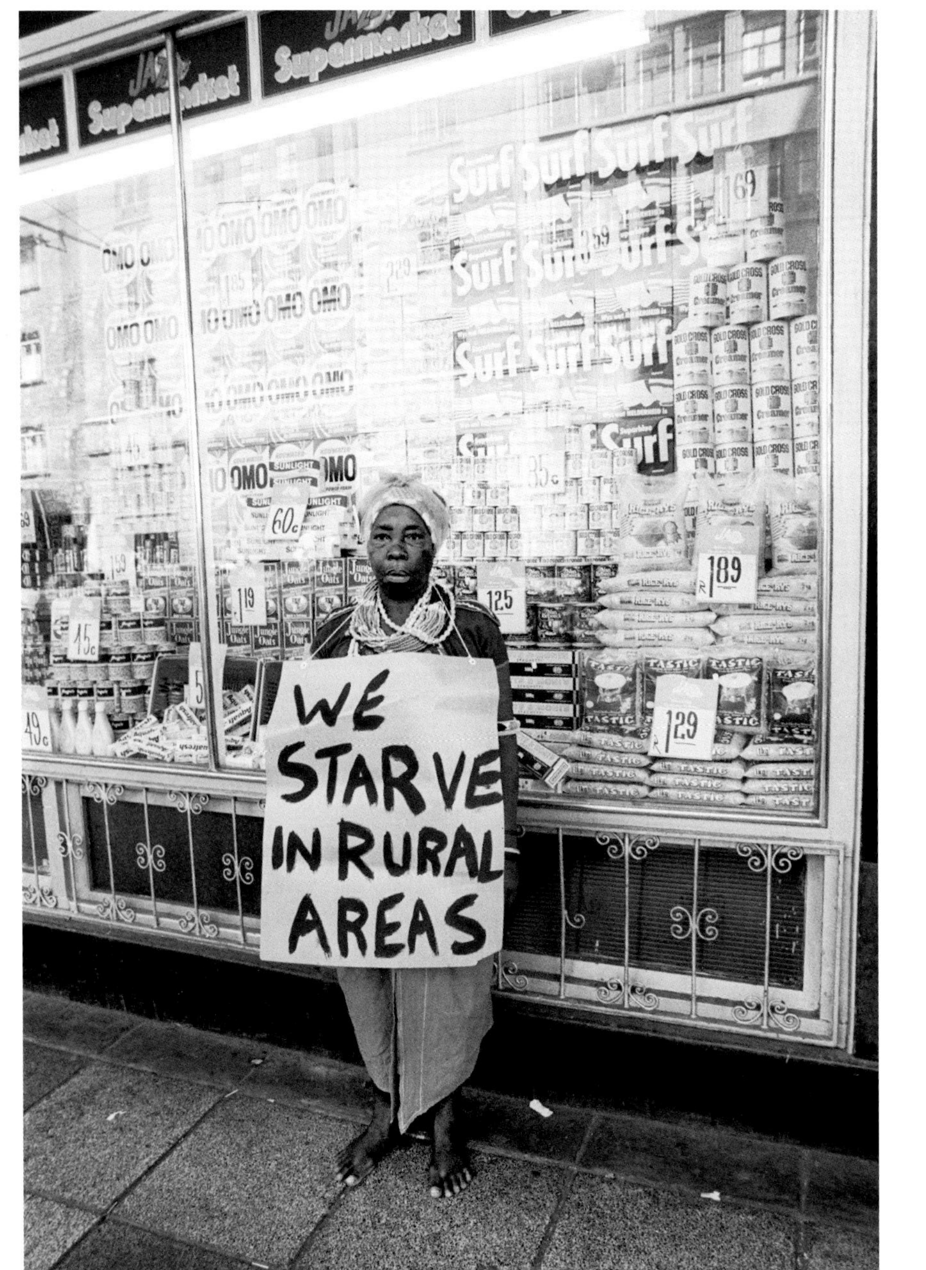
WE
STARVE
IN RURAL
AREAS

a few years later, the campaigns waged by photographers, artists, writers and activists of every age and stripe were slowly coming to fruition.

With apartheid's fall and the country's first democratic elections in 1994, the documentary imperative changed tracks, and photography's possibilities as a creative medium with a limitless range of subject and aesthetic possibilities gained force.[71] The past five decades of resistance photography forged some of the world's most notable and tenacious photographers; many of them have moved towards more personal projects, while others continue to document the continent's most troubled areas, carrying on in an activist mode predicated on documentary photography's potency.[72]

four

Painting, Printing and Photography

Photography's introduction across the continent was never a matter of simple importation: foreign technologies were constantly adapted and taken up in ways that suited African local and cosmopolitan frames of perception and usefulness. Photographers of the nineteenth and twentieth centuries relied on the medium's quality of verisimilitude to convey their subjects as records, whether for official surveillance, didactic purposes, in popular media or as objects of civic and personal memory. The characteristics of photography which have been deemed useful or appealing by photographers, artists, patrons and their audiences on the continent are as much about underlying aesthetic criteria and particularities of political and historical context.

The objects and visual traditions in this chapter, several of which come from west Africa, consider the intersections of photography, portraiture and likeness. In particular, the 'iconicity' of a photograph – its tangibility, its portability, its connection to a lived presence – is transmitted into other forms and materials. It may be that the link to a photographic moment is in some ways as important as the photograph itself. Other examples suggest how select qualities of a photograph are rendered by artists in a number of ways. Verisimilitude is widely considered central to a photograph, yet what is considered to be truthful in a representation turns out to be a rather circumscribed thing. So, different kinds of truths are distilled, and they require a reconsideration of what verisimilitude entails.[1]

These discussions flag photography's ubiquity: the enormous array of means by which photography and its qualities were taken up in a larger creative practice.[2] Considering aspects of painting, oral history, funerary arts, adorned urban environments and even tailored clothing, these examples illuminate the particularities of photography's iconic and veristic capabilities, and their insertion into new visual and performative spaces. Further, they remind us to step back from isolating photography too much, because it has always been interwoven with creative modes across a spectrum of media.

Merina Courtly Portraiture in the Colonial Era

The confluence between painted and photographic portraiture, and royal patronage of European colonial artists in the Merina kingdom poses a number of fascinating questions. The Merina, who consolidated their power over much of Madagascar in the nineteenth century, had their highland court at the capital city, Antananarivo. The court is one of the few places on the continent known thus far where there was an established tradition of painted portraiture in place before the first European photographers arrived. Through the nineteenth century, a procession of French and English artists settled on east Africa's Indian Ocean islands, a result of the region's strategic colonial importance. From Europe came a flow of illustrated press, books, artists, missionaries and colonial institutions comprising a diverse visual economy.[3] In Madagascar, this material was mainly accessible to royalty, local elite and mission-educated people, and painted portraiture traditions were exclusively the prerogative of rulers. So when photography entered onto the scene, Malagasy rulers had long appreciated how evocative and portable portraits were in compelling the attention of distant audiences. Royal Malagasy portraiture suggests that photography's early trajectory was successful only to a degree, in this case driving commissions of painted works for courtly display.

In nearby Port-Louis, Mauritius, the French *lycée* (opened in 1799) had French art instructors, and by 1810, when the colony was transferred to British hands, the renamed Royal College matriculated students from neighbouring islands, India and Indonesia. In Antananarivo, waves of British missionaries set up schools that included instruction in the arts,[4] including the London Missionary Society in 1818 and the Society of Friends in 1867. These institutions brought novel techniques of easel painting to a select cosmopolitan audience.

King Radama I (*r.* 1810–28) was the earliest of Antananarivo royalty to commission a painting. In 1816, while his brothers were attending school in Mauritius, Radama commissioned their portrait from the resident painter Colombet.[5] Pleased with the results, in 1825 Radama asked André Baptiste Copalle, a professor of art at the Royal College, to paint his own likeness. The resulting painting was apparently less than satisfactory to Radama's desires, particularly the rendering of his face, but larger interest in portraiture remained.[6] Other portraits in oil, situated in the palace and painted on the walls of the prime minister's country house, were probably the work of local artists (so far unidentified) who were encouraged by Copalle's visit.[7] By the 1830s, oil paintings apparently were integral to display in the palace. Western emissaries to Antananarivo were aware of the Merina court's history of commissioning local resident painters, and indeed, diplomats and visitors to the royal seat noted local interest in naturalistic painting techniques from the mid-nineteenth century. Before his arrival at Antananarivo, the British missionary William Ellis had gathered that portraits of the French Emperor and Empress were on view at the Antananarivo palace, gifts from French visitors. When Ellis met with Queen Ranavalona I (*r.* 1828–61) in 1856, he followed his French rivals' example by presenting coloured engravings of Queen Victoria and the Prince Consort, and of Windsor Castle.[8]

The appeal of the early royal portraits derived in part from the effect of their brilliance and visibility. By comparison, dark and diminutive early photographs were less than compelling portraits in their own right.[9] Some of the earliest photographs taken at the court were models for oil paintings, notably Ellis's photograph of King Radama II (*r.* 1829–63) taken in 1856. During his return trip to England, Ellis commissioned a painting based on the albumen print portrait he had produced. He described its unveiling in Madagascar in 1862:

> The king and queen came to look at it, and I watched with interest the effect it produced . . . He smiled and looked again and again,

and then came . . . and pressed my hand very warmly, saying, 'I
remember all this', pointing to the different parts of the picture.
He then gazed again and smiled with great satisfaction . . .[10]

The enthusiasm for photography was connected to its possibilities for
even grander portraits in oil: the queen asked for a painting based on
her photograph, while the king went so far as to inquire if the next
painting could be life-size. Photographs captured the density of fine
details, offering lush visions of imported lace and brocades, intricate
embroidery, medals of state and swords, imported furniture and finely
crafted regalia.

An 1862 photographic portrait of Radama II commemorates his
coronation, a collaborative effort between the king and Ellis (illus. 67).
Taken on Ellis's porch as fashioned into a makeshift studio, the king wore
the British field-marshal's uniform given to him by Queen Victoria. On
the table rests a new crown fashioned for the occasion and at his feet is
the plumed hat worn for his coronation. Imported fashions were among
the flow of gifts between European and Antananarivo courts and marked
the display of wealth, but more importantly allude to Radama II's larger
political strategy of creating a more outward-looking and modernizing
kingdom.[11] Paintings of later monarchs, such as a portrait of Queen
Ranavalona III by the British painter Arthur Trevor Haddon, hung in
the palace and were based on carefully arranged photographs that dwelt
on the finery as much as the royal figure herself. The latest European
fashions on display satisfied the prerogatives of majestic iconography:
the photograph was not tinted, but Haddon's portrait shows the queen
in red, a colour reserved for the Merina monarchy.[12]

The Antananarivo monarchy's preference for paintings over photography endured, even as photographic portraits of the rulers and ex-rulers
circulated in Europe, printed as souvenir images and on postcards.[13]
The Malagasy painter Philibert Ramanankirahina was sponsored at the
Ecole des Beaux-Arts in Paris in 1888. He returned to create a series of oil
portraits of Merina rulers from the founder of the kingdom, Andrianam-
poinimerina (*r.* 1787–1810), to Queen Ranavalona II (*r.* 1868–83), of which
the later rulers' portraits were almost certainly based on photographs.

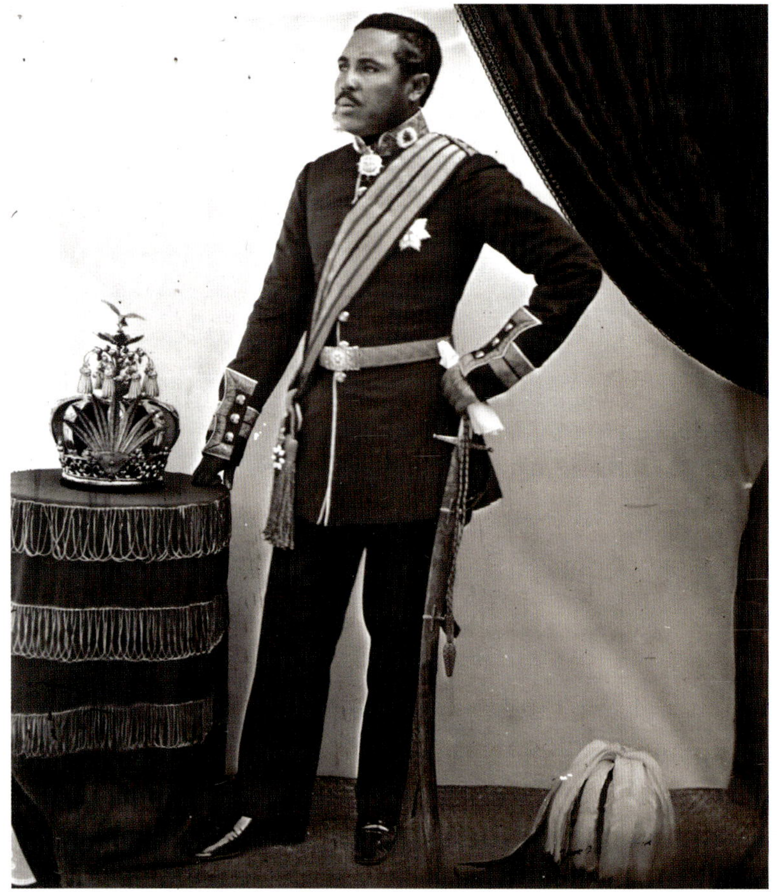

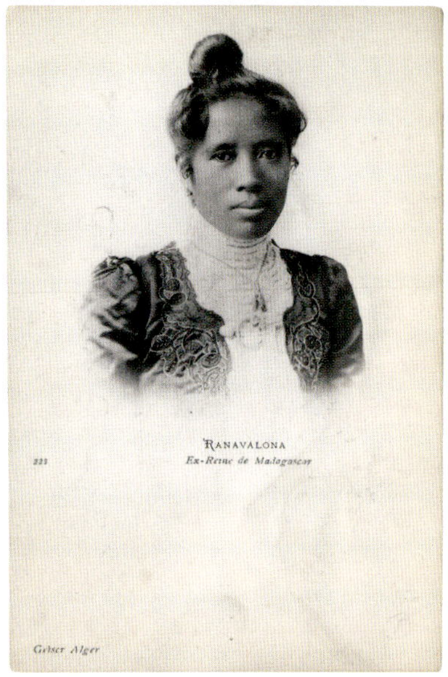

68 Unknown photographer, *Ranavalona. Ex-Queen of Madagascar*, c. 1905, collotype postcard.

67 William Ellis, *Radama II*, *King of Madagascar*, 1862, albumen print from collodion negative.

These were commissioned for and displayed in the palace from 1890.[14] Other Malagasy painters and students trained with foreign artists established on the island, and local elite patronage for these painters hints at this interest. Genre scenes by James Rainimaharonsoa (1860–1926), a missionary-trained painter and lithographer, were adapted from existing photographs he exhibited in the 1905 International Exposition in Paris.[15] Meanwhile, nearly contemporary with the sponsorship of painting students, the first known Malagasy photographers emerged to record important events for the elite, 40 years after the introduction of the medium to the island. One wonders if the royal and elite preference for naturalistic painted portraiture, which for so long held sway, helps account for the rather late emergence and popularity of local portrait studios in Madagascar.

Aina Onabolu's Improvements

Photography's connections with the arts of drawing and easel painting are little understood around most of the continent,[16] but some records illuminate the work of the first known easel-painter of west Africa,[17] Aina Onabolu (Nigeria, 1882–1963). A well-known portrait painter and pioneer educator, Onabolu considered himself a history painter in an era of rising African nationalism. He was self-taught and later received academy training in Europe, wrote about European art-historical subjects and academic painting traditions, and on art pedagogy within the Nigerian colonial education system.[18] Onabolu's was a critical voice on the relationship between painting and photography, defined in part by his position as a west African artist with academic European credentials. His work is imbricated in the emerging artistic culture fashioned by photographic traditions.

As a child, Onabolu taught himself to draw from illustrations and photos in books, newspapers and magazines, images he initially considered the exclusive domain of European production.[19] He attended secondary school in Lagos and stayed with a family friend, J. K. Randle, a prominent nationalist.[20] Despite an education that emphasized 'crafts' rather than drawing, Onabolu trained his eye in verisimilitude and one-point perspective; skills presumed to be inherently superior (and impossible for any African to master) during an era of rising racism within the colonial ranks. He continued to work in this revolutionary manner, or still-life scenes, landscapes and portraits from memory and from photographic models.[21] A 1901 exhibition of Onabolu's drawings in Randle's home may now be considered an early landmark in modern Nigerian art.[22] He quickly won a number of private portrait commissions from middle-class Lagos society.

Onabolu's virtuosity took him to London's St John's Wood School of Art and the Royal Academy of Arts, and to Paris. As a teacher in Lagos, he fomented a significant formal trend of naturalism in early twentieth-century Nigerian artistic practice. In this regard, Onabolu's legacy is controversial: he considered his mastery of pictorial realism and 'European' techniques of painting to be a personal and political rebuke to colonial notions of purported African inferiority. Onabolu wrote:

> the West African Negro has been reproached with his failure to develop any high form of civilization, that he has never painted a picture nor sculpted a statue . . . [I] felt that this was a reproach on the African. I was therefore determined to refute the statement and wipe off the reproach.[23]

On the other hand, Onabolu's adherence to pictorialism was not considered radical by contemporary European standards, or by later Nigerian artists exploring non-representational methods of the art academy.

From early on, Onabolu found that drawing from photographic models did not produce satisfying effects, and he preferred to draw from life, memory and imagination, and encouraged the same in his students. Yet while he asserted the superiority of his painted portraits over photographs, the Lagos milieu of the late nineteenth and early twentieth century already had strong traditions of local portraiture in place that had been shaped by cosmopolitan African photographers and their patrons.

Though an assessment of locally run studios in Lagos – and the photographic record has yet to be completed – it is certain that the city's photographic culture was well-established by Onabolu's early days. Itinerant photographers included J. P. Decker, J. G. Harding, members of the Lutterodt family from the 1870s onwards, and others.[24] Shops such as T. A. King offered cameras, technical books and 'amateur outfits' in Lagos by 1886. N. Walwin Holm of Accra worked on government commissions in the Lagos Colony since 1891 and ran the Adela Portrait Studios in Lagos by 1894, as did T. Maclean Bell in 1899 and George S. A. Da Costa in 1895, and Herzekiah Andrew Shanu trained at the Lagos C.M.S. Grammar School before he opened his studio in Boma, Congo in 1893.[25] Onabolu's subjects would have had something similar in mind when arranging themselves for a modern painted portrait.

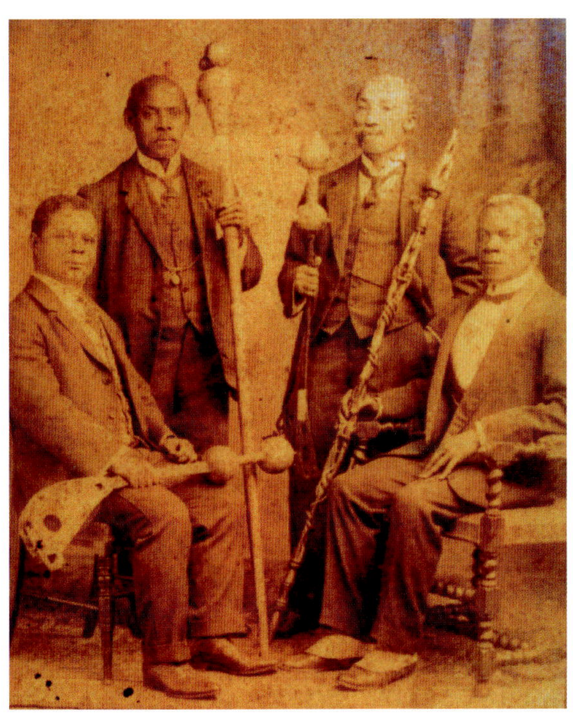

Although the body of Onabolu's work is scattered across family collections, his notes, commentaries and lectures situate the painting and photography of the era. His celebrated position as a portraitist meant that kings, chiefs, celebrities, prominent Africans, missionaries and colonial officials sat for him, earning him the nickname 'Joshua Reynolds'.[26]

Onabolu's work dovetailed with the west African nationalists' use of portrait photography to witness political activism. Imagery of African deputations to London were common from the 1890s on, such as the members of the Gold Coast Aborigines' Rights Protection Society (left), or a 1913 delegation of Nigerian rulers (illus. 70).[27] Onabolu's studies at St John's Wood coincided with a visit of the 1919 West African Congress to London, where some of its delegates visited him and expressed their surprise and delight with his mastery of 'this foreign form'.[28] Onabolu was dismissive of photography, flawed by its rendering of minutiae – wrinkles, veins, stray hairs – whereas his paintings conveyed idealized personages via mood, pose, gesture and gaze.[29] Yet as with photographic portraiture, Onabolu equally amplifed his subjects' place in society, attending to the prestigious embroidered clothing worn by a chief, or the Bible held by a Christian.

As with photographs, Onabolu's portraits were a means of inserting the memory of notable personages into the realm of physical, tangible, visible posterity. Key African and European personalities who worked for nationalist causes and against British colonial rule, pan-Africanists and members of the National Congress of British West Africa, all counted as worthy and inspiring subjects.[30] For Onabolu, their portraits verified their worth within local cultural and political judgments and equally in larger world history, and he considered their portraits to be less particular, more in the genre of history paintings. Unlike oral histories, the 'words written upon the surface of water all of which in a moment vanished away',[31] paint on canvas ensured a more substantial material legacy.

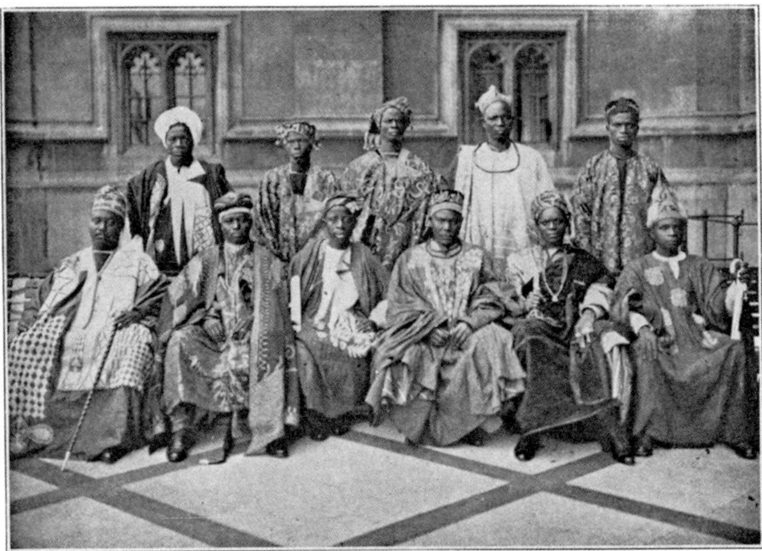

Commissioning a painting was a weighty action, loaded with recognition of ascent into a larger social memory. It is difficult to imagine Onabolu's oeuvre, portraits-as-history, emerging in such sharp relief as idealizing monumental works, without the backdrop of longstanding cosmopolitan photographic traditions.

Gold Coast's Honorary Photographs

Photography's exceptional histories in Africa extend beyond notably early local patronage or the medium's intermingling with other artistic forms. The material manifestations of photographic objects in African collections suggest photography's prominence in certain quarters, and the way in which there is value attached to the ease with which a photograph is transformed and layered by many creators and viewers. Images from nineteenth-century Gold Coast family collections illuminate some of these social and private dimensions in a photograph's unstable existence.[32]

Prosperous trading centres like Accra fostered many wealthy families, such as the Wulff family of Osu, whose fortune in the nineteenth century

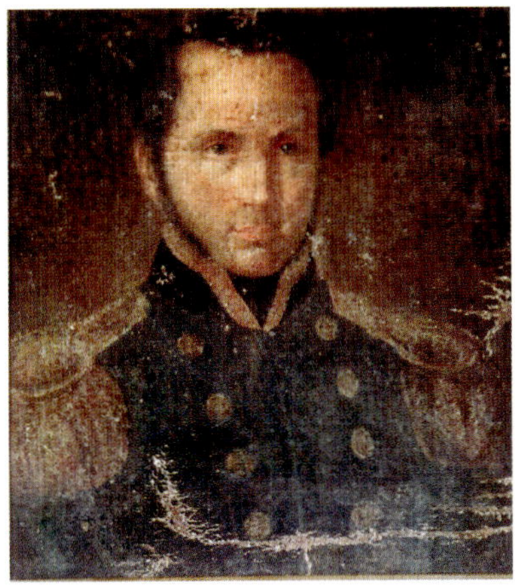
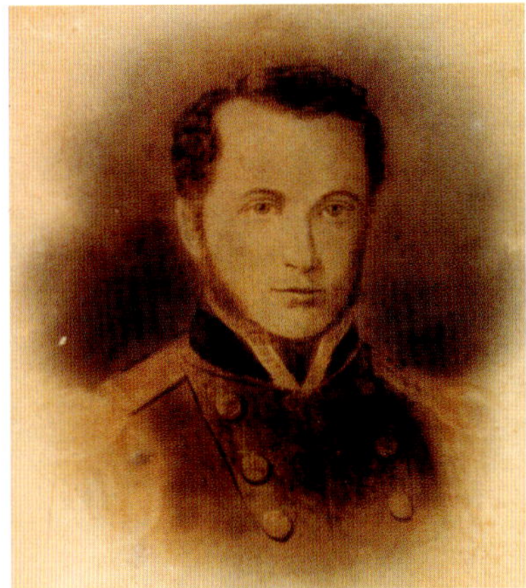
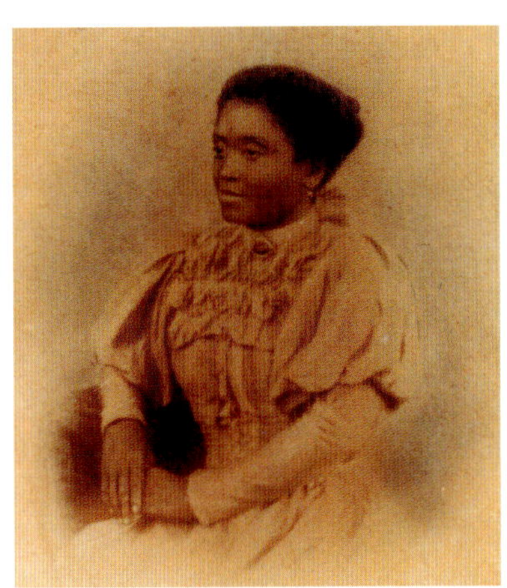

71 David Monies, *W. Joseph Wulff*, 1835, painted portrait.

72 Unknown photographer, *W. Joseph Wulff*, c. 1890, unknown media.

73 Unknown photographer, *Florence Wulff*, c. 1890, unknown media.

derived from trading and plantations. W. Joseph Wulff was a Danish trader who settled in Osu in 1836, married into a prominent Afro-Danish family, and started a family in the house he built near the trading fort. After he died, Wulff's portrait, painted in Denmark in 1835, was sent to his Accra family, and presently it hangs in his house, in which some of his descendants live, and is surrounded by photographic portraits of Wulff descendants. Another branch of the Wulff family descendants keep a collection of ancestral portraits, among them is another version of this painted W. Joseph Wulff portrait (illus. 72). While it appears to be done in charcoal and wash, its owners referred to it as a photograph.[33] Formally, it echoes the appearance of his granddaughter's photographic portrait made around that time, *c.* 1890, in its large scale (40 x 50 cm), vignette format, muted tones and soft edges (illus. 73). This creation of a forbearer's portrait relies on the verisimilitude of the Danish painting, and also its iconic connection to the lived presence of W. Joseph Wulff. It has been deliberately created to reflect the photographic style and iconography of the other family portraits, matching the subtle framing and printing techniques of an Accra photographic studio in the 1890s. While it is certainly not another painting, and probably not a photograph *of* the painting, it is based on a portrait from a pre-photographic era and incorporated into the modes of photographic portrait display within elite family houses in the last quarter of the nineteenth century.

Two portraits of Joseph Wulff's sons (right), dating from the 1880s,
have been adjusted towards entirely different reasons and ends. The
durability of different printing techniques is obvious for the two roughly
contemporary images: the clarity of the carbon print process contrasts
with the crayon portrait, a faintly printed photographic likeness over
traced with charcoals or pastels. Others in the Wulff family collections
are in various states of disrepair. The story of these assembled nineteenth-
century portraits, ranging in manufacture over the course of 60 years,
highlights some of the problems of photographic qualities, and the ways
in which owners have addressed them. There is the ongoing problem of
impermanence in tropical conditions:[34] the more recent photographs are
not in a better shape, and one needs a durable photographic print (if
the negative's long lost) in order to reproduce and disseminate ancestral
photographs among family branches. So the creative interventions to
preserve, protect, repair and disseminate the oldest photographs include
a variety of media, enacted by a number of creators and owners beyond
photographic studios. Underlying this is the significance of the medium
of photography, including these layered intercessions, which are central to
the display of family history in private spaces.

The means of preserving photographic imagery may extend beyond
the photographic plane entirely, as is the case with the painted portrait
of J. M. Cooke, a title-holder in Cape Coast from 1929 to 1962. It is a particularly compelling rendering of a photograph, painted on board, and in
its scale, clarity and durability, has overcome some of the shortcomings
of its photographic antecedent. It is large, yet kept hidden away in the
private rooms of the Ebiradze royal family house. No one remembered
who commissioned it, but the artist, in keeping to monochrome, suggests
that this work has entered the ranks of an honorary photograph.[35] As
with many other kinds of interventions on photographs, their derivations
and iterations, the owners and viewers of these old photographs change
the qualities of an image and of its many receptions. They are, in effect,
creative audiences. So the boundaries between artist and owner, photographer and subject, and photograph and milieu must be redefined
to consider these creative practices in all their expansiveness.

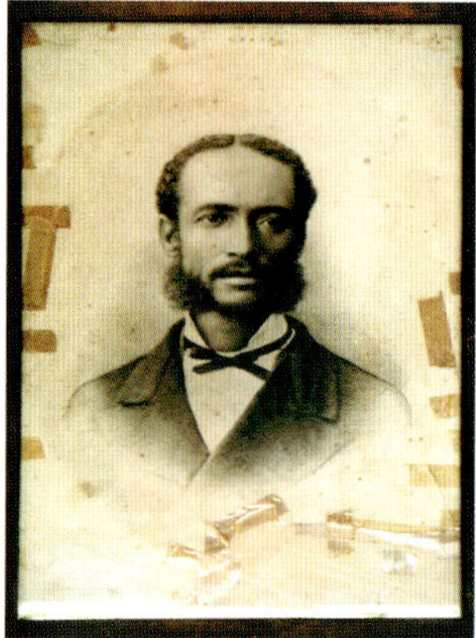

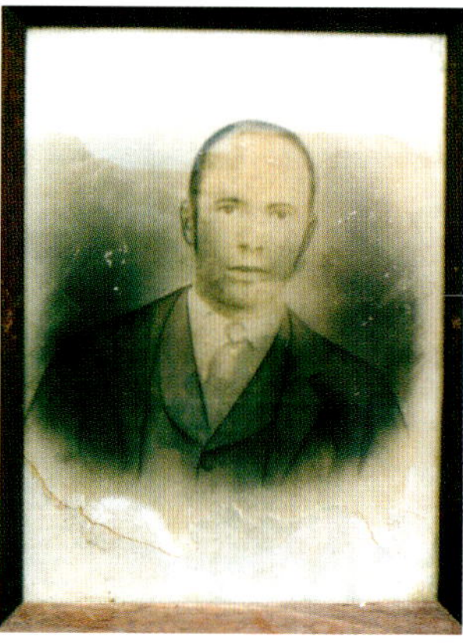

74 Unknown photographer, *Theodore Wulff*, c. 1880s, carbon print.

75 Unknown photographer, *Frantz Wulff*, c. 1880s, crayon and mixed media.

Twentieth-century painting traditions on the continent moved alongside, and occasionally were sparked by photography's growing popularity. Two distinct traditions of painting in Senegal have been influenced by the scarcity of easily reproduced photographic objects, suggesting quite different ways in which image reproduction worked in these contexts.

Sous-verre (also called *sur-verre*), paintings date from at least the late nineteenth century in the Sahel, appearing in Senegal, as well as Côte d'Ivoire, Mali, Tunis (present-day Tunisia), Niger and Nigeria. This glass-painting technique was likely imported by north African artists crossing the Sahara. The rise of *sous-verre* painting in Senegal's cities was initially spurred by the introduction of Muslim devotional images, inexpensive chromolithographs printed on paper, which were imported by Moroccan, Lebanese and Syrian merchants. These came to the attention of French colonial authorities in Senegal, who, alarmed at the possibility of the expansion of Islam in the colony, outlawed these images. Yet the demand for them remained high, and as photographic reproduction was still expensive, the religious images were duplicated by hand on glass.[36]

During the same period, artists began to embellish photographs which were covered in glass.[37] In some early examples, black-and-white photographic portraits were framed with painted decorative motifs, where animal, floral and geometric motifs might on occasion surround the image. Later, artists drew inspiration directly from styles of photo studio portraiture: one notable example is the proliferation of portrayals of elegant idealized women by artists such as Gora Mbengue (1931–1988) and others from the 1950s, which were based on Mama Casset's (1908–1992) accomplished photographic portraits.[38] *Sous-verre* painting was taken up as a means of replacing damaged or faded photographic portraits that had deteriorated over time. It was also a means of enlarging images for better public view – and so *sous-verre* images depicted both actual and idealized portraits.[39] More recent sous-verre painters, such as Babacar Lô, have reproduced a photograph on glass so many times that the once-recognizable portrait has become an icon of 'sentimentalized' old-fashioned feminine glamour. A photograph of the famous

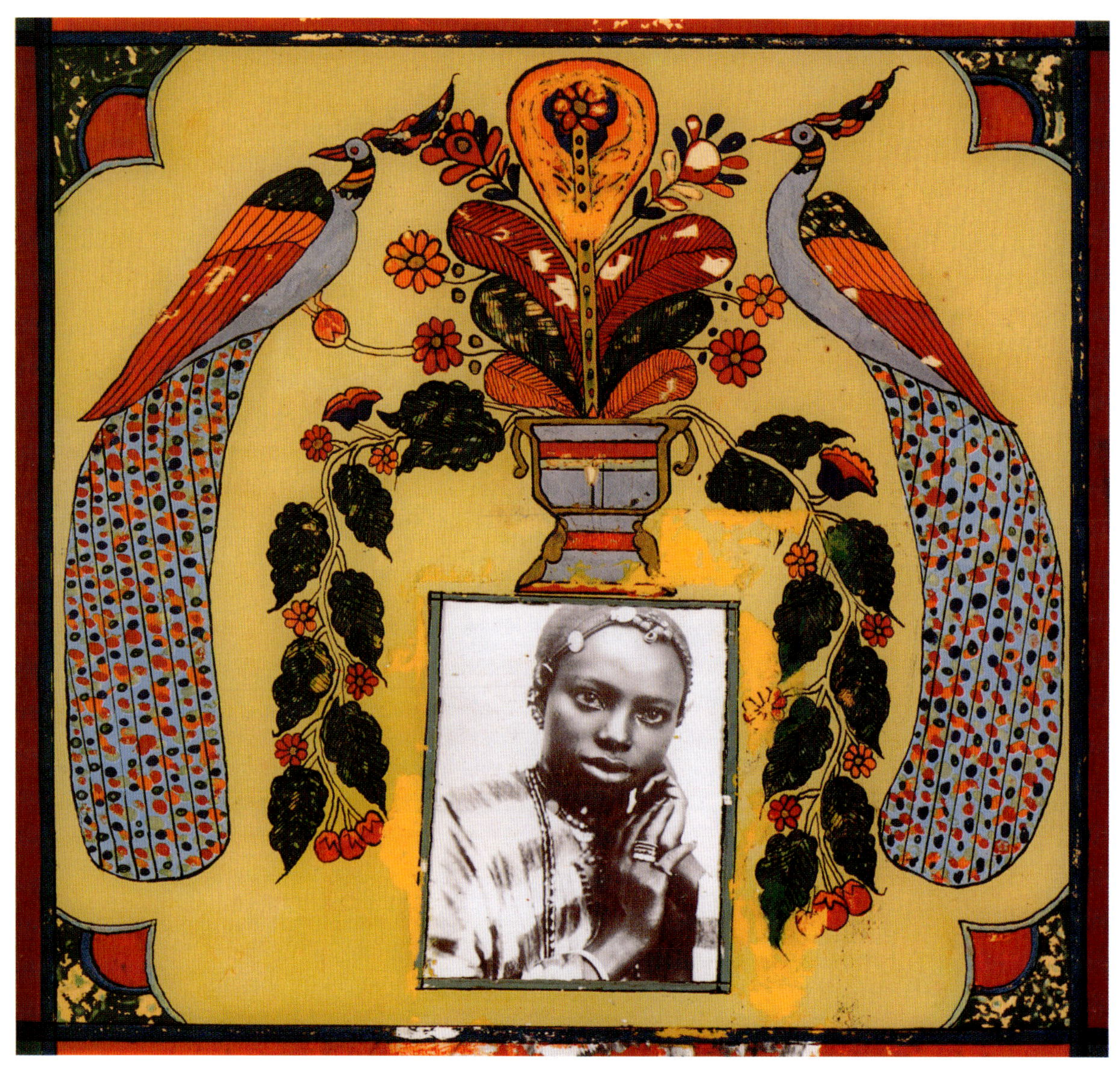

Aba Segou, known early in the twentieth century, was painted on glass first by Lô (according to him; see right) and later copied by other painters.[40] The repetition of subject matter still allows for pictorial freedom within *sous-verre* techniques, and the flat painted surfaces tend towards abstraction and idealization distinct from the detailed photographic plane.

76 Unknown artist and photographer, early 20th century, photographic portrait with painted decorative background.

From a different Senegalese creative tradition altogether, we consider how a wealth of imagery generated from a single poorly reproduced photograph, has spawned a pervasive visual culture of devotion. Images of the Sufi saint, Sheikh Amadou Bamba are all in a sense descended from a 1913 photograph, taken without ceremony by a French colonial officer (and which is now lost) but has nevertheless proliferated through the visual world of Bamba's followers.[41] In this case, the efficacy accorded to these images underscores the irrelevance of photographic reproduction via original negative, or even an adherence to pictorial fidelity.

Sheikh Amadou Bamba (1853–1927) was a mystic whose teachings spawned one of the four Sufi Muslim movements in Senegal, called Mouridism, and his image has since become an icon to devotees. Mourides consider reproductions of Bamba to be particularly potent: a sacred image which actively generates 'a blessing power called a *baraka* (or *barkê*)'.[42] The mystic's original photograph was taken in front of a mosque in Diourbel, Senegal (illus. 78); Bamba was living under house arrest following his exile as an accused dissenter. It is less a physiognomic trace and more an unsuccessful mug shot: details of Bamba's face are obscured by the strong sunlight's contrast, and his body is not captured in its entirety. During the eight decades following its creation, the image

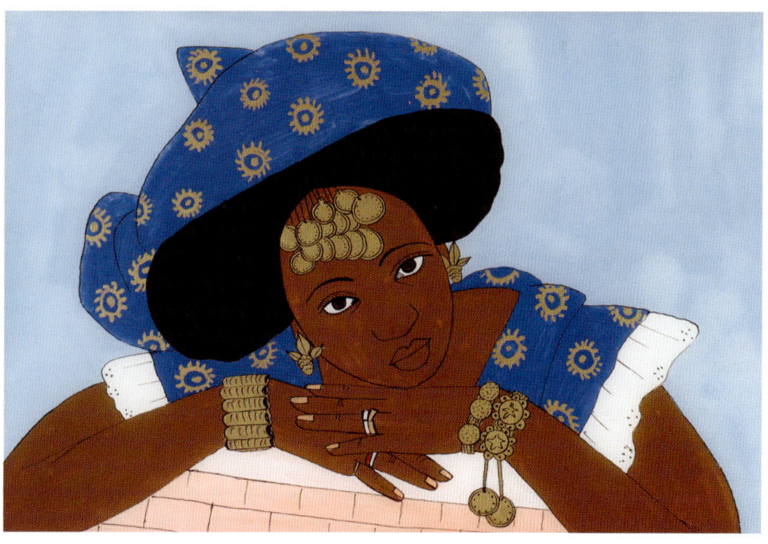

77 Babacar Lô, *Woman with Libidor, sous-verre* painting based on a photograph of Aba Segou, n.d.

of Bamba published in a 1917 book has been lithographed, photocopied, painted on walls of homes and businesses, buses, trees, portable objects, the interiors of homes and devotional webpages. The process of creating Bamba's image and its presence for believers, acts as a talisman that protects and inspires those who see it.[43] The appearance of Bamba's figure in paint is rendered by Mouride and non-Mouride artists, and posters and murals signal communities of faithful on the walls of shops and places of work, the interiors of homes, over entrances, and on banners and calendars. Crucially, the fact of Bamba's pictorial mass reproduction by photocopying, by painters, sculptors, jewellery makers and graphic artists does not lessen the image's strength or efficacy. One Dakarois Mouride explained the connection between imagery and devotion:

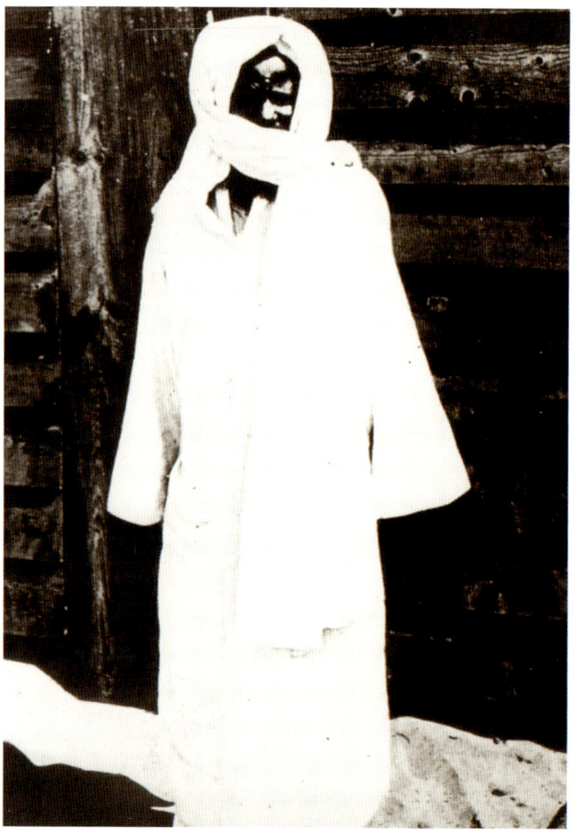

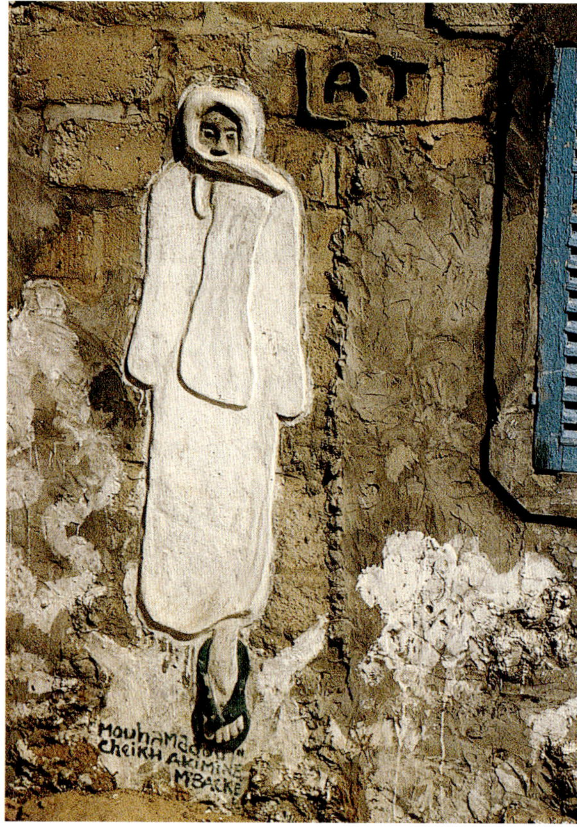

78 Unknown photographer, *Amadou Bamba*, c. 1913, photogravure.

79 Mary Nooter Roberts and Allen F. Roberts, *Low Relief of Amadou Bamba on a Wall, Saint-Louis*, before 1996, medium unknown.

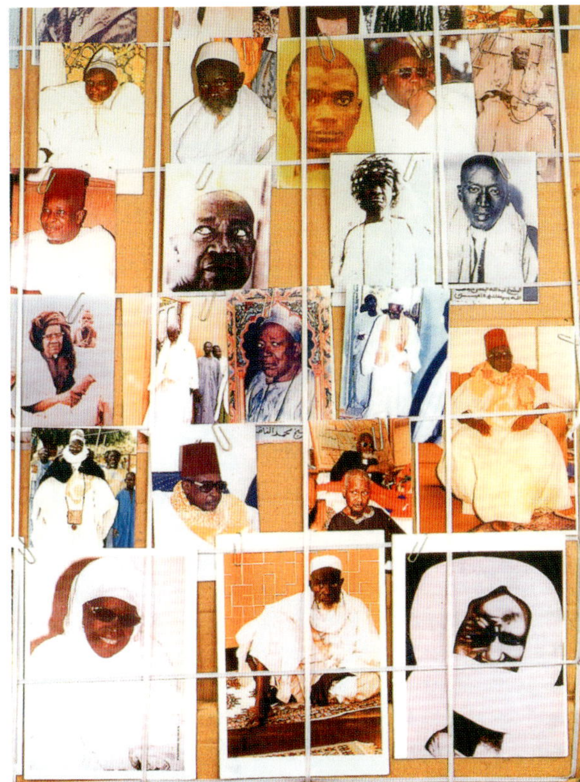

80 Unknown photographer, Photostand from Dakar, Senegal, before 1996, of images sold for shrines including Assane Dione's image of Bamba, lower right.

Wherever Mourides are, they must put pictures of the Holy Man because the images give them hope of Paradise. Their hope resides in him . . . [He] has come to us to bring Happiness. Therefore, everything related to him will help us, for example, his picture, his writings, everything. [He] is an integral part of my life.[44]

Indeed, the idea of the immediacy and fidelity of a photographic image would not seem to apply here at all: a particularly well-known series of oil paintings of Bamba by Assane Dione, were later photographed without the artist's consent and sold by street picture vendors.[45] Photographers, sculptors in wood, potters, calligraphers, creators of all kinds generate a devotional and multivalent visual scope, where the multiplicity of Bamba imagery enlivens the sense of personal interpretations. Dione created a more intense and closely cropped image of Bamba, one which omits the body and fills in aspects of his face not visible in the original photograph. His series of images amount to a new and powerful revisioning of the early photograph. Dione's iconic image and all the other thousands of versions that comprise the realm of Bamba imagery, were inferred from a photograph and do not rely upon verisimilitude nor fidelity to the old photographic image. Instead, their efficacy derives from the beliefs of the intended audience, their status as icons and their recognizability to a specialized and global audience.

'African' Fancy Prints and Wearable Portraits

Photography has long been integral to the look of immensely popular printed textiles in west Africa. Printed cloth is ubiquitous there, remaining for many a treasured and expensive adornment. How cloth is worn conveys aspects of one's personal and political sensibility, rooted in space and time.[46]

What are often referred to as African-printed cloths – the brightly
coloured textiles sold in markets across the continent, not to mention in
the diaspora cities – are textiles which came about over the last century
or so. In the late 1800s, Dutch textile designers produced cloth meant to
emulate Indonesian batiks, in a bid to undercut local textile production
in their colony, but the results did not appeal to their intended Indonesian audience. They instead found an interested market for the cloth
in another of their main trading partners, in the Gold Coast. These
cloths combined a Dutch-designed aesthetic, based on impressions
of Indonesian batiks, but were quickly geared to southern Gold Coast
preferences for the visual depiction of proverbs.[47] Other patterns included
objects from Indonesian patterns, English letters and numbers, objects
of royal authority that were taken to Britain as part of the Asantehene's
(king of Asante) banishment in 1896, and *adinkra* symbols.[48]

In the 1910s, the technique of printing on one side of the cloth allowed
for the inclusion of photographic imagery. One of the earliest includes a
photo-based portrait of a Gold Coast trader from 1929.[49] Shortly after this,
cloths illustrated with images of west African rulers appeared. The earliest
commemorative cloth dates to 1936, which shows Nene Nyarku Eku v, the
Omanhene (king) of Agona, pictured with the Twi expression of mourning,
'*Damirifa Due*' (an expression of farewell to the deceased). These cloths contributed a new dimension to the public spectacle of mourning in southern
Ghana. Wearing cloth emblazoned with a portrait of the departed was
probably one of the earliest instances in which mourners could wear the
image of the deceased on their persons, and this practice would broaden
and find diverse new forms throughout the twentieth century.[50]

Shortly thereafter, cloth design included images celebrating anni-
versaries of schools, churches, missions and mosques, and the visits
by leaders of African and European nations and religious leaders on the
occasion of their visits. After the Second World War, with the decline of
colonial power and the shifting of 'African print' textile production from
European factories to factories in Africa, a new kind of cloth emerged
which marked independence celebrations. Early examples include those
marking Ghana's independence, the first in sub-Saharan Africa in 1957,
which incorporate the image of Kwame Nkrumah, the first president, with

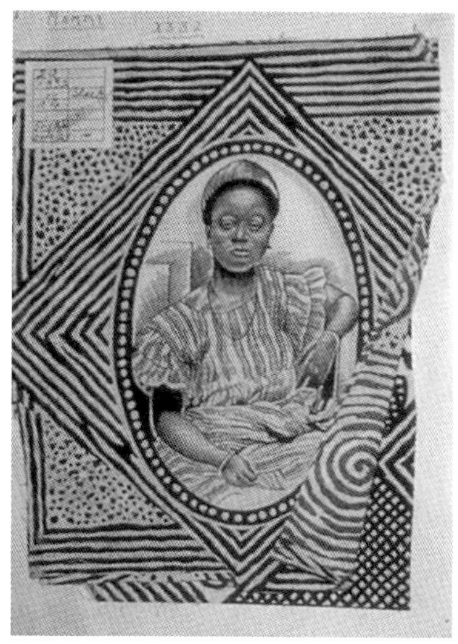

81 Unknown designer, United Africa
Company fancy prints sample book based
on a photograph of an unknown Gold
Coast woman, 'Mammy', 1929.

82 Factory printed cloth, Ivory Coast, n.d.

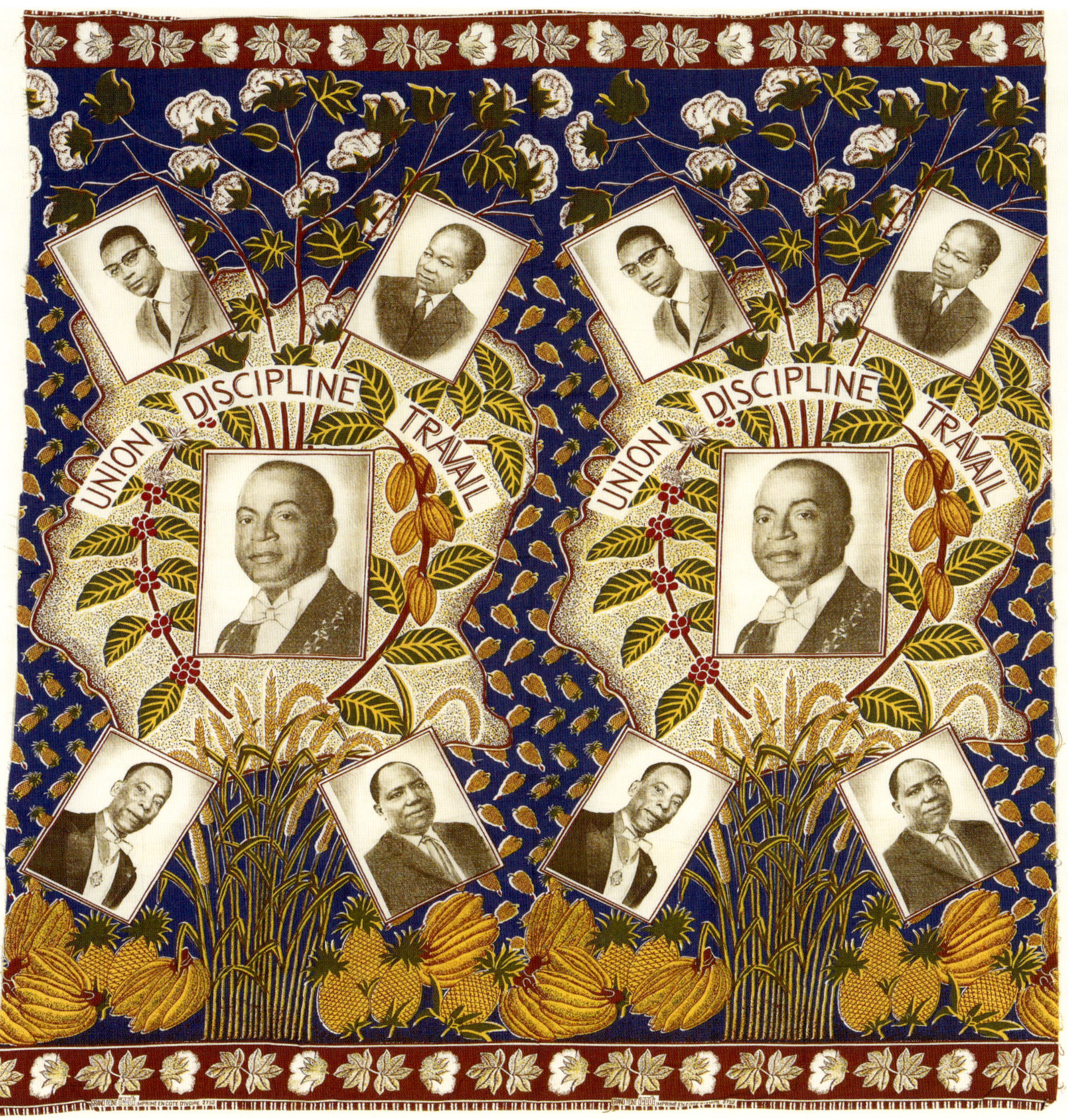

UNION DISCIPLINE TRAVAIL
UNION DISCIPLINE TRAVAIL

the words 'Freedom and Justice'. A cloth honouring
northern Nigeria's independence in 1959 is printed
with rows of photographic framings of local rulers,
men on horseback and camel, and the architectural
landscape, captioned in English and Hausa. Two Sierra
Leone cloths, created before and just after its 1961
independence celebrations, substitute elements in a
popular design: the portrait of Queen Elizabeth was
replaced with that of Prime Minister Sir Milton Margai,
and the British coat of arms was swapped for a Sierra
Leone landscape scene.

Cloth was another avenue of conveying political
or civic allegiance, but also marked in time a sense of
the political moment and emerging nationalist fervour.
Whether celebrating local religious figures or new
presidents, photographic imagery on cloth circulated
the iconography of African leadership within the
imaginaries of local and national consciousness.[51]
Durable and vivid, wearing these cloths often merited
a visit to the portrait studio.

Commemorative Sculpture, Funerary Objects and Processions

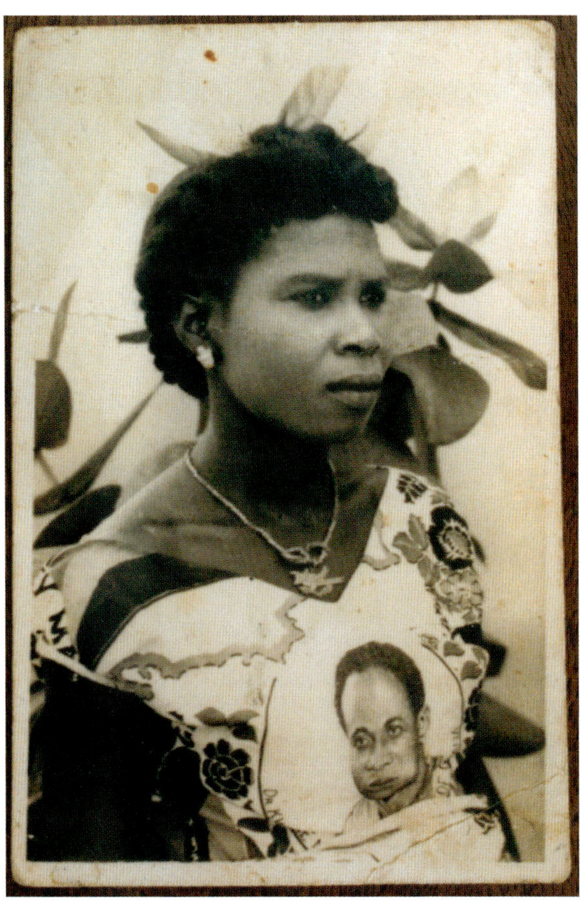

83 Unknown photographer, *Sahadata Naa-ajeley Botchway*, after 1957, black-and-white print.

Across the continent, photography quickly featured in all manner of
funerary and commemorative celebrations, and brought about new ways
to document individual posterity. The pageantry of funerals has long
been a photographic subject in West Africa, where mourning ceremonies
are among the most showy of spectacles. J. A. Green's portrayal of the
obsequies of an unknown Calabar dignitary (opposite),[52] stages the
slaughter of a cow, surrounded with mourners, attendants, wives and
children. Photographing certain rites and views of funerals, in addition
to mortuary photography, continue to be a pervasive phenomenon in
West African photographic traditions. Portraits, often quickly altered to

reflect their new status as commemorative images, comprise fundamental elements in the matrix performances and displays that eulogize the dead.

The full-length, roughly sculpted portrait of Christiana A. Ansah, a grave monument in southern Ghana (illus. 85), echoes conventions of early twentieth-century photographic portraiture, while the face and body are generalized in the tradition of earlier funerary terracotta sculpture.[53] It reflects the ordered body language of respectability, the local preference for showing a person in his or her entirety, with calm demeanour, seated with hands on knees, and dressed in woven cloth rather than imported attire.

This approach to depicting the commemorated person is strikingly similar in painted funerary monuments by the Ankrah Brothers of Aflao, eastern Ghana, who painted life-sized images based on photographs, protected under a small grave shelter. Relying on a photograph, the artist

84 Jonathan Adagogo Green, *'Funeral ceremony of a chief at Old Calabar, NCP'* (Niger Coast Protectorate), *c.* 1897, albumen print.

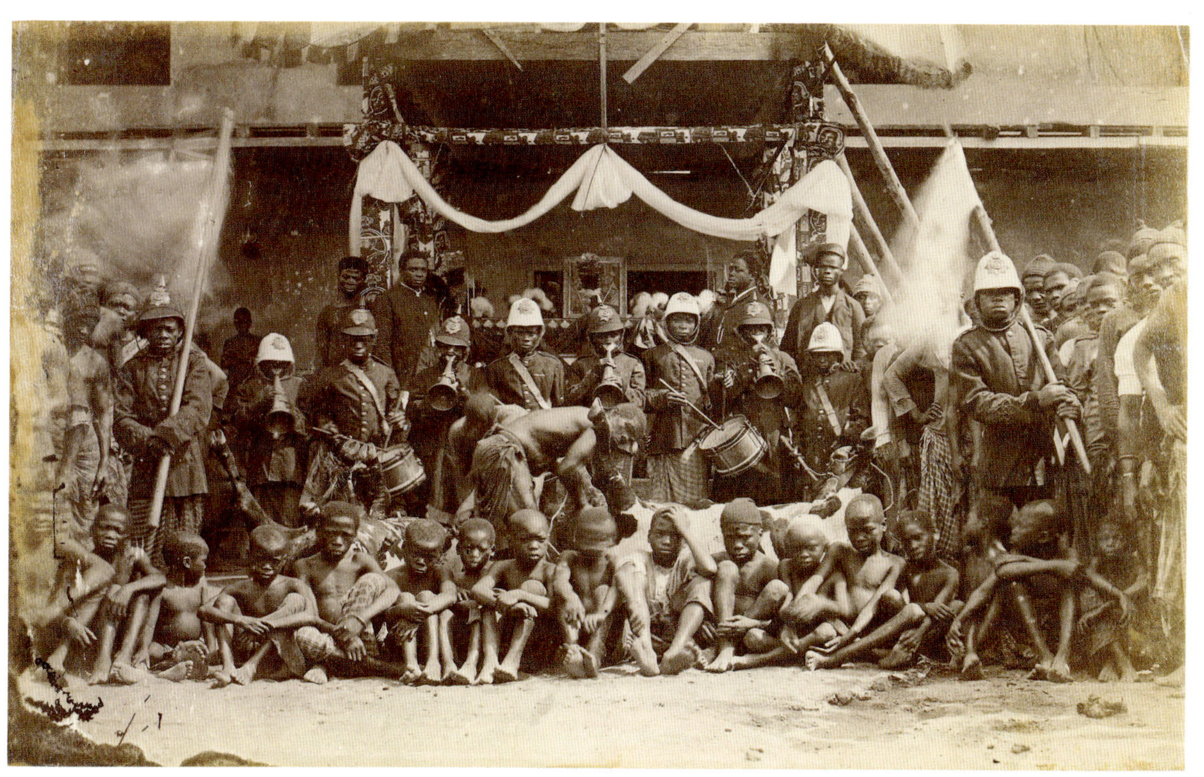

added details of the body and costume as the family required.[54] In the same area, Stephen Zanoo's grave monuments were also rendered from photographs, but Zanoo addressed the subject of the commemorated individual beyond the scope of what was deemed suitable for a photographic portrait. On one grave is a sculpted man, seated and wearing cloth, who in turn looks at his carved double, who wears shorts and swings a hoe, commemorating his life as a successful farmer.[55]

Photography's expansion has played a crucial role in the elaboration of commemorative arts. In parts of Ghana, Nigeria and elsewhere, when a relation dies it is incumbent on the family to find their best photographic portrait, which is then sent off and reprinted as an integral part of the obituary posters that are later plastered on walls, poles and gates of the neighbourhood. These posters list the chief mourners, the dates of funeral celebrations. Punctuating the urban landscape, they are ubiquitous visual reminders of the attention lavished on the dead at the time of their 'transition'. Many accoutrements of funerary and commemorative ceremonies are inscribed with images of the deceased: mourners pin on illustrated paper badges, and families who can afford it print commemorative bulletins and publications filled with biographical notes, hymns, poetry, numerous eulogies and several portraits.[56] Some people also use photographs to mark friends and family members who have died by inscribing an 'x' on the body or above the head, and occasionally words written on photographs also record the moment of personal loss.

While photography helped drive new creative forms of commemorative objects and practices, photographic portraits themselves also become the focus for a range of performances. In Ijẹbu, Nigeria, Margaret Thompson Drewal has described public funeral processions by family mourners which include bands of musicians, dancers and others singing praises to the family, while a photograph of the deceased is held aloft; the entire ensemble and its actions comprise a multifaceted performed portrait of the deceased (illus. 87). The concern for posterity is connected not only with the idea of

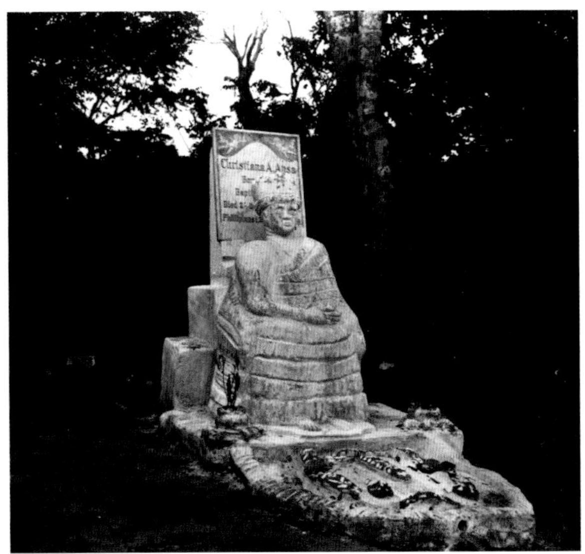

85 Rudolf Fisch, '*Memorial on the grave of a deceased native*' (Christiana A. Ansah, Gold Coast), before 1911, print from gelatine dry plate.

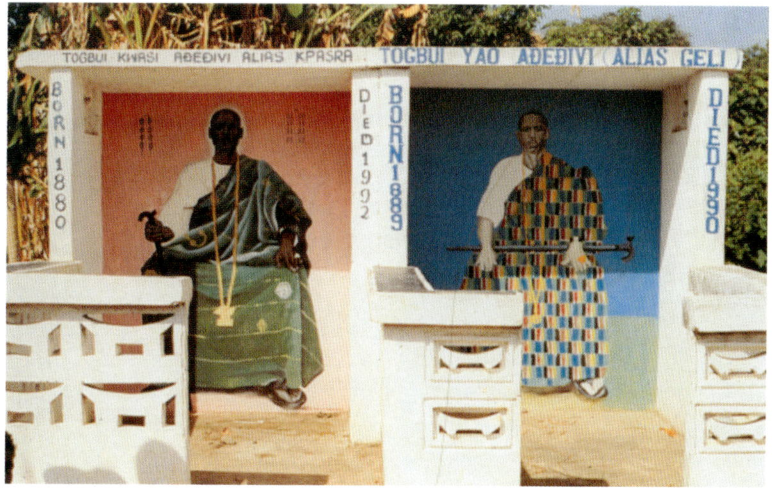

86 Ankrah Brothers of Aflao, funerary monuments of Togbui Kwasi Adedivi and Togbui Yao Adedivi, *c.* 1990–92, painted portraits on concrete based on unattributed photographs.

leaving a praise-worthy 'image' behind for the living to remember, but also an image that when looked at, connects to this memory of personal achievement. The diviner Kolawole Ositola articulated this concern for posterity in public memory:

> [Mourners] think dancing and enjoying after the death will depict the deceased's achievements on earth, how he or she was able to behave to the community . . . If they don't do it then the deceased who is joining the ancestors will be . . . unhappy . . . because he has not been remembered. The deceased will have to answer queries [that is, from the ancestors]. 'Why are you not properly initiated, or sent to us? Perhaps you have not performed well, have not achieved well? If you have performed well, why is posterity forgetting you?' The only way for us on earth to judge the deceased is to know how much honor was given to him by his descendants.[57]

Photographs amount to an integral part of ensuring and shaping this sense of posterity, which extends from a person's earthly life and into the next realm.

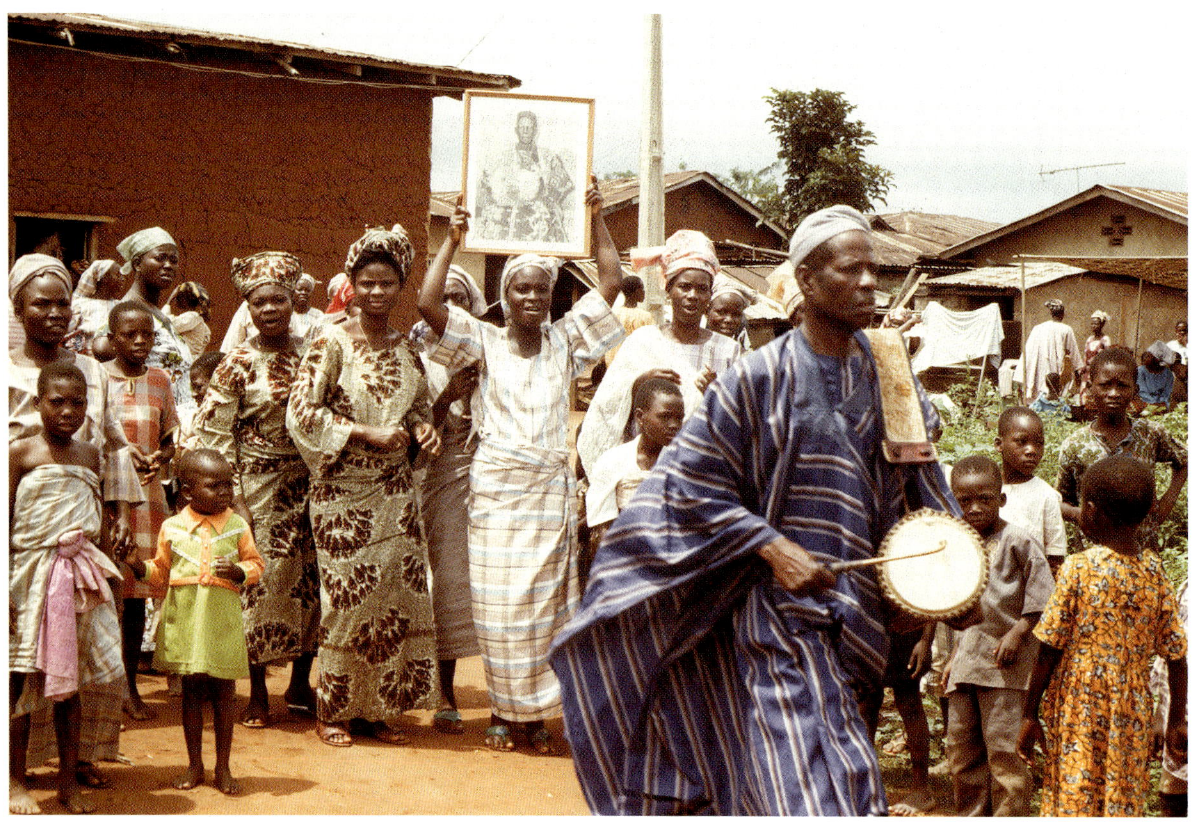

Post-Photographic Painting Traditions

Across the continent, urban landscapes sparkle with painted works by commercial artists. Painters' commissions range from signage for local enterprises, to murals and storefronts advertising restaurants, mechanics, tailors, grocers, barbers, internet cafes and money changers; painters create designs for taxis and buses, and banners for churches, mosques and civic events. Paintings on board, canvas and paper are sold in street stalls, in galleries, and in markets for local and international patrons or foreign markets. While some painters are self-taught, others apprentice with artists or learn in workshop settings, while others attend trade schools or university level art schools.

87 Margaret Thompson Drewal, 'A funeral "play" (ere) travels about the town, a member of the family carries aloft a photograph of the deceased, Ìjẹbu area, village of Imọsan, 13 September 1986.'

Much of this painting can be referred to as post-photographic, in that photographs and other forms of mechanical or digital reproduction form the basis for much of the models for training and commissions. Painters gather subjects from the press, other published imagery, photographic portraits and art-historical subjects from local and international spheres. The Congolese painter Tshibumba Kanda Matulu's historical paintings of central African political history, commissioned by anthropologist Johannes Fabian, draw on aspects of press photography of Patrice Lumumba, but their compositions rely on the artist's sense of history.[58] Chéri Samba's paintings run a commentary on all aspects of the social universe, captioned and titled, with his subjects at times seeming awkwardly frozen, as if caught in the camera's flash.[59]

The relationship between the most deliberate career painters and their photographic source material has rarely been explored in depth. Kumase realism, a genre of painting that emerged in the 1950s in Ghana (dubbed 'Kumase realism' by the artist and scholar Atta Kwami), is a style which attends to the sheen and contour inscribed on a photograph's glossy surface. Its artists are usually based in workshops, and range from the self-taught to school-trained. Painters in Kumase and elsewhere employ the images of public figures in order to exploit shaded contours of skin and textiles' surfaces as well as the chance to arrange their subjects in fantastical contexts.[60] The most newsworthy celebrities rub shoulders: Bill Clinton and Nelson Mandela share billboard-scaled space with Ghana's President John Atta Mills and Barack Obama; local beauty queens and Osama bin Laden are other subjects. Adherence to aspects of the photographic marks the work of a master painter, while juxtaposing subjects, adding new backgrounds and ornamentation, and playing with scale, all detach subjects from their veristic realm. The conventions imbed the subjects in an intense imaginary, discarding the photographic frame in order better to magnify the skills and imagination of an exceptional painter.

The great variety and evocation of photographs in African spaces and creative practices pushes us to move beyond considering photography as a medium unto itself. From its African inceptions these examples illustrate how multiples in film and other media proliferated and expanded across time, those interventions only occasionally being the work of photographers. They invite an acknowledgement of their tangibility and their fragility, of the social, political and physical effects of their immediate environment. In Madagascar's courtly painting and in Onabolu's larger-than-life portraits, photography provided a rarefied visual milieu which patrons and painters saw as something to be improved on and surpassed. Portraits from Ghana and Senegal evoke the tangible alterations that mark out each iteration. Photographs are these traces that mark each new creation. Meanwhile, on cloth, billboard or tree, photographic reformulations invite touch and public perusal, and stave off destruction and decay for a little while longer.

88 St Baffour Studio, *Former President of Ghana John Kuffuor, Kanda, Accra, Ghana*, 2002, pigment on plywood.

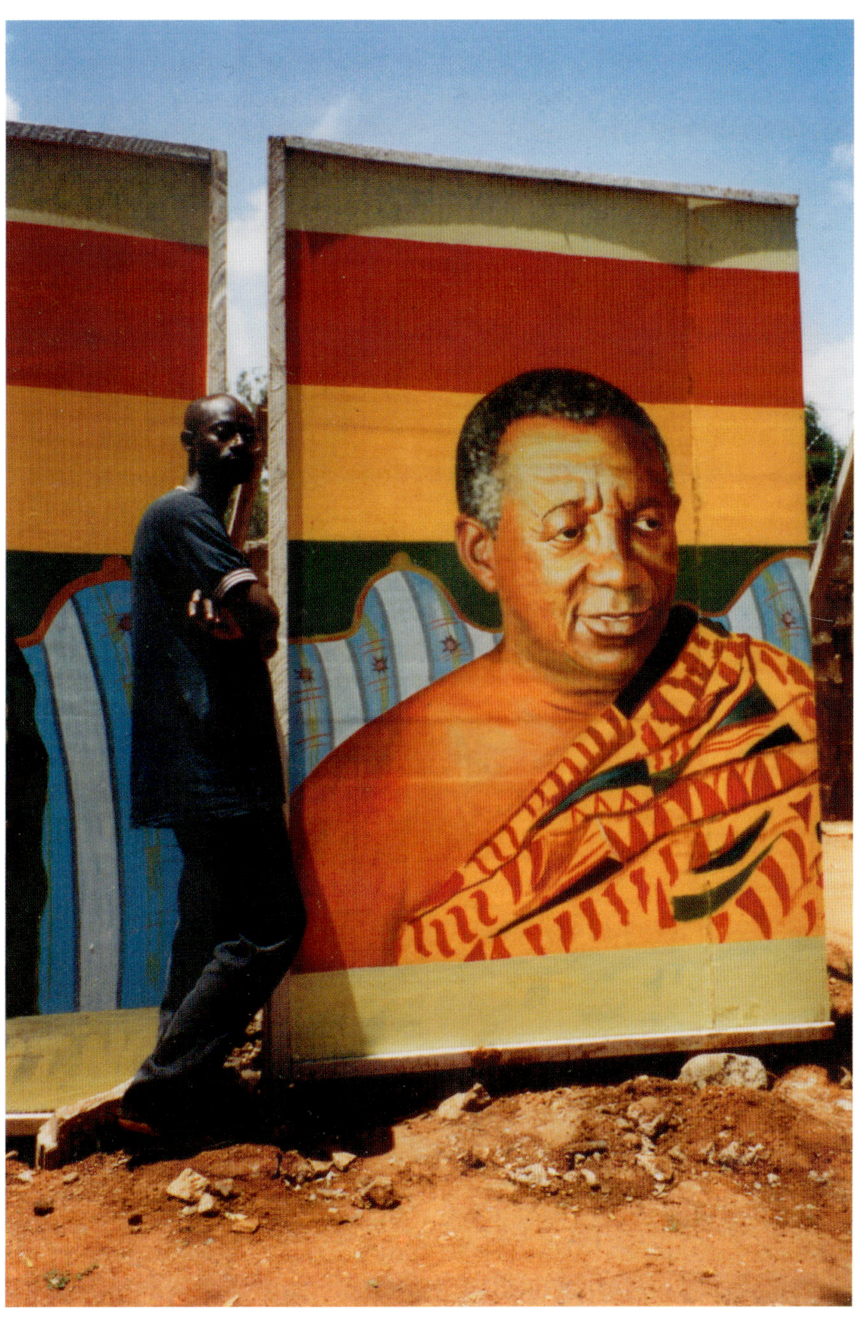

five

Intimate Views

Among the revelations of recent photography from Africa and its diaspo-ras is the built-in presumption of a curious and plugged-in pan-geographic audience.[1] In the narratives these images evoke, there is little elaborate justification or explanation. Indeed, they amount to provocative deliveries of unapologetically intimate views. These photographers have shifted the burden of knowledge and inquiry, rigorous looking and calling out old fictions, onto the viewer. The effect is dramatic.

Such projects draw in part from the presence of creative photo-graphic traditions. Although photography has only recently arisen as an academic subject taught in African universities and other spaces, its artistries and pasts inform larger visual culture and are passed on via personal and professional tutelage. To be sure, contemporary projects cannot be disentangled from the breadth and depth of historical creativity on the continent and its diasporas. This may seem a fairly banal point, except for the fact that we are still only beginning to come to terms with the continent's distinctive photographic traditions. It makes sense to bear in mind some of the narrative particularities of place, history and identity in the mix with a larger sense of this vast creative dimension.

Meanwhile, certain facts remain: many parts of Africa are exceedingly poor and people survive in spite of political unrest and corruption. Migration is commonplace. Artists and photographers persevere despite the lack of patronage, academic and commercial arts institutions, and reliable access to materials, electricity and technology.[2] Photography is predominantly a trade education for much of the continent, yet this continues apace with the time-honoured practice of apprenticeships, the recent flourishing of photography workshops from the late 1990s, and the unique history of workshops in South Africa. Though the reality of deeply variegated photographic practice may seem universal, we must pay attention to its particularities with regard to African contexts. It is perhaps not surprising that there is a thread of humanism pervading the work of many contemporary photographers from Africa, and it is this that ties the work considered in this chapter.

Disturbances

Activist photography over the past two decades has carried on in many guises, underscoring a new breadth of subjects brought to local audiences and less familiar ones abroad, chiefly by means of online and print media, books and to a much lesser extent in exhibitions.

Gideon Mendel's landmark *A Broken Landscape: HIV and AIDS in Africa* (1996) broached the problem of the present overwhelming pandemic. He moved beyond depicting the stark physicality of the ill and their families, to detailing the efforts of healthcare workers, orphanages, volunteers,

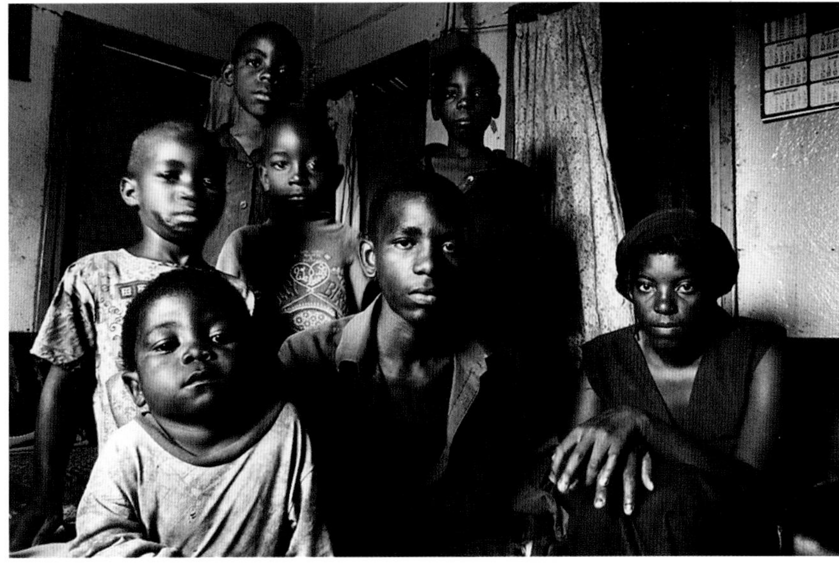

89 Gideon Mendel, *Janet Mbulo and Family, Copperbelt, Zambia*, c. 2000, black-and-white photograph.

'My name is Janet Mbulo and I am 20 years old. Since our father died on the 17th of November 1997 things have been very difficult for us. He was the one earning an income. Our mother then died in 1998. Even from long before then because our parents were ill the older children had to take care of the younger ones. We have all managed to stay together in our family home in Kwacha Compound but now we struggle to survive. We used to bake scones to sell at the market but we could not continue as our electricity was disconnected after we did not pay the bill. We make a bit of money by making doormats to sell and we are helped by an organization which gives us some maize meal every month and pays the school fees for Joyson, Joshua and David. Monica Musonda and Christopher stay home with me.'

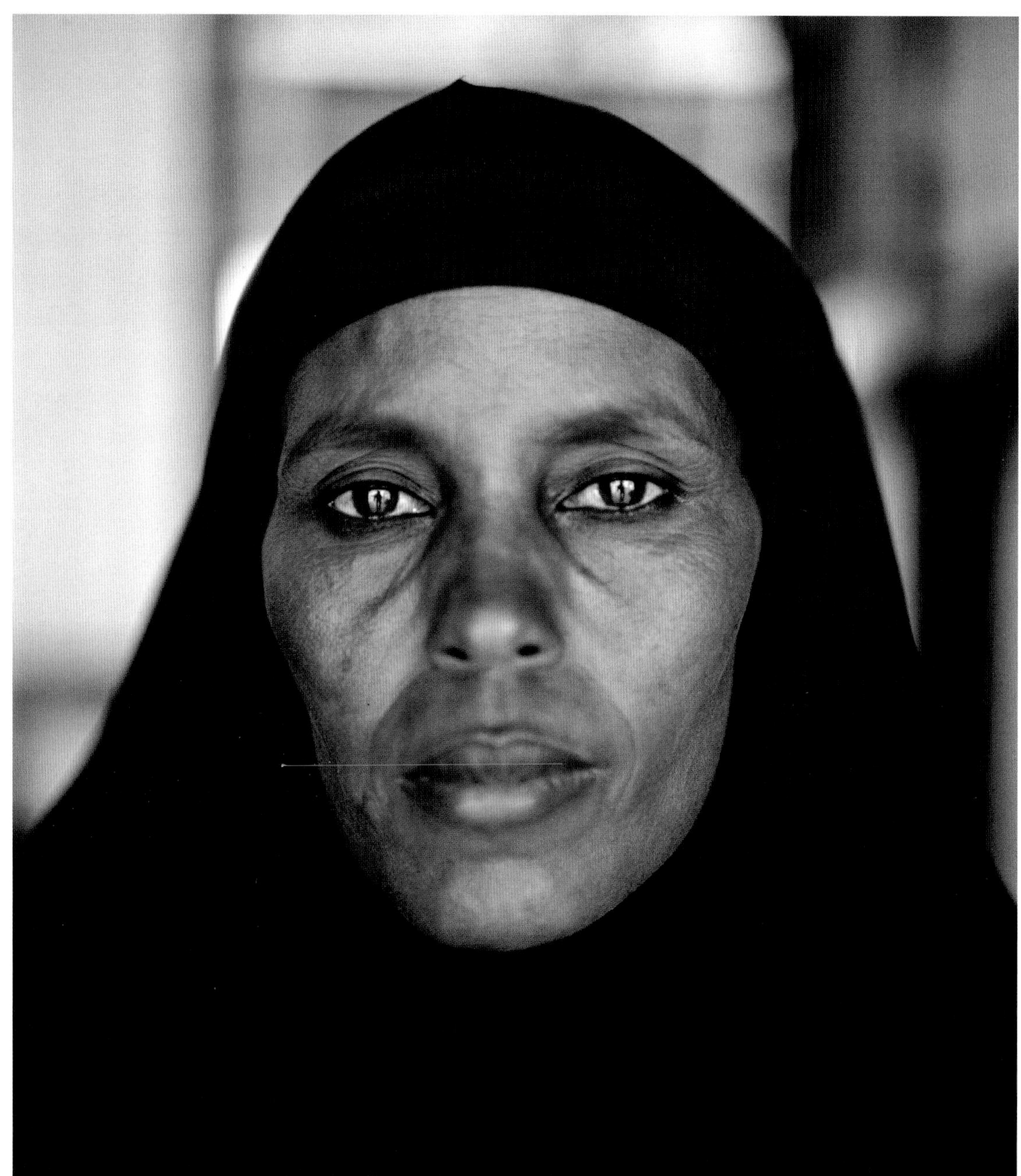

scenes of educational plays and activist parades, all to a devastating effect. Personal statements accompany each portrait, and many trace the efforts of individuals, some at their deaths and during their funerals. It is a complex project, humour and outrageousness pervading the imagery of grieving communities working in educational workshops, and the scenes of political advocacy in the streets. *Broken Landscape* illustrated the stigma of acknowledging HIV/AIDS within a social frame, and detailed in frame by frame, barriers to public conversation at a crucial moment in that pandemic's trajectory.[3]

It is rare to gather the resources to move beyond the short-term in photojournalistic approaches. Mendel and other photographers take on intensely complex and difficult subjects by tying their depictions with names and direct quotations that illuminate a larger narrative beyond anonymous victimhood and dispossession. Fazal Sheikh's sustained activist approach, such as his *A Camel for the Son* (1992–2000), combines intensely poignant formal portraits of Somali women and children living in Kenyan refugee camps.[4] Depictions such as the one opposite are imbued with a universalizing respectability. They are efforts to remove people from the 'socially inflicted ugliness' of their political deprivation,[5] and the tracks of damaging visual depictions and deliberate blind spots. Sheikh juxtaposes the portraits with his subjects' personal narratives, translated in first person, and these are framed with imagery of the dramatically altered landscapes of the camps' situation in northern Kenya. The meditative portraits are paradoxically structured within urgent human rights' crises, stories which only occasionally merit mention in press coverage of the continent, beyond the borders of occasional headlines.

Yto Barrada's work moves away from individual subjects, but they equally hinge on political and personal themes. As such, Barrada poses circumspect questions formulated in remarkably wide-ranging and non-judgmental images. In the *Strait Project* (1998–2004),[6] Barrada's uneasy observations of her Morocco home town, Tangier, inscribe sensations of waiting and longing that suffuse those who are intent – or just imagining – on crossing the Strait of Gibraltar into Spain. They underline a desperation running along the corridor connecting the African and European frontiers in a fraught era of migration after 9/11. The project is an expansive and dynamic photo-collage, framing scenes of citizens looking across, during the decade when parts of Europe's borders were drawn tight, making the Strait into what was essentially a one-way route.[7] Barrada's later works, such as *Iris Tingitana* (opposite), and video *The Botanist* (2007) illuminate connections between Morocco's transforming economic and political landscape and that of weeds and blooms. Playful and lush, these works attend the national government's projects to transform public spaces and protected forests into a tourist-driven beach paradise. Tangiers' rapid development is geared towards supporting the social infrastructure of the country, but as historic buildings, marketplaces and beaches succumb to this homogenous terrain, Barrada notes that public debate about land use is absent. So local fauna is reduced to folk-loric picturesque scenery, and it is this vegetal transformation to which Barrada turns her eye. Flowers yield a metaphorical underpinning, and suggest an optimistic vista where plant life offers an example and mode of quiet resistance.[8]

Photojournalistic work by a number of photographers blurs the edges of reportage, for audiences both international and national. Mikhael Subotzky is a young South African whose dazzlingly accomplished work, including a formidable complex of work on post-apartheid prisons, *Die Vier Hoeke* (The Four Corners, 2005), won several international prizes and gained him admittance as the youngest member of Magnum photo agency in 2007.[9] 'Bonita Sings' (illus. 92) comes from his 2007–8 series *Beaufort West*. The project focuses on the stymied possibilities for the citizens of a town known as a way-station on a busy highway, and for its prison which is situated at the centre of an enormous roundabout. Subotzky's descriptions footnote the economic realities and everyday moments of his subjects, such as his note that the family, reliant on a daughter's work as a prostitute and another's disability pension, is commonplace and distressing. At the core of this image are individual silences crossing in communal space: the overworked young mother listens, subdued, and a grandmother stares pensively, while they listen to a cousin singing an Afrikaner hymn.[10]

The vast oeuvre of Jodi Bieber's formidable photojournalistic work in South Africa and around the world attends to the violent processes

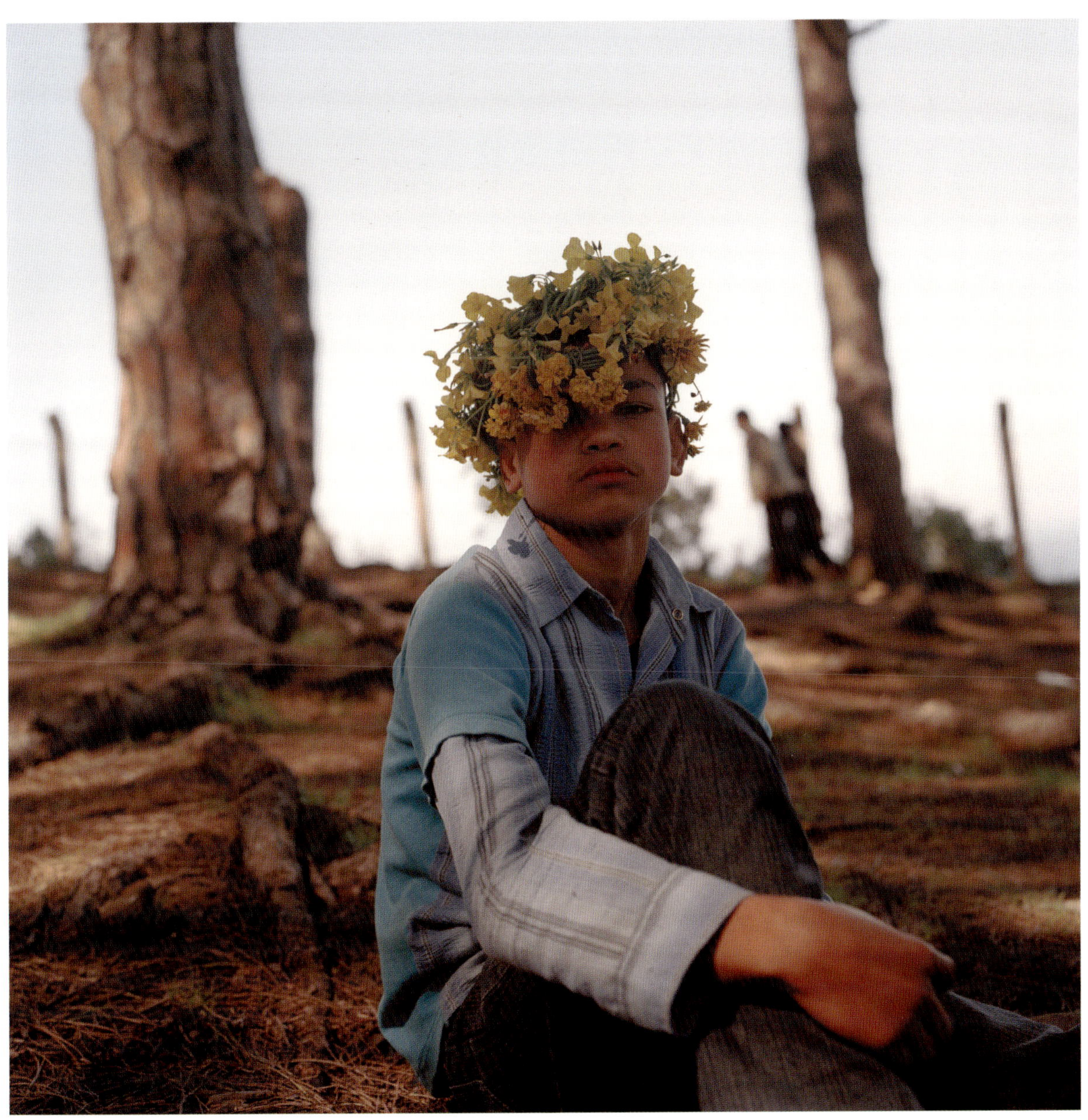

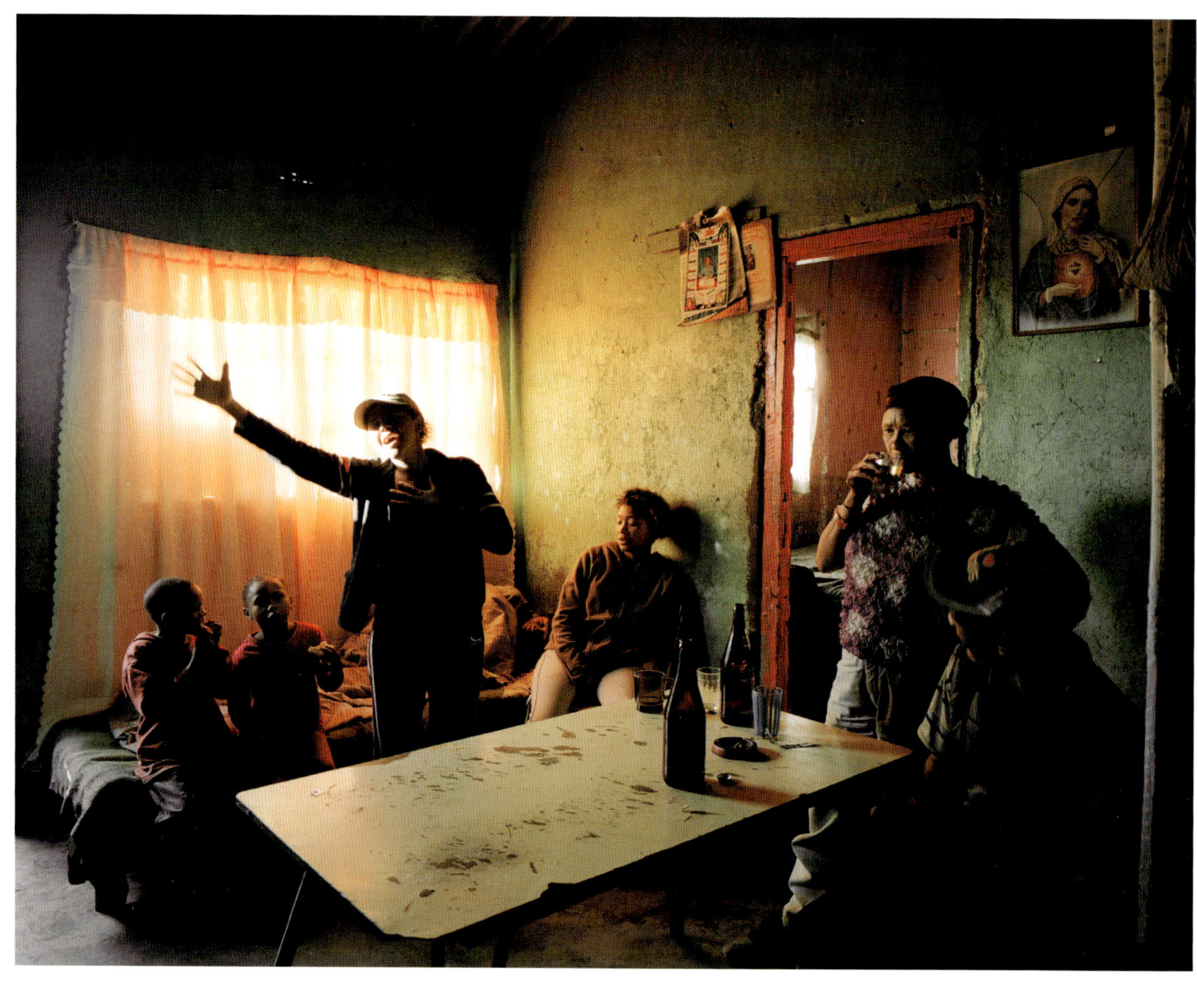

and histories of political confrontation and disenfranchisement. She has merited wide acclaim. The remit of Bieber's assignments trace the most marginalized of subjects: drug addicts, abused women and children, survivors of atrocities in the Congo, the Aceh conflict, post-invasion Iraq, and Zimbabwean migrants detained in South Africa.[11] Other photo-journalists quietly document the lovely and the unspectacular, and in doing so make important documents which resonate locally but may surprise international audiences with the insights they turn up. Attuned

92 Mikhael Subotzky, 'Bonita Sings', Mallies household, Rustdene township, South Africa, from the series *Beaufort West*, 2006, c-print.

to the historicities of Cairo, Randa Shaath's wide-ranging camera illustrates the city's *Al-Ahram Weekly* in ongoing assignments, such as her portraits of Egyptian intelligentsia and artistic communities. In her personal work, she surveys the space of rarely-viewed worlds, such as the roof-top towns of shanty structures built on the firmament of Cairo's magnificent architecture.[12] Mamadou Gomis's recordings of Dakarois sights punctuate that city's *Le Journal* six days a week. Gomis closes in on the pace and everyday performances through his meanderings of the city, whose citizens are both his audience and his subjects.[13]

The recent work of Ethiopian artist Aida Muluneh is very much inflected by the personal dimension, and which reveals her gifts for connecting with her subjects. Muluneh is ever-mindful of the egregious imbalances in mass-media depictions of the continent, and regarding her home country in particular. Muluneh's low-key photographic work, stories and video projects delight in mundane satisfactions – a father and daughter in a car, men sharing lunch inside a shop (illus. 93), gathering celebrants for religious festivals – as part of her larger projects that reveal facets of larger narratives of Ethiopia and its diasporas rarely put to international audiences.[14]

As with many approaches considered here, the depth of local photographic traditions sustain many of today's creative projects, and in the case of South Africa since 1994, there has not been a turning away from documentary photography so much as an acceptance of other genres into the spotlight. While political engagement threads through much contemporary work, photographers grapple with the personal, autobiographical and conceptual themes, the politics of identity, gender and sexuality, present-day economic realities, and the nature of personal and social memory. One important theme that resonates through the work of several artists is the depiction of and contestation over land and inhabited spaces. David Goldblatt's formidable oeuvre spanning three decades rings with subtlety and wide-ranging attention: *The Structures of Things Then* (1998) gives weight to the memory of labour and migration inscribed upon disrupted earth, social spaces, and built and modified landscapes. Others broach topography as metaphor and as formal subject, with astonishingly powerful effects, as with Guy Tillim's *Jo-burg* series (2004), Jo Ractcliffe's *Johannesburg Inner City Works* (2000–4), works by Andrew Tshabangu

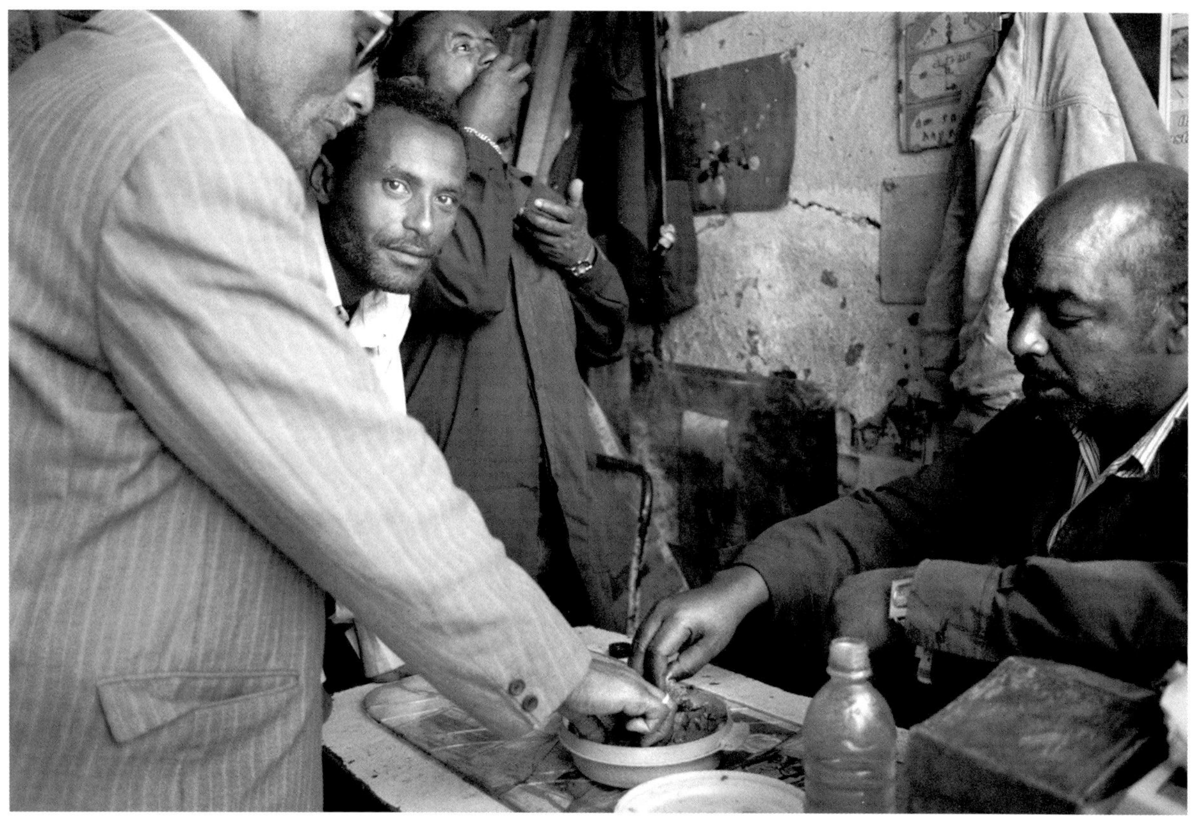

and installations by Jean Brundrit. They attend to the legacy of land as experience and as vision, smiting the long-simmering vision cultivated in the country's salon landscape paintings, utterly unpopulated, of the early- and mid-twentieth century.[15]

Geography is almost a centrifugal force in renderings by the Lagos artists' collective *Depth of Field*. Drawn to the aesthetic and public dimensions of their megalopolis home, in the works by these photographers the present-day flattens the historical. *Depth of Field*'s collaborative union reflects a zeitgeist of new patronage and new potential for sustaining a critical conversation among artists away from more formal institutions. In 2001, Kelechi Amadi-Obi, Uchechukwu James-Iroha, Amaize Ojeikere and Toyin Sokefun-Bello formed their collective in the absence of accessible

93 Aida Muluneh, *Tin Shop, Addis Ababa*, 2000, black-and-white digital print.

structures for artistic collaboration there; later Emeka Okereke and Zaynab Toyosi Odunsi joined them. Collectively, their imagery has been informed by vibrant strands of art making: music, film, video and television, fashion, design and the kaleidoscopic theatre of public display. Documenting the city streets is an inherently provocative act, and they have often been hassled, mugged or suspected of troubling governmental or press affiliations. The six photographers mentor and critique each other, and when required, manipulate and negotiate the scene while another makes the 'aggressive' gesture of pointing a camera in public. Amaize Ojeikere's work is at first glance apparently mundane, taken with the rhythmic compositions of watch bands, or shoes which mark the compositional elegances of street-vendors' arrangements. Kelechi Amadi-Obi's panoramic cityscapes contain sweeps of dense life compressed under a wide-format sky. In Uchechukwu James-Iroha's images, taken under the cover of night, light from lorry parks and night markets meld to paint glowing abstractions.[16]

Homes

Several artists who descend from various recent African diasporas, explore the subjectivities of personal and familial biography as manifested in the physical world. In their works, depictions of land and private space are remote, yet loaded with the poetic implications of family memory in the post-colonial present. Zarina Bhimji's intense photos and films render her explorations of the Ugandan landscape as beautiful ruins and surfaces, unpeopled, richly coloured and imbued with loss. Her family left Uganda during President Idi Amin's 1972 expulsion of Indians, and her return years later registers grief and emptiness: vacated rooms, disarranged cemeteries, an anti-homecoming.[17] Allan deSouza, a fellow exile of Indian descent from east Africa, puts forward questions about memory, loss and photographs in his *The Lost Pictures* series (2004). He took images of his family's Nairobi snapshot archive, reprinted them and literally lived among them: family portraits were adhered to shower walls and sinks and floors, scuffed and obscured and covered with detritus. They are the

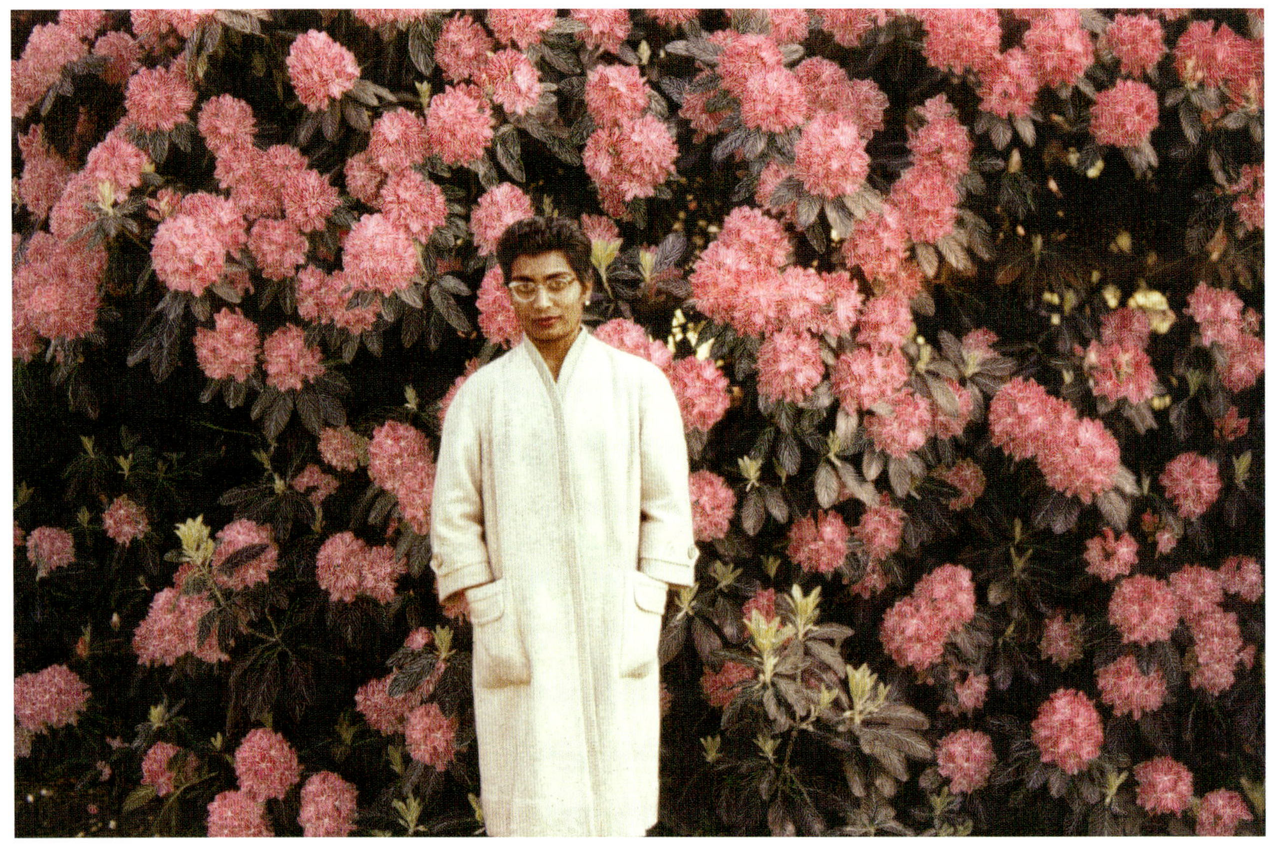

deposits of different layers and speeds of family and personal memory, and reliquaries of the artist's use. *Blossom* (2004), a portrait of the artist's mother, was painstakingly hand-traced and blurred, a tribute of inscription that signals the impossibility of return and a persistently shifting nostalgia.[18] Theo Eshetu's stills and images from *Trip to Mount Ziqualla* (2005) records a pilgrimage in Ethiopia, formalized by rhythmic angles: he is both a fascinated visitor and oblique witness.[19] For Eshetu, home is never recognizable, but the attempts to interpret it are a seductive visual pleasure. Bhimji, deSouza and Eshetu's projects take up journeys infused with personal and familial particulars, and in different ways mark the very familiar and recognizable sense of home's disruption.

94 Allan deSouza, 'Blossom', from *The Lost Pictures* series, 2004, digital C-print.

By contrast, Akinbode Akinbiyi's work is insistently nomadic. Long resident in Berlin, he has roamed through the sprawls of Cairo and the tiny avenues of Bamako (where he has recently curated exhibitions for the biennale). His project *Lagos: All Roads* began in the early 1980s, documenting the relentless polarities of sprawl, dystopia and aggression in the hub of the continent's most populous nation. The open-air drama in the city transfixes Akinbiyi, whose camera makes critical note in oddly askance views.[20] His *Sea Never Dry* series reveals beaches as social thoroughfares and as the spaces where the poor live in a teeming, ill-equipped megalopolis. Residents of the beach are cheek by jowl with visitors enjoying a hired horse ride, while celebrants in religious services go about their devotions (illus. 95).

As from the medium's beginning, artists continue to expand the boundaries of portraiture, swerving through political, conceptual and historical narratives, and invoking the personal. Emeka Okereke's 2007 series *Unspoken Hero* is a sustained documentary portrait that unexpectedly recorded his subject's last year of life; pushing forward in time the memorial imperative implied in his photographs.[21] Okereke's commemorative project was forced to jump lanes: originally intending to describe scenes in his uncle's exceptional life, his subject suddenly died. Okereke's photographs, as if by rote, convey the obligatory photographic moments that ceremonialize funerary proceedings. As is the case with many kinds of portraiture and memorialization, a funeral is not an end but a series of points that describe and recreate the socially inscribed personal identity: 'death is seen as the birth into a new life that is of a different consistency than the earth life – a spiritual consistency . . .'.[22] A lace shroud surrounding the mourner's room alludes to this liminal state (illus. 96); another image from the series registers the shock and ordinariness of the news with an obituary portrait on university halls, and an empty chair. The intent of tribute within his portrait essay resonates in local registers of past and of the present-day audience.

Other photographers' recent projects explore subjectivities and political moods underpinning everyday visual worlds. The prosaic textures of familiar and intensely personal terrain are tended to in formal, and sometimes deadpan gazes. Moshekwa Langa's impressionistic images of

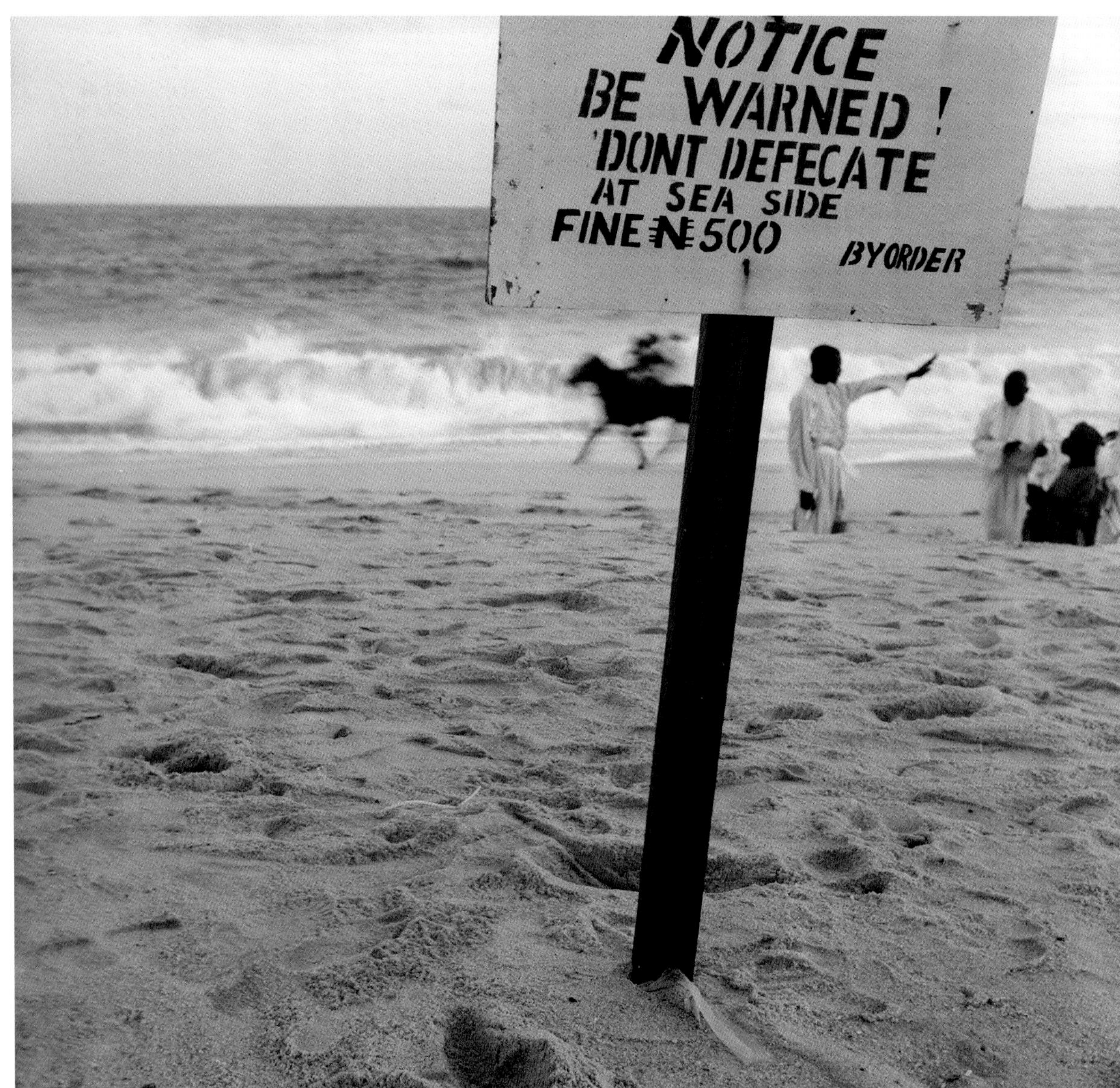

NOTICE
BE WARNED !
DONT DEFECATE
AT SEA SIDE
FINE ₦ 500
BYORDER

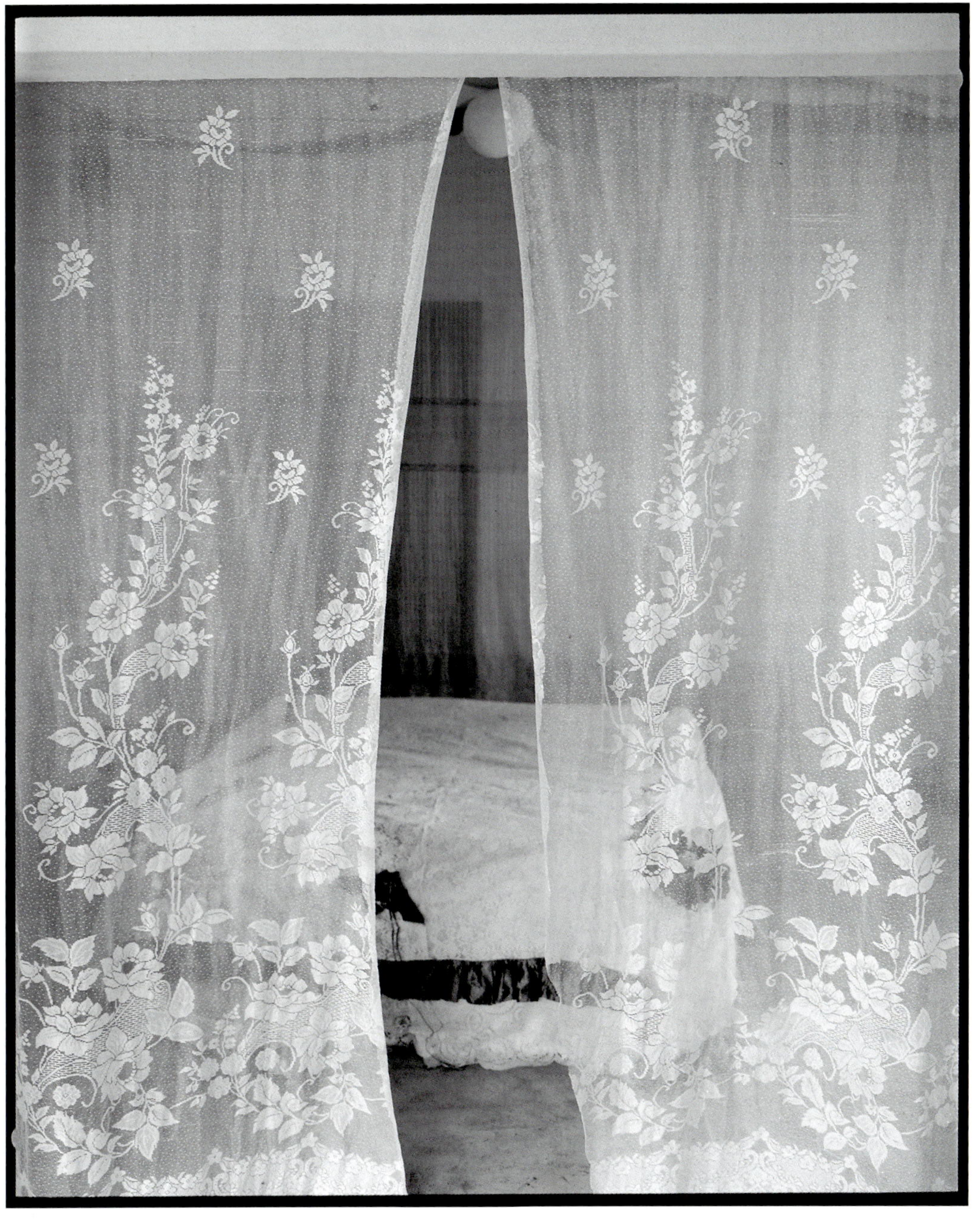

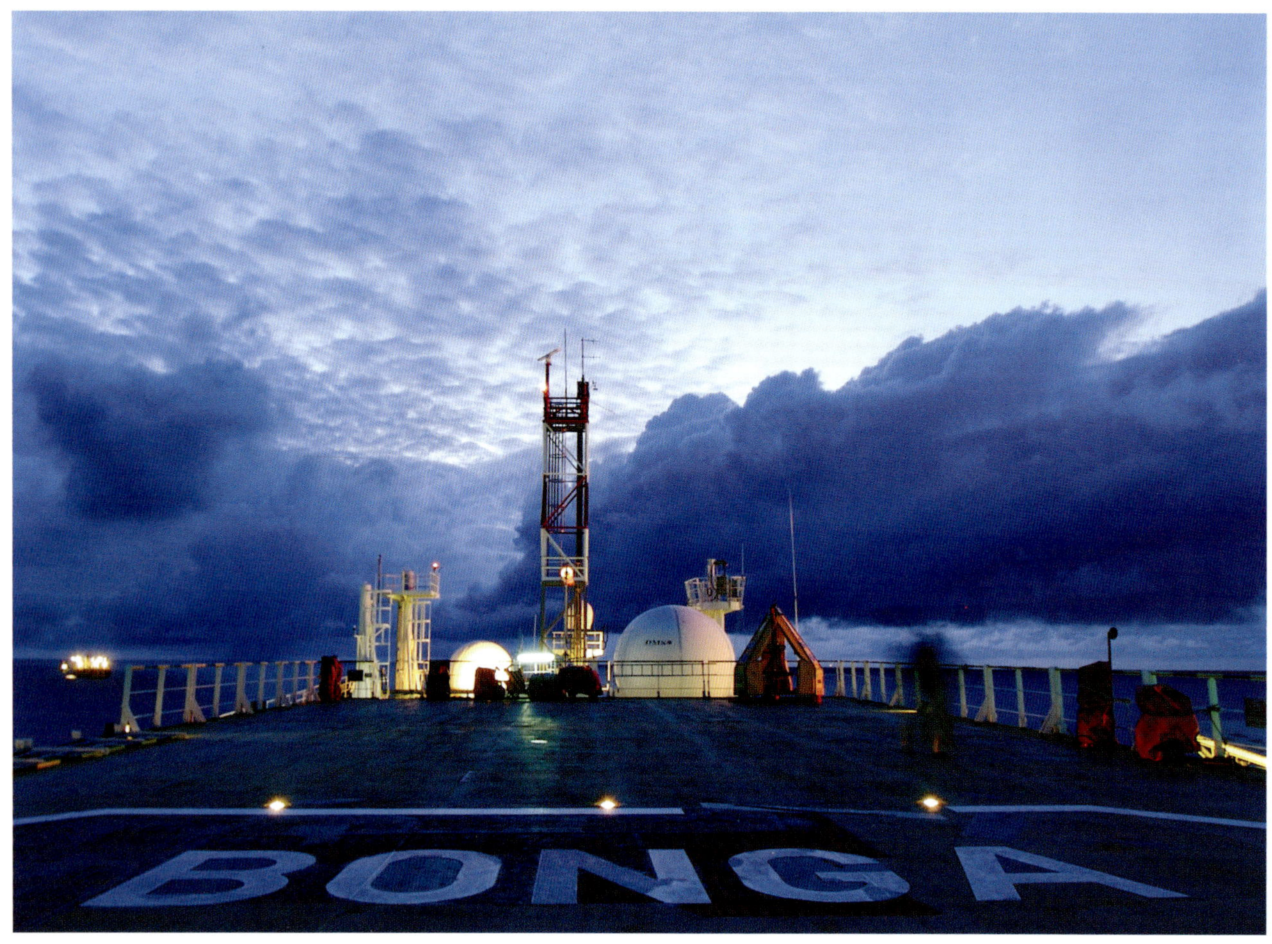

light, surfaces and objects in South Africa, where he spent time as a child, elude narrative, and defy sentimentality, as in his *Untitled* 2005 series. A visual devotion to everyday objects – a cabinet topped with a sewing basket and an ordinary glass vase and grubby rug – oddly frame the tangibility and transience of domestic views.[23]

For Jide Adeniyi-Jones, momentary visual wonders are imbedded in provincial knowledge and political realities. His works manifest a painterly, expressionist approach, and the views are as vivid and singular as his accompanying texts, which are elegantly constructed ruminations on

97 Babajide Adeniyi-Jones, *Bonga*, 2005, colour digital C-print.

previous page: 96 Emeka Okereke, 'Untitled', from *Unspoken Hero*, 2006, digital print.

a subject. Much of Adeniyi-Jones's work begins with a documentary stance, and he selects images of emotional intensity rooted in metaphor and symbols. Such is the case with his images of mourners at the wake-keeping for the king of Opobo; nocturnal festivities are smoothed in the gestures, sparkling cloth and radiant adornment of dancing mourners. Yet Adeniyi-Jones's purview is ultimately political and wide-ranging. Under an obliviously glorious sky sits the surreally efficient, tidy and unpeopled Bonga oil platform (opposite). Situated just off the coast of Lagos, it 'supports a political and economic system that is the antithesis of those attributes'.[24] The image carries a powerful after-effect, recalls what we normally see: masked men in the Niger delta, powerboats carrying oil executives, pipelines in flames.

Manipulations

The strength of artists exploring the conceptual and formal qualities of photographic and digital media have proliferated from the 1990s. South African artists Penny Siopsis, Jean Brundrit, and Tracey Rose's images, installations and video work are among the most distinctive and compelling ruminations on race, gender, origin, sexuality and place. Jane Alexander has created a particularly intricate corpus of photomontages, wherein jarring dissonances allude to a larger ethical framework of depictions of black bodies.[25] Her 1995 *Fragmented Group* contrasts a lightly clad African mannequin, stuck in a museum box, as if viewed by a haloed and pregnant black Virgin Mary. Many of Alexander's works from this series feature imagery of the disturbing sculpture-installations *Butcher Boys*, and the series of childlike figures *Bom Boys*, with adult and children's bodies sprouting sinister animal heads, horns, beaks. Their mutated bodies insinuate the physiological depth of apartheid society's damaging effects.

Fatimah Tuggar's digital photomontages and video pieces reverberate between the realms of domesticity and exoticism, and play along with photography's verism and sense of reliable narrative. *Village Spells* (1994–2005) are still-life sets, and *Fusion Cuisine* a video (*c.* 2004) which

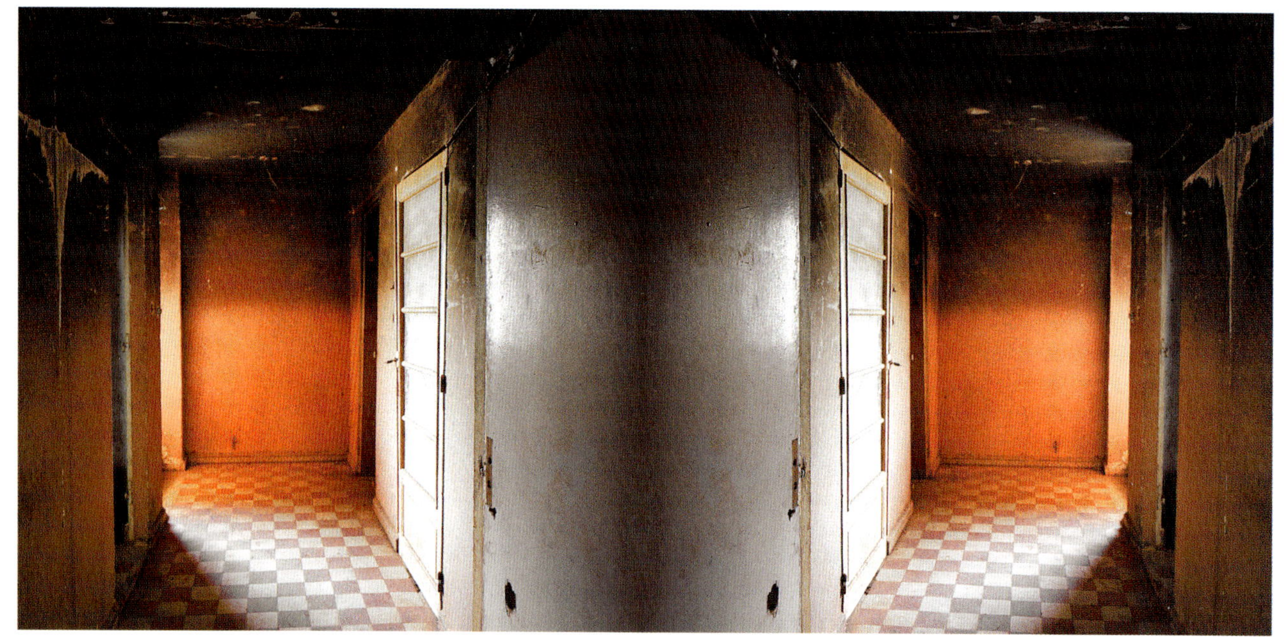

reference the geographic disparities of modern technology. Robots cook over charcoal-stoves, and skyscrapers rise out of calabash rims. Tuggar sends up the omnipresent codes of advertising and portrayals of Africans in Europe and North America, situating domestic encounters with stereotyped imagery, playing with the authority of media rendering more broadly, and teases out the oblique and the wry in these conjunctions.[26]

Lara Baladi's attention to mass visual culture is equally mindful of the art history generated of Egypt as *Oum el Dounia*, or 'Mother of the World'. Works such as *Al Fanous el Sehry* (2002) and *Perfumes and Bazaar* (2005), Baladi cuts and pastes a wealth of images, escorting family portraits, paintings, book illustrations and magazine fodder into an inviting technicolour garden; in doing so she riffs upon old Orientalist standards which persist in various guises today. Formally, Baladi heightens the sense of connection between photographic sheen and the substance of her subjects. The overwhelming scale of her montages, pastiches and installations, running to dozens of metres, stream candy-colours in high definition.[27]

Harandane Dicko's recent works ruminate on obsolete spaces: abandoned factories, warehouses, corridors (opposite). Unlike other artists who dwell on ruined interiors as *loci* of memory, Dicko interprets their otherworldly aspects, tricking the space with mirrors and light, and revealing another melancholic dimension with his refracted views. His subjects in the *Désaffections urbaines* series (2007) are anti-picturesque, an antithesis of the 'scenes and views' genre, and their dislocations dazzle.[28] Whether by accident or intention, they evoke the double-vision stereo slides from an earlier century, as well as a range of doubling traditions in photography across west Africa.

Close Up

Many South African photographers during the 1980s were driven by what was implied in the act of making an image: the political defiance or creative gesture implicated therein. Santu Mofokeng's range of approaches during that era reflect an attention to the histories of photographs as objects. Mofokeng's worked as a street photographer in Soweto and with the Afrapix collective, a guiding principle of which was that activist photographers were ethically bound to override the prerogatives of their subjects on behalf of the greater good of exposing apartheid's conditions. Frustrated that his representations of 'struggle' did not resonate with people in townships, Mofokeng changed tactics by reconsidering 'the work that people actually keep for themselves'.[29] The discrepancy between political and desirable portrayals suggested an expansion of photography's use as an act of political intervention, leading to the *Look at Me/Black Photo Album* project.[30] Photographing old family portraits, writing down any information the owners recalled, and later digitally 'repairing' parts of them, *Black Photo Album* became a respectable and subversive pictorial social memory. Shown as a slide show interspersed with names, histories and his own questions, they are a testimony and an archive, a counterpart and defiant complement to the archives and catalogues of African people predominating in South Africa's photographic legacy in public archives.

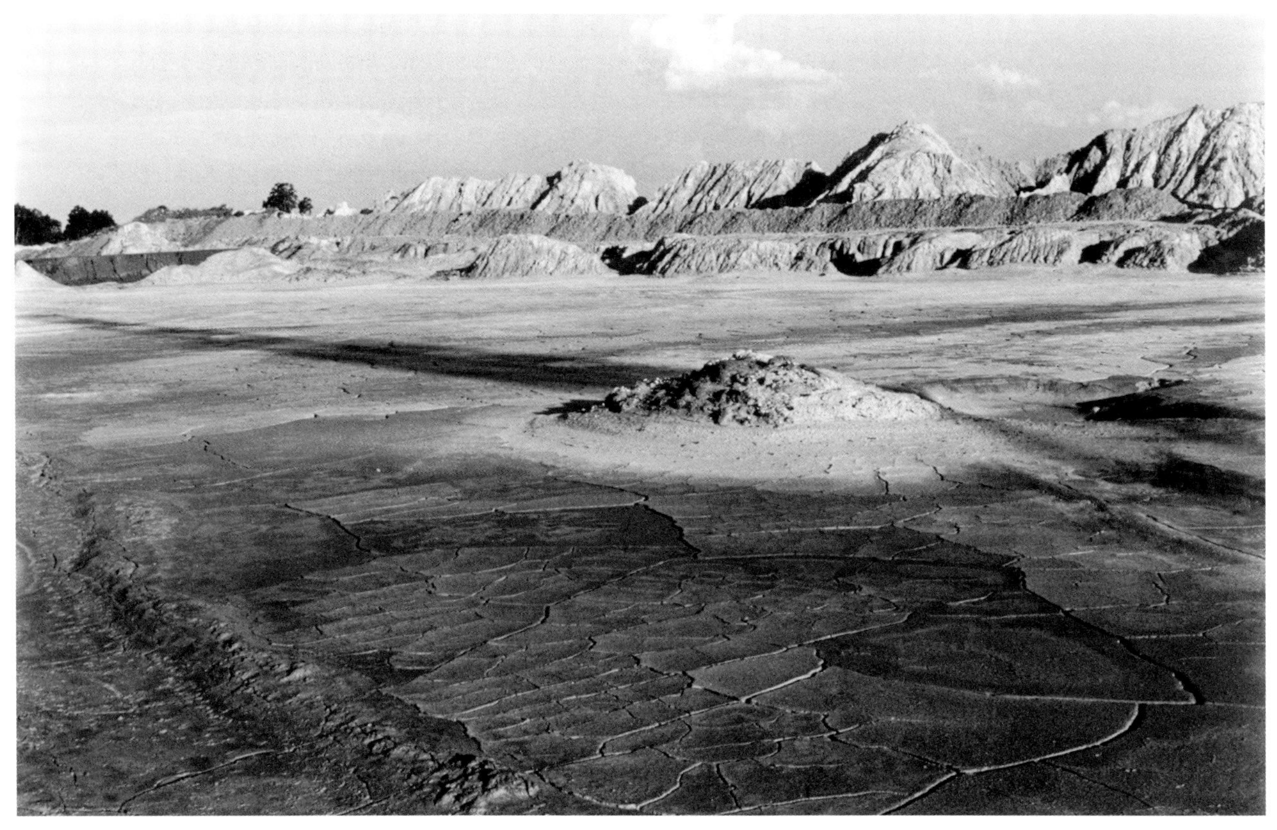

Since the early 1990s, the ethics and imperatives of making documentary photographs have changed and grown even more complex. Mofokeng turned his attention to intense religious devotions that some have sought in the aftermath of apartheid's official end, as seen in his series *Chasing Shadows* at Motouleng cave (1997–ongoing). Another set of works in progress draw attention to the use of land, such as juxtapositions of billboards in township landscapes. His *Germiston Mine Dumps* (above) manifests the country's wealth as a site overlaying human and mineral capital, and is at the same time a twist on a pictorialism of land use, ownership and desolation, and part of a larger series on multiple histories overlaying such contested topography.[31] Mofokeng's recent projects include work on climate change and HIV/AIDS;[32] aware of the 'industry'

99 Santu Mofokeng, *Germiston Mine Dumps*, 1990s, black-and-white photograph.

sustained by the health crisis in southern Africa, he turned away from
making distressing narratives and the stigma implicit in creating such
depictions. Instead he moved in a more oblique and circumspect manner,
considering the spaces and homes as they are run by orphaned children,
observing how home, land, environment and roles change once adults
have gone.[33]

Another artist whose work has drawn on the possibilities of tracing
contours of society's divisions – in this case, Lagos – Zaynab Toyosi
Odunsi's work is also attuned to the problematic ethics of depiction, as
a personal and public act, and in the resulting objects. Her attention to
disconcerting subjects could not have been managed without the benefit
of slowly developed relationships. In her projects, the trace of her presence,
a long negotiation, and deliberate arrows drawn to subject/space/time
frame all reference this guardedness and protection in her depictions.
Odunsi made essayistic images of a nine-year-old girl managing a stall as
she cared for her three younger siblings in *Khadija* (2003). She has also
turned her camera to teenagers working as dancers, DJs and prostitutes
at Varieties nightclub, living on Kuramo beach (illus. 100). These register
Odunsi's formal virtuosity in capturing mood, playing with the light,
visibly revealing her connection with these subjects; her empathetic
and non-judgmental stance gathers together a multifaceted and complicated view of people's poverty and resilience into the frame. So despite
the exhaustion and damage they register, Odunsi's works veer away from
anonymity and towards individual stories.[34]

As Odunsi has travelled for work, her projects have grown more conceptual while examining relationships and interior life. Odunsi explores
stereotypes of encounters of African-ness and French-ness, hospitality
and marginality in Paris; she inserts herself, a self-invited Nigerian
dinner guest, into various 'host family' portraits as part of her approach-
ing an assortment of strangers.[35] The results are full of humour and defy
expectations. Odunsi presently works as a lecturer and photographer
in Saudi Arabia, and there she has intensified her engagement with the
interior feminine worlds she is privy to; and the inviting possibilities
more conceptual and contemplative work for an artist accustomed to
moving freely in public. Her recent works delve into this expansion of

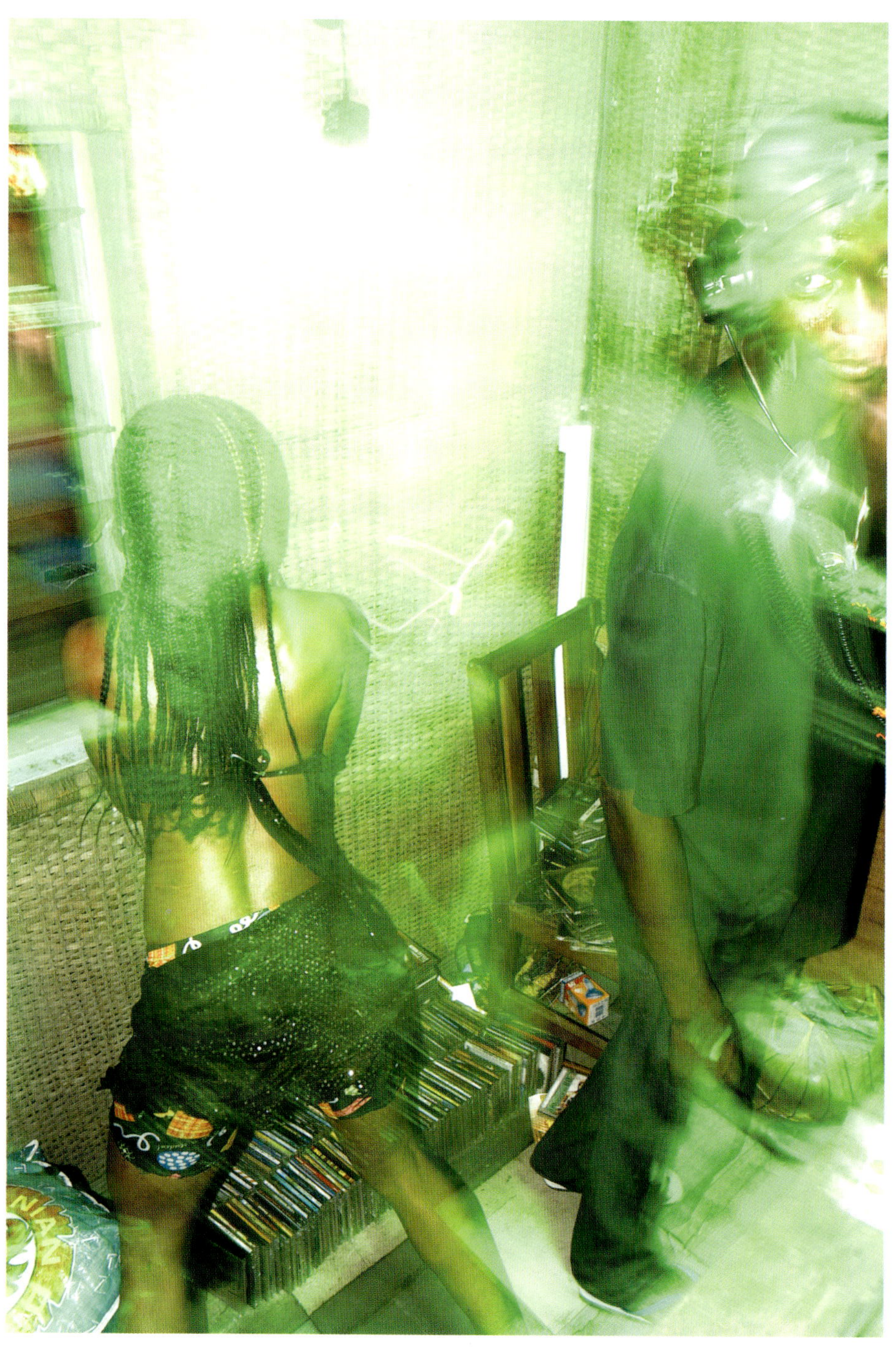

the social and intellectual dimensions of photographic practice, and feminine subjecthood as a Muslim woman photographer.[36] She seems intrigued by the challenges of picturing facets of life in the face of such privacy, and holds her subjects in a manner that's both guarded and complex, underlining the element of surprise, working against the formulaic and moralistic. Her clear-eyed ethical lens is a contrast to so much voyeuristic work; her images credit the viewer with a nuanced grasp of interaction across dissolved frontiers. Odunsi's work, like the best of her contemporaries, demands we jettison the fantasy of sealed cultural worlds. There are few relevant distinctions between photographs as art and as socially useful intervention.

Exhibitions beyond Africa

Optimism and interest in African photography's historic and current vibrancy is dotted across the continent, most predominantly in its urban centres. Photographers are well represented in the galleries and museums of South Africa's comparatively sturdy economy. On the other hand, perhaps because it is staged in one of the continent's poorest countries, the circumstances of Rencontres Africaines de la Photographie biennale at Bamako, Mali, brings into sharp relief the different economic registers of practitioners across the continent. The Rencontres has endeavours to be geographically inclusive and wide-ranging in its selection of photographers. Yet often, those who exhibit and who can attend are a relatively elite affair of people with significant financial means or sponsorship. As is true with many arts festivals, its organizations have done little to support local photographers, institutions or Bamakois audiences.[37] Indeed, the dearth of substantive patronage on the continent inflects the framing of most contemporary photographers working today, and encourages many to migrate for better access to resources. Without meaning to, many exhibition programmes bring into sharp relief the unevenness of access to the infrastructure photographers (and their exhibitions) require.

 That said, many of the activist and humanist impulses in these present-day artists take for granted that a focus on the intimate reverberates beyond

100 Zaynab Toyosi Odunsi, 'Shimmering Lights', from *Kuramo Nights*, 2003, digital C-print.

the local geography. As examples throughout this volume attest, the flow
of ideas, technologies and inspirations are not phenomena of a one-way
movement. They defy pervasive assumptions we often face about notions
of 'Africanness' and authenticity. In the works mentioned here, artists
expect that there is a multivalence inhering in their projects, the awareness of sharply divided worlds of access and opportunity. The venues for
display, publication and exhibition are vastly different once one enters
the market tracks of the global north. These divisions ripple into the
public discourses and critical writing that attend these photographs.

Before the late 1980s, very few photographic exhibitions on the
continent drew international attention; the increasingly commonplace
inclusion of contemporary African and diaspora photographers in
exhibitions in the USA and Europe is a very recent phenomenon. This
development is due in no small part to the efforts of writers and curators
who produced Revue Noire's publications from 1991, the exhibition
In/Sight: African Photographers, 1940 to the Present (Guggenheim Museum,
New York, 1996), and the journals *Nka*, *Art South Africa* and *Third Text*
among many other critical and exhibition projects. Recently, museum
and gallery audiences have glimpsed African contemporary photography
beyond studio portraiture; to wit, the Lion d'Or prize at the Venice
Biennale went to Bamako studio portraitist Malick Sidibé in 2007.
Okwui Enwezor's 2006 *Snap Judgments: New Positions in Contemporary
African Photography* was another confirmation of the arrival of global
Africa in New York's art establishment, The International Center for
Photography. Elizabeth Harney has suggested that Enwezor's project
was an activist effort to set contemporary photographers at the intersection of engaging with larger African photographic histories. For her,
it evoked the 'possibility of commonality beyond geography and race
that lays its claim to Africa as a cosmopolitan entity within a globalized
world'.[38] Indeed, for most publics, coming to terms and appreciating
African cosmopolitanism and the history of its creative modernities and
modernisms would comprise a long-overdue and dramatically political act.

Africa's photographic histories are exceptional; they have formidable
roots and have proliferated in places and in ways that have amplified and
cross-fertilized the continent's arts over an astonishing depth of time.

101 Uche James-Iroha, *Osodi* (Lagos),
2005, digital C-print.

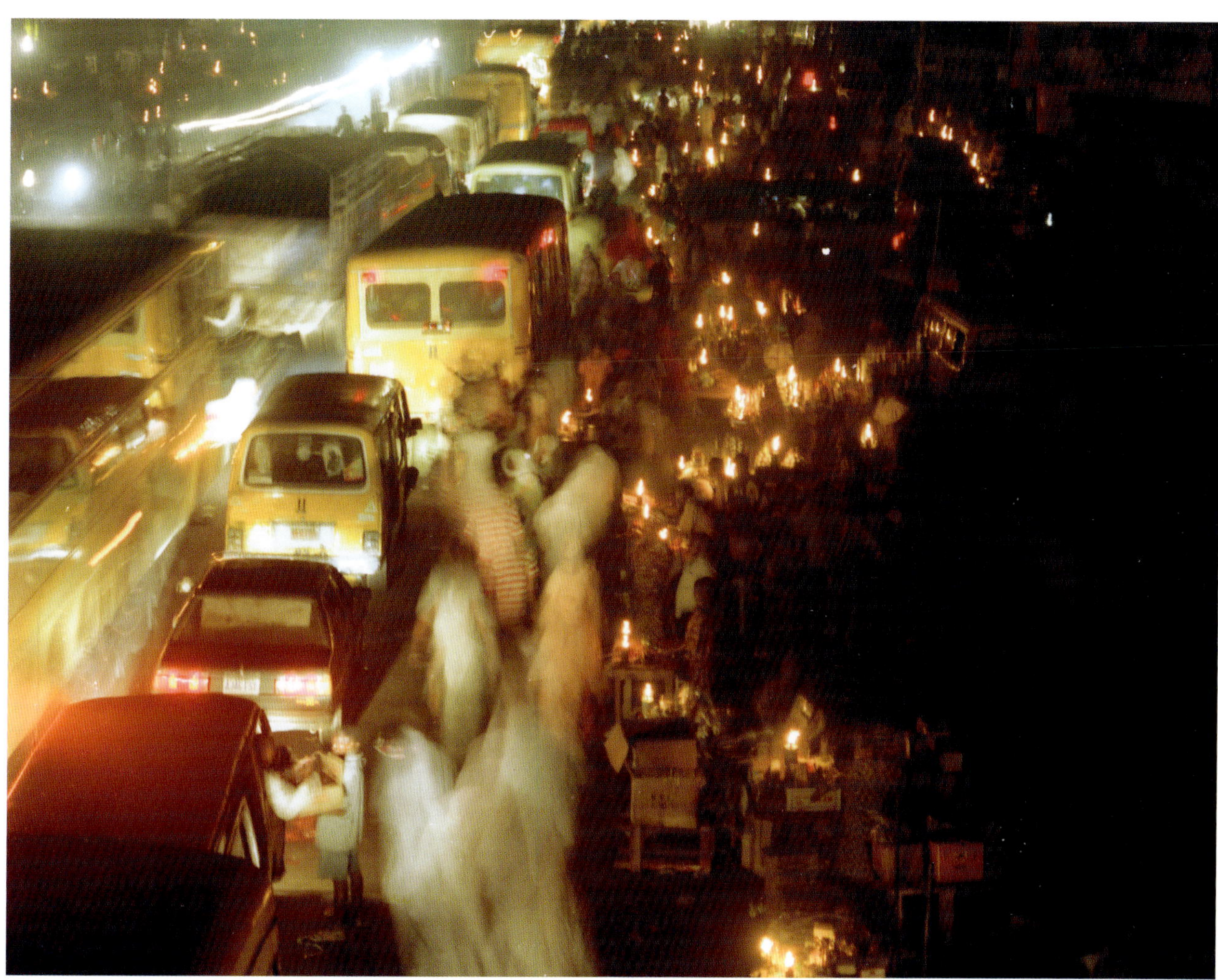

The question is, how best to take account of what is happening now and of what has been inherited? Even as ethnicity, place and shifting senses of belonging and identity weave in and out of artists' work and narratives, new framings will demand that audiences question and engage with what they see in more finite terms. While we endeavour towards a more complete account of African photographic histories – and what their dispersal and existence mean for 'art' and 'photography' and 'Africa' – we can move away from these broad constructs which do little to elucidate them.[39] Contemporary works force viewers towards the finer grain of history and narrative. The most compelling of them tune the eye to what is new and unfamiliar, and to subjects which defy constrictive visualities of space and race. While those far away hope to see more of what these new photographers engage with, those who are fitting the fullness of life within their frame presume their audiences are up to the challenge.

References

Introduction

1 Holm was from Accra, and with his son would own branches in Accra and Lagos, which is why he also advertised in the *Gold Coast Chronicle*, Accra, v/165, 11 August 1894.

2 The persistent notion of a unity beyond the geographic is informed by European notions of race, and the fiction of Africa's insulation from the rest of the globe. V. Y. Mudimbe argued that the notion of 'Africa' was created by non-Africans as a paradigm of difference, through which Europeans in particular have fashioned images of an exotic 'other', see Mudimbe, *The Invention of Africa: Gnosis, Philosophy, and the Order of Knowledge* (Bloomington, IN, 1988).

3 Chinua Achebe's interview, in Kwame Anthony Appiah, *In my Father's House, African in the Philosophy of Culture* (Oxford, 1992), p. 173.

4 Okwui Enwezor and Octavio Zaya, 'Colonial Imaginary, Tropes of Disruption: History, Culture and Representation in the Works of African Photographers', in *In/Sight: African Photographers, 1940 to the Present*, exh. cat. Guggenheim Museum, ed. Clare Bell (New York, 1996), p. 20.

5 Ibid., p. 29.

6 Olu Oguibe, 'Photography and the Substance of the Image', in *In/Sight*, p. 233; Nicolas Monti, *Africa Then* (New York, 1987).

7 John Picton, 'From Lagos Island to the Picasso Bar, or: How African Art Is as African Artists Do', paper presented at the Pan African Circle of Artists conference, Enugu, Nigeria, May 2002; I thank him for sharing his draft with me.

8 Jennifer Bajorek, remarks at workshop 'Creating the Global Image Archive', Goldsmiths, London, 16 February 2009.

9 See research done on private local collections on the continent by Erika Nimis, *Photographes de Bamako de 1935 à nos jours* (Paris, 1998); Frédérique Chapuis, 'The Pioneers of St Louis', in *Anthology of African and Indian Ocean Photography*, ed. P.M.S. Léon and N. Fall (Paris, 1999); Santu Mofokeng, 'The Black Photo Album/Look at Me: 1890–1950', *Nka: Journal of Contemporary African Art*, 4 (1996), pp. 54–7; Tobias Wendl and Heike Behrend, eds, *Snap Me One! Studiofotografhen in Afrika* (Munich, 1998); Liam Buckley, 'Objects of Love and Decay: Colonial Photographs in a Postcolonial Archive', *Cultural Anthropology*, xx/2 (2005), pp. 249–70.

10 Elizabeth Edwards, *Raw Histories, Photographs, Anthropology and Museums* (Oxford, 2001); Elizabeth Edwards and Janice Hart, eds, *Photographs Objects Histories: On the Materiality of Images* (London, 2004); Christopher Morton, 'The Anthropologist as Photographer: Reading the Monograph and Reading the Archive', *Visual Anthropology*, xviii/4 (2005), pp. 389–405; Buckley, 'Love and Decay'; Erin Haney, 'Film, Charcoal, Time: Contemporaneities in Gold Coast Photographs', *History of Photography*, xxxiv/2 (May 2010).

11 Edwards and Hart, eds, *Photographs Objects Histories*; Deborah Poole, *Vision, Race and Modernity: A Visual Economy of the Andean Image World*, (Princeton, NJ, 1997); Christopher Pinney, *Camera Indica: The Social Life of Indian Photographs* (London, 1997); Haney, 'Film, Charcoal, Time'.

12 See Andrew Roberts, ed., *Photographs as Sources for African History* (London, 1988); David Killingray and Andrew Roberts, 'An Outline History of Photography in Africa to ca. 1940', in *History of Africa: A Journal of Method*, xvi/1 (1989), pp. 197–208; Vera Viditz-Ward, 'Photography in Sierra Leone, 1858–1918', in *Sierra Leone: Two Centuries of Intellectual Life*, ed. M. Last, P. Richards and C. Fyfe (Manchester, 1987); much of the work by Christraud Geary, especially *Images from Bamum: German Colonial Photography at the Court of King Njoya, Cameroon, West Africa, 1902–1915*, (Washington, DC, 1988) and *In and Out of Focus, Images from Central Africa, 1885–1960* (Washington, DC, 2002); numerous compilations by *Revue Noire*, particularly the *Anthology of African and Indian Ocean Photography* (Paris, 1998); the exhibitions and writing of Okwui Enwezor, Olu Oguibe, Erika Nimis, Michael Godby, Kathleen Grundlingh, Patricia Hayes, Omar Badsha, Elizabeth Edwards, forthcoming by Jennifer Bajorek, and forthcoming by the author; and conversations with Jide Adeniyi-Jones, Jennifer Bajorek, Liam Buckley, Julie Crooks, Christraud Geary, Elizabeth Harney, Jessica Levin Martinez, Akinbode Akinbiyi, Erika Nimis, Jürg Schneider, John Parker, John Picton and Vera Viditz-Ward.

one: Towards a Wider History

1 Nissan N. Perez, *Focus East: Early Photography in the Near East 1839–1885* (New York, 1988), p. 196. Frédéric Goupil-Fesquet's account states otherwise, that the Pasha called it the work of the Devil: See Frédéric Goupil-Fesquet, *Voyage d'Horace Vernet en Orient* (Brussels, 1844).

2 This notion of visual economies and flows of imagery comes from Deborah Poole, *Vision, Race and Modernity: A Visual Economy of the Andean Image World* (Princeton, NJ, 1997).

3 Vera Viditz-Ward, 'Photography in Sierra Leone, 1850–1918', *Africa*, lvii/4 (1987); Liam Buckley, 'Objects of Love and Decay: Colonial Photographs in a Postcolonial Archive', *Cultural Anthropology*, xx/2 (2005), pp. 249–70; Erin Haney, 'If These Walls Could Talk! Photographs, Photographers and their Patrons in Accra and Cape Coast, Ghana, 1840–1940', unpub. PhD thesis, University of London, 2004.

4 See Perez, *Focus East*; Kathleen Stewart Howe, *Excursions Along the Nile: The Photographic Discovery of Ancient Egypt*, exh. cat., Santa

Barbara Museum of Art (Santa Barbara, CA, 1993); Douglas R. Nickel, *Francis Frith in Egypt and Palestine: A Victorian Photographer Abroad* (Princeton, NJ, 2004).

5 François Arago, quoted in Louis Figuier, *Exposition et Histoire des Principales Découvertes Scientifiques Modernes* (Paris, 1858), pp. 80–81.

6 *Bulletin de la Société de Géographie*, II/12 (1839), p. 223.

7 Howe, *Excursions*, pp. 26–7.

8 Percy Bysshe Shelley, 'Alastor; Or, the Spirit of Solitude', *The Norton Anthology of English Literature*, vol. II, 5th edn (New York, 1986), p. 671.

9 A. D. Bensusan, *Silver Images: The History of Photography in Africa* (Cape Town, 1966), p. 80; Nicolas Monti, *Africa Then* (New York, 1987); F. Musso, *L'Algérie des Souvenirs* (Paris, 1976); and albums in the Getty collection.

10 The literature has expanded on this topic immeasurably; for two early articles see Raymond Corbey, 'Alterity: The Colonial Nude', *Critique of Anthropology*, 8 (1988), pp. 75–92; Malek Alloula, *The Colonial Harem* (Minneapolis, 1986).

11 See Perez, *Focus East*, for biographies of many of these photographers in Egypt.

12 One recent programme which seeks out private archives of old photography from this region is the Arab Image Foundation, based in Lebanon and online at www.fai.org.lb

13 Viditz-Ward, 'Sierra Leone'; Ann Shumard, *A Durable Memento: Portraits by Augustus Washington, African-American Daguerreotypist*, exh. cat., National Portrait Gallery, Washington, DC (1999); Erin Haney, 'If These Walls Could Talk'; Jürg Schneider, 'The Topography of the Early History of African Photography', *History of Photography*, XXXIV/2 (May 2010).

14 Larry W. Yarak, 'Early Photography in Elmina', *Ghana Studies Council Newsletter*, 8 (1995), pp. 9–11, citing *Elmina Journal*, 19 January 1840.

15 Yarak, 'Early Photography'; NBKG 366: *Elmina Journal*, 30 January 1847.

16 Though none have been recovered, Daniel West's journal indicates he gave a number of daguerreotype images to his subjects, see Daniel West, *The Life and Journals of the Rev. Daniel West, Wesleyan Minister on Deputation to the Wesleyan Mission Stations on the Gold Coast, Western Africa* (London, 1857), p. 193.

17 Shumard, *Durable Memento*; by 1860, Washington was in Saint-Louis, Senegal, see Frédérique Chapuis, 'The Pioneers of St Louis', in *Anthology of African and Indian Ocean Photography* (Paris, 1999), p. 51; Viditz-Ward noted Washington's advertisement in the Freetown *New Era*, see 'Photography in Sierra Leone, 1858–1918', *Africa*, LVII/4 (1987).

18 Schneider, *Topography*; J. Schneider, 'Francis W. Joaque: An frican Photographer Between Freetown and Libreville', *Visual Anthropology*, forthcoming 2010; J. Schneider, 'Francis W. Joaque, Photographer, Sierra Leone, Fernando Po, Gaboon: Eine Fallstudie zur Geschichte der Fotografie in West- und Zentralafrika, 1840–1890', unpub. PhD thesis, University of Basel, forthcoming 2010.

19 John Falconer, 'African Photographs in the Royal Commonwealth Society Library', *African Research and Documentation*, XXXI (1983), pp. 12–19; Christopher Fyfe, *A History of Sierra Leone* (London, 1962), p. 362; Vera Viditz-Ward, 'Studio Photography in Freetown', *Anthology of African and Indian Ocean Photography* (Paris, 1999); Haney, 'If These Walls Could Talk'.

20 Haney, 'If These Walls Could Talk'; Barbara Frey Näf and Jürg Schneider, pers. comm., 26 October 2006.

21 *The Illustrated London News*, 20 December 1873; Haney, 'If These Walls Could Talk', ch. 1.

22 Schneider, *Topography*; see also the discussion of a related photographic commission to photographically survey the Empire's peoples by Elizabeth Edwards, *Raw Histories: Photographs, Anthropology and Museums* (Oxford, 2001).

23 Tobias Wendl and Heike Behrend, eds, *Snap Me One! Studiofotografen in Afrika* (Munich, 1998); T. Wendl, 'Portraits and Scenery', *Anthology of African and Indian Photography* (Paris, 1999); Haney, 'If These Walls Could Talk', ch. 3.

24 *The Gold Coast Times*, 10 May 1884.

25 Erin Haney, 'Film, Charcoal, Time: Contemporaneities in Gold Coast Photographs', *History of Photography*, XXXIV/2 (May 2010); Haney and Schneider, guest eds, *Visual Anthropology*, special issue on West African photographic histories, forthcoming January 2011; manuscript on the Lutterodts in progress.

26 Frédérique Chapuis, 'The Pioneers of Saint-Louis', *Anthology of African and Indian Ocean Photography* (Paris, 1999), p. 51.

27 Xavier Ricou, *Trésors de l'iconographie du Sénégal colonial* (Paris, 2007); Ricou notes that most nineteenth-century photographers and postcard producers in Senegal were French, although there were also military, itinerant professionals, travellers and enthusiasts; see Ricou's website at http://senegalmetis.com.

28 Important sources include L'Association Images et Mémoires: www.imagesetmemoires.com/index2.html; Images du passé en Afrique de l'Ouest: http://idpao.com/index.php; and Ricou's site – Patricia Hickling, pers. comm., 5 January 2008.

29 Opinion cited, Hickling, 5 January 2008; Philippe David has completed an exhaustive survey of Fortier's postcards and estimated that two thirds of West African postcards are of Senegal; Philippe David, *Inventaire Général des Cartes Postales Fortier* (Paris, 1986–8); see David's postcards at www.imagesetmemoires.com/index2.html; see also Christraud Geary, 'Different Visions? Postcards from Africa by European and African Photographers and Sponsors', *Delivering Views: Distant Cultures in Early Postcards*, ed. Christraud Geary and Virginia-Lee Webb (Washington, DC, 1998); Patricia Hickling, 'The Early Photographs of Edmond Fortier: Documenting Postcards from Senegal', *African Research and*

Documentation, CII (2007), pp. 37–51.

30 Haney, 'If These Walls Could Talk'; Haney, 'Going Forward'.

31 Haney, 'If These Walls Could Talk'; *The Gold Coast Times*, 12 May 1883; *The Gold Coast Times*, 23 April 1884.

32 Allister Macmillan, ed., *The Red Book of West Africa* (1920; reprinted London, 1968), p. 132; David Killingray and Andrew Roberts, 'An Outline History of Photography in Africa to *ca.* 1940', in *History of Africa: A Journal of Method*, XVI/1 (1989), pp. 197–208.

33 Donald Simpson and Peter Lyon, *Commonwealth in Focus: 130 Years of Photographic History* (Victoria, Australia, 1982), p. 118.

34 Ibid., pp. 34–5.

35 A. D. Bensusan, *Silver Images: The History of Photography in Africa* (Cape Town, 1966), pp. 2–3.

36 Quoted in the *Grahamstown Journal*, 28 November 1846; Bensusan, *Silver Images*, p. 10.

37 Bensusan, *Silver Images*, p. 15.

38 James R. Ryan, *Picturing Empire: Photography and the Visualization of the British Empire* (London, 1997), p. 37.

39 Kirk made notable images of coastal towns in the 1860s from Sena, Mozambique through Mombasa, Kenya; see Bensusan, *Silver Images* and Ryan, *Picturing Empire*.

40 Stereographs were commercially available from the 1850s, and representations of Africa were primarily limited to North African views and South Africa until 1909, when Underwood & Underwood introduced a series of 100 African views; see Geary, *In and Out of Focus: Images from Central Africa, 1885–1960* (Washington, DC, 2002); Rick VanderKnyff, 'Parlor Illusions: Stereoscopic Views of Sub-Saharan Africa', *African Arts*, XL/3, pp. 50–63.

41 Henry M. Stanley, *How I Found Livingstone: Travels, Adventures and Discoveries in Central Africa, Including Four months' Residence with Dr. Livingstone* (London, 1872); *Through the Dark Continent: or, The Sources of the Nile Around the Great Lakes of Equatorial Africa, and Down the Livingstone River to the Atlantic Ocean* (New York, 1878).

42 See my ch. 3; and Felix Driver, 'Henry Morton Stanley and His Critics: Geography, Exploration and Empire', *Past and Present*, CXXXIII (November 1991), pp. 134–66.

43 Patrick Brantlinger, 'Victorians and Africans: The Genealogy of the Myth of the Dark Continent', *Critical Inquiry*, 21 (1985), p. 166.

44 James Augustus Grant, *Photographs of Zanzibar by James Augustus Grant, 1860: Moobarik Bombay* (Cambridge University Library: Royal Commonwealth Society Library, 1860), Y3047C.

45 Elizabeth Edwards, 'Photographic Types: Pursuit of Method', *Visual Anthropology*, III/2–3 (1990), p. 235.

46 Portraits were part of Grey's collection now held in the photographic archive of the South Africa National Library.

47 Gustav Fritsch, *Die Eingeborenen Süd-Afrika's ethnographisch und anatomisch beschrieben* (Breslau, 1872).

48 P. Hayes, W. Hartmann, J. Silvester, eds, *The Colonising Camera: Photos in the Making of Namibian History* (Cape Town, 1998); Karel Schoeman, *The Face of the Country: A South African Family Album, 1860–1910* (Cape Town, 1996).

49 Edwards, *Raw Histories*, ch. 6. The much discussed Bleek and Lloyd archive came about in an effort to record knowledge of the fast-dwindling San population, who were driven off their lands, starved and enslaved as a result of Boer trekkers' migrations. See also Pippa Skotnes's *Miscast: Negotiating the Presence of the Bushmen* (Cape Town, 1996); Andrew Bank, *Bushmen in a Victorian World: The Remarkable Story of the Bleek–Lloyd Collection of Bushman Folklore* (Cape Town, 2006).

50 Jill R. Dias, 'Photographic Sources for the History of Portuguese-speaking Africa, 1870–1914', *History in Africa*, 18 (1991), p. 67; Killingray and Roberts, *Outline History*, p. 199; J. A. da Cunha Moraes published the four-volume *Africa Occidental* (Lisbon, 1885–1888); see also the Falkenstein collections (1876) at the Royal Geographical Society, London.

51 Dias, 'Photographic Sources'; Andrew Roberts, ed., *Photographs as Sources of African History* (London, 1988).

52 Geary and Webb, *Delivering Views*.

53 Santu Mofokeng, *The Black Photo Album/Look at Me: 1890–1910s*, installation (1996). See also similar recuperative projects and writings by Hayes et al., *The Colonising Camera*; Skotnes, *Miscast*; and Marjorie Bull and Joseph Denfield, *Secure the Shadow: The Story of Cape Photograph from its Beginnings to the End of 1870* (Cape Town, 1970).

54 *Le Cernéean*, 27 February 1840; Tristan Bréville, 'En route to India', *Anthology of African and Indian Ocean Photography* (Paris, 1999), p. 319.

55 *Le Cernéean*, 16 June 1840; Bréville, 'En route to India', p. 320.

56 More research is in progress; many of these may have been French; Bréville has a more extensive list.

57 See Musée de la Photographie du Maurice, http://musee-photo.voyaz.com.

58 See ch. 4 of this volume for a fuller discussion, and Bréville, 'En route to India'.

59 For instance Chambay invented a method of transferring colour to paper positives; after nine years operating studios on Mauritius, he left to open two commercial studios in Paris.

60 William Zitte, 'The Anthropometry of Memory', *Anthology of African and Indian Ocean Photography* (Paris, 1999), p. 351; examples in the Archives Départmentales de La Réunion, La Bibliothèque Nationale de France, and the Centre des Archives d'Outre-Mer.

61 Marc Kichenapanaïdou, 'Les Photos Lontan de Jean Legros', *Témoignages du mardi*, 25 Septembre 2007, www.temoignages.re/article.php3?id_article=24969; Jackie Ryckebusch, *Louis Antoine Roussin et ses précurseurs: historique de la lithographie sur la Réunion* (Paris, 1994). http://iconotheque-de-l-ocean-indien.org

62 Louis Antoine Roussin, *L'Album de l'île de la Réunion: Recueil de Dessin et de Texts Historiques et Descriptifs* (Saint-Denis, Réunion,

published in portfolios 1856–1876); Jackie Ryckebusch, *Louis Antoine Roussin et ses Precurseuers les Debuts de la Lithographie et de la Photographie à la Reunion* (Paris, 1994); exhibition *Louis Antoine Roussin*, Musée Léon Dierx, Saint-Denis, 2008–9, see http://lycee-antoine-roussin.ac-reunion.fr/IMG/pdf/roussin-dossier-documentaire.pdf

63 Zitte, 'Anthropometry of Memory'.

64 Ibid., p. 352; amateurs included Octave Dumesnil, Zampierro, Eruida, Claude Marion and several Indian photographers; this significant photographic legacy has recently been the subject of interest, for example, see the online archive in progress: http://iconotheque-de-l-ocean-indien.org.

65 Simon Peers, *The Working of Miracles: William Ellis: Photography in Madagascar 1853–1865* (London, 1995).

66 Ibid.

67 Frédéric Izydorczyk, 'The Great Island', *Anthology of African and Indian Ocean Photography* (Paris, 1999).

68 Isolde Brielmaier, '"Picture Taking" and the Production of Urban Identities on the Kenyan Coast, 1940–1980', unpub. PhD, Columbia University (2003), ch. 1.

69 Heike Behrend in Robin Lenman, ed., *The Oxford Companion to the Photograph* (2005), p. 11.

70 See Killingray and Roberts, *Outline History*.

71 Although his daguerreotypes have not survived, engravings based on them have been published: Henry Aaron Stern, *Wanderings Among the Falashas in Abyssinia: Together with Descriptions of the Country and its Various Inhabitants* (London, 1862).

72 Richard Pankhurst and Denis Gérard, 'Court Photographers', *Anthology of African and Indian Ocean Photography* (Paris, 1999), pp. 119–33.

73 Richard Pankhurst, 'The Political Image: The impact of the Camera in an Ancient Independent African State', in Elizabeth Edwards, *Photography and Anthropology 1860–1920* (New Haven, CT, 1992), p. 234.

74 Pankhurst and Gérard, 'Court Photographers'; Pankhurst, 'The Genesis of Photography in Ethiopia and the Horn of Africa', *British Journal of Photography*, CXXIII/44 (1976), pp. 952–3.

two: Portraits in the World

1 'Ethiopia', *The African Times*, 23 February 1863, cont'd. 23 March 1863.

2 The Gambian photographers Liam Buckley met, moved from cities to rural hinterlands in the dry seasons; personal communication, January 2008.

3 Deborah Poole's notion of visual economies suggests that all kinds of imagery-photographs, postcards, posters, book and newspaper illustrations, paintings and the like comprise an image-world, and the circuits through which these images travel are uneven and often one-sided; these manifestations matter as much as the images themselves. Deborah Poole, *Vision, Race and Modernity, A Visual Economy of the Andean Image World* (Princeton, NJ, 1997). I thank Jennifer Bajorek and Claire Colebrook, who with workshop presenters encouraged rethinking of these circuits during their 'Creating the Global Image Archive', Goldsmiths, University of London, 16 February 2009.

4 *The Trader: A Monthly Commercial Record and Trade Review*, Freetown, 28 February 1891.

5 Erin Haney, 'If These Walls Could Talk! Photographs, Photographers and their Patrons in Accra and Cape Coast, Ghana, 1840–1940', unpub. PhD thesis, University of London, 2004.

6 Ibid., ch. 3.

7 The Lisk-Carew studio in Freetown also produced Sande and Bondu society portraits, see Christraud Geary, 'Different Visions? Postcards from Africa by European and African Photographers and Sponsors' in *Delivering Views: Distant Cultures in Early Postcards*, ed. Christraud Geary and Virginia-Lee Webb (Washington, DC, 1998); and Julie Crook's discussion of A. Lisk-Carew's Susu and Bondo society portraits in her thesis on 'Lisk-Carew and Photography in Sierra Leone', forthcoming, University of London.

8 More research is underway on photographic collections in West Africa; it is clear from collections considered thus far in southern Ghana that these portrait traditions were quite variegated through the early twentieth century.

9 Poole, *Vision, Race and Modernity*, p. 112; Peter Hamilton and Roger Hargreaves, *The Beautiful and the Damned: The Creation of Identity in Nineteenth-Century Photography* (London, 2001).

10 See Christraud Geary, 'The Black Female Body, the Postcard, and the Archives', in *Black Womanhood, Images, Icons and Ideologies of the African Body*, exh. cat., ed. Barbara Thompson, Hood Museum of Art, Hanover, New Hampshire (Hanover, NH, 2008). This topic has been considered in a number of quite ideological essays: Mieke Bal, 'A Postcard from the Edge,' in *Double Exposures: The Subject of Cultural Analysis* (London, 1996); Achille Mbembe, 'Regard d'Afrique sur l'image et l'imaginaire coloniale', in *Image et Colonies*, ed. Pascal Blanchard and Armelle Chatelier (Paris, 1993).

11 Isolde Brielmaier, '"Picture Taking" and the Production of Urban Identities on the Kenyan Coast, 1940–1980', unpub. PhD, Columbia University, 2003; Prita Meier, 'Selfhood on the Edge, Portrait Photography in 19th-century Zanzibar', paper delivered at the Boston University symposium, November 2008.

12 Geary, *Delivering Views*, p. 154; Raymond Corbey, 'Alterity: The Colonial Nude', *Critique of Anthropology*, VIII/3 (1988), pp. 75–92.

13 Philippe David published many studies on postcards, see especially on the voluminous Fortier corpus, *Inventaire Général des Cartes Postales Fortier (*Paris, 1986–8); Terence Dickinson, *Gold Coast Picture Postcards, 1898–1957* (Dronfield, UK, 2003).

14 Christraud Geary, *Images from Bamum: German Colonial*

Photography at the Court of King Njoya, Cameroon, West Africa, 1902-1915, exh.cat., National Museum of African Art, Smithsonian Institution (Washington, DC, 1988); Richard Pankhurst and Denis Gérard, 'Court Photographers', *Anthology of African and Indian Ocean Photography* (Paris, 1998), pp. 119–33; Simon Peers, *The Working of Miracles: William Ellis: Photography in Madagascar 1853–1865* (London, 1995); Haney, 'If These Walls Could Talk', ch. 4.

15 Eliot Elisofon, Photographic Archive, National Museum of African Art, Smithsonian Institution; Ghana Photographs Album, 1995–0018. The date is based on Michel Doortmont's research into Gyan's history.

16 Pers. comm., John Picton, 20 July 2006 and 29 June 2007.

17 See Geary's formidable tracing of courtly photography in *Images from Bamum*.

18 Christraud Geary and Joseph Nevadomsky, eds, *African Arts*, XXX/3 and 4, special issue, Benin Centenary.

19 Flora Kaplan's research on the Benin court photographer S. O. Alonge is forthcoming; personal communication with Amy Staples, 19 October 2008.

20 Charles D. Gore, 'Commemoration, Memory and Ownership: Some Social Contexts of Contemporary Photography in Benin City, Nigeria', *Visual Anthropology*, XIV (2001), pp. 321–42.

21 Seydou Keïta, André Magnin, ed., *Seydou Keïta* (Zurich, 1997); Erika Nimis, *Photographes de Bamako de 1935 à nos jours* (Paris, 1998); Elisabeth Bigham, 'Issues of Authorship in the Portrait Photographs of Seydou Keïta', *African Arts*, XXXII/1 (Spring 1999); Jennifer Bajorek, '(Dis)locating Freedom: The Photographic Portraiture of Seydou Keïta', in *Critical Interventions: Journal of African Art and Visual Culture*, special issue on 'Interrogating African Modernity' (2009).

22 Seydou Keïta, in *Seydou Keïta*, pp. 10–11.

23 Unidentified portrait and photographer, collection of El Hadj Adama Sylla, Saint-Louis, Senegal. I am very grateful to Mr Sylla and Dr Jennifer Bajorek for correcting Frédérique Chapuis' estimated date of this image, and for their discussions of this image.

24 Fatma Bassiouni, 'Van-Leo's Unrivaled Images of Cairo's Belle Epoch', *The Middle East Times*, 2–8 December 2000; Pierre Gazio, *Portraits of Glamour: Van Leo, Photographer*, trans. Colin Clement (Cairo, 1997).

25 In 1994 the first *Rencontres de la Photographie Africaine* was held in Bamako, Mali; Bernard Descamps met Samuel Fosso whilst seeking photographers in Bangui; Maria Francesca Bonetti and Guido Schlinkert, *Samuel Fosso*, exh. cat., Calcografia (Rome, 2004).

26 Artist interview with Guido Schlinkert, *Samuel Fosso*, p. 51.

27 Erin Haney, 'Bringing Art up to Date: Photographic Modernities in Time', presented at the Mbanefo Conference, *Interrogating African Modernity*, University of California, Santa Barbara, April 2007.

28 Ibid.

29 Liam Buckley, 'Studio Photography and the Aesthetics of Postcolonialism in The Gambia, West Africa', unpub. PhD, University of Virginia, 2003; Liam Buckley, 'Self and Accessory in Gambian Studio Photography', *Visual Anthropology Review*, XVI/ 2 (Fall–Winter 2000–1), pp. 71–91.

30 Heike Behrend, 'Fragmented Visions: Photo Collages by Two Ugandan Photographers', *Visual Anthropology*, XIV (2001), pp. 301–20.

31 Heike Behrend and Tobias Wendl, eds, *Snap Me One! Studiofotografen in Afrika* (Munich, 1998).

32 Ibid.

33 Tobias Wendl and Nancy du Plessis, *Future Remembrance: Photography and Image Arts in Ghana*, VHS, 55 minutes (1998).

34 Behrend, 'Fragmented Visions', p. 318.

three: 'Observers are worried . . .'

1 Max Kozloff, *Photography and Fascination: Essays* (Danbury, NH, 1979).

2 There were many such projects in this area, among them: European explorer and travel photography, souvenir and postcard imagery of 'types', views, personages, towns, commercial and labour scenes, colonial infrastructure, mission enterprises, and later, images of slaves and prisoners, the Force Publique and European enforcers, and atrocity imagery; all of these moved through different registers of dissemination in the region and overseas. A good overview of this breadth of photography and imagery of this region is Christraud Geary's *In and Out of Focus, Images from Central Africa 1885–1960*, exh. cat., National Museum of African Art (Washington, DC, 2002); see also Kevin Grant, 'Christian Critics of Empire: Missionaries, Lantern Lectures and the Congo Reform Campaign in Britain', *Journal of Imperial and Commonwealth History*, XXIX/2 (2001), pp. 22–57, and Nicholas Mirzoeff's 'Photography at the Heart of Darkness', in *Bodyscape: Art, Modernity and the Ideal Figure* (London, 1995).

3 The photomontages of Sammy Baloji's 2006 series 'Memory' recuperate old photographed Congolese subjects, positioning them in present-day mine sites, very much based in this concern with framing, representation as acquiescence and labour; there is also the political painting traditions by artists such as Tshibumba Kanda Matulu, see Bogumil Jewsiewicki, 'Painting in Zaire: From the Invention of the West to the Representation of the Social Self,' in *Africa Explores: Twentieth Century African Art*, exh. cat., ed. Susan Vogel and Ima Ebong, Center for African Art (New York, 1991), pp. 130–51. For a discussion of local resistances, see A. Isaacman and J. Vansina, 'African Initiatives and Resistance in Central Africa, 1880–1914', in A. Adu Boahen, ed., *General History of Africa*, vol. VII (Paris, 1985).

4 James R. Ryan, *Picturing Empire, Photography and the Visualization*

of the British Empire (Chicago, IL, 1997), p. 223; J. H. Harris, *Rubber is Death* (London, 1906).

5 It has been argued that this nineteenth-century exploration entailed a kind of Western mass amnesia of centuries' worth of accumulated knowledge and exchange between Europe and central Africa, including the Atlantic slave trade, replaced by a vision of an untouched, uninhabited wilderness; see Nicolas Mirzoeff, 'Transculture: From Kongo to the Congo', in *An Introduction to Visual Culture* (London, 1999).

6 Stanley described his actions as necessary to complete his journeys; he wrote of how deserters 'were well flogged and chained' – see Stanley, *How I Found Livingstone* (London, 1872), p. 318 – and said of his African entourage: 'when mud and wet sapped the physical energy of the lazily-inclined, a dog-whip became their backs, restoring them to a sound – sometimes to an extravagant – activity'. John Bierman, *Dark Safari: The Life behind the Legend of Henry Morton Stanley* (New York, 1990), p. 97. Piloting his boat on Lake Tanganyika, Stanley privately recorded that 'the beach was crowded with infuriates and mockers . . . we perceived we were followed by several canoes in some of which we saw spears shaken at us . . . I opened on them with the Winchester Repeating Rifle. Six shots and four deaths were sufficient to quiet the mocking.' *The Exploration Diaries of H. M. Stanley*, ed. Richard Stanley and Alan Neame (New York, 1961), p. 125, records the desertions, illnesses and deaths rarely included in his published accounts. See also Frank McLynn, *Stanley: The Making of an African Explorer* (London, 1989).

7 Henry Morton Stanley, *The Congo and the Founding of its Free State: A Story of Work and Exploration*, 2 vols (New York, 1885); *Through the Dark Continent: or, The Sources of the Nile, Around the Great Lakes of Equatorial Africa, and Down the Livingstone River to the Atlantic Ocean*, 2 vols (New York, 1878). Not all readers were impressed, and protesters included the Aborigines Protection Society and the Anti-Slavery Society; see Adam Hochschild, *King Leopold's Ghost* (New York, 1999), p. 50.

8 See A. Isaacman and J. Vansina, 'African Initiatives'; Jean Stengers and Jan Vansina, 'King Leopold's Congo, 1886–1908', in *Cambridge History of Africa*, ed. Roland Oliver and G. N. Sanderson (Cambridge, 1985), vol. VI; Jean Stengers, 'The Congo Free States and the Belgian Congo before 1914', in L. H. Gann and Peter Duignan, eds, *Colonialism in Africa 1870–1960*, 5 vols (Cambridge, 1969).

9 Stengers and Vansina, 'King Leopold's Congo', pp. 324–7.

10 Geary's *In and Out of Focus* (2002) is an extensive and meticulously researched cataloguing of photography and popular imagery from Central Africa in postcards, photo collections, magazines and commercial and trade imagery. Ethnographic imagery by resident photographers Jean Audema, Robert Visser and Emile Gorlia illustrated local dress, material culture, and those treasures of increasing interest to expanding European museum collections such as ivory tusks, sculpted figures and kingly portraits; see also J. Vansina, 'Photographs of the Sankuru and Kasai River Basin Expedition undertaken by Emil Torday (1876–1931) and M. W. Hilton Simpson (1881–1936)', in *Anthropology and Photography*, ed. Elizabeth Edwards (New Haven, CT, 1992), pp. 193–205; Paul S. Landau, 'Empires of the Visual: Photography and Colonial Administration in Africa', in *Images and Empires, Visuality in Colonial and Postcolonial Africa*, ed. Paul S. Landau and Deborah D. Kaspin (Berkeley, CA, 2002), pp. 141–71.

11 Geary, *In and Out of Focus*, ch. 2; David MacDougall, 'Staging the Body: The Photography of Jean Audema', in *The Corporeal Image: Film, Ethnography and the Senses* (Princeton, NJ, 2006).

12 Emile Gorlia's sizeable collection of lantern slides, glass and stereograph negatives and prints are housed at the Eliot Elisofon Photographic Archive, National Museum of African Art, Smithsonian Institution, Washington, DC; I am indebted to Xavier Couroble who catalogued this collection and I am grateful for his knowledge of this world; see also Geary, *In and Out of Focus*, ch. 2.

13 Katrin Adler and Christine Stelzig, 'Robert Visser and his Photographs from the Loango Coast', *African Arts*, XXXV/4 (2002); Christine Stelzig, 'Altar of Maloango: Being, Nonbeing and Existence of an Object of West Africa', *Baessler-Archiv*, XXXVI/2 (1998), pp. 369–428.

14 Jules Marchal, *L'État Libre du Congo: Paradis Perdu, L'Histoire du Congo 1876–1900*, vol. I (Borgloon, Belgium, 1996), p. 212.

15 Journal of Louis Chaltin (an officer of the Force Publique), 16 July 1892, quoted in David Northrup, *Beyond the Bend in the River: African Labor in Eastern Zaire, 1865–1940* (Athens, OH, 1988), p. 51.

16 Report by a British Vice-Consul, 15 September, 1899; Pultaney to FO, FO 10/731, no. 5, in S.J.S. Cookey, *Britain and the Congo Question: 1885–1913* (London, 1968).

17 George Washington Williams, 'An Open Letter To His Serene Majesty Leopold II', reprinted in John Hope Franklin, *George Washington Williams: A Biography* (Chicago, IL, 1985); see also Bernard Porter, *Critics of Empire: British Radical Attitudes to Colonialism in Africa, 1895–1914* (London, 1968).

18 Other efforts included those of the Baptist Missionary Society; see H. R. Fox Bourne, *The Aborigines Protection Society: Chapters in Its History* (London, 1899); Catherine Ann Cline, *E. D. Morel 1873–1924: The Strategies of Protest* (Belfast 1980); E. D. Morel, *King Leopold's Rule in Africa* (London, 1904); J. H. Harris, *Dawn in Darkest Africa* (London, 1912).

19 Hochschild, *King Leopold's Ghost*, p. 233; Daniel Vangroenweghe, *Du Sang sur les Lianes* (Brussels, 1986), p. 10.

20 University of Chicago anthropologist Professor S. Frederick Starr was an apologist for the Congo regime, and his account of travels in the colony were published with Manuel Gonzalez's photographs in Starr's books, the *Chicago Tribune*, and the widely-sold ethnographic stereograph slides by Underwood & Underwood and

its successor the Keystone View Company; see Geary's account, *In and Out of Focus*, pp. 40–43.

21 Ibid., p. 50; Francis Ramirez and Christian Rolot, 'Histoire du Cinéma Colonial au Zaïre, au Rwanda et au Burundi', *Annales-Série IN-80-Sciences Historiques*, 7 (Tervuren, 1985); Françoise Morimont, 'Herzekiah Andrew Shanu', in *Les Photographes de Kinshasa*, ed. N'Gone Fall (Paris, 2001), pp. 12–16.

22 From Mark Twain's 1905 pamphlet, wherein Leopold was imagined to have cursed 'the incorruptible *Kodak . . .* the only witness I have encountered in my long experience that I couldn't bribe'. *King Leopold's Soliloquy: A Defense of his Congo Rule*, ed. E. D. Morel (London, 1905).

23 Ryan, *Picturing Empire*, p. 223; Joseph Conrad, *Heart of Darkness, with, The Congo Diary*, ed. and intro by Robert Hampson (London, 1995); John Peffer, 'Snap of the Whip/Crossroads of Shame: Flogging, Photography and the Representation of Atrocity in the Congo Reform Campaign', *Visual Anthropology Review*, XXIV/1 (2008), pp. 55–77.

24 Beginning with the work of Nigerian-born photographer Herzekiah Andrew Shanu, see Morimont, *Shanu*; Geary, *In and Out of Focus*; and the work of Sammy Beloji, *Septièmes Rencontres Africaines de la Photographie: Dans La Ville et Au-dela*, exh. cat., ed. Simon Njami, Musée National du Mali, Bamako (2007).

25 A. D. Bensusan, *Silver Images: The History of Photography in Africa* (Cape Town, 1966); M. Bull and J. Denfield, *Secure the Shadow: The Story of Cape Photography from its Beginnings to the End of 1870* (Cape Town, 1970); P. Hayes, W. Hartmann and J. Silvester, eds, *The Colonising Camera: Photos in the Making of Namibian History* (Cape Town, 1998).

26 The African National Congress and the South African Indian Congress (ANC) stepped up a pan-racial set of nationalist strikes, boycotts and civil disobedience, the largest of its kind, in response to the rash of apartheid legislation by the all-white Congress. The 1958 Treason Trial followed the South African Congress Alliance, where a Freedom Charter was signed by delegates as part of a movement advocating a non-racial South Africa, calling for democracy, equal rights for land, education, fair labour laws and nationalized governance. The Trial imprisoned, held, and/ or banned the leadership of the ANC and other Congress parties, (including ANC President Chief Albert Luthuli and Nelson Mandela) and marked a new phase of conflict between the national government and anti-apartheid groups. The 1976 Soweto riots began with youths marching in the township to protest the dire injustices and imbalances of the Bantu education system and forced instruction in Afrikaans, but turned violent once police started shooting at the young marchers.

27 Bensusan, *Silver Images*, pp. 103–5; Kathleen Grundlingh, 'The Development of Photography in South Africa', *Anthology of African and Indian Ocean Photography* (Paris, 1998), p. 244.

28 Patricia Hayes, 'Southern Africa', *The Oxford Companion to the Photograph*, ed. Robin Lenman (Oxford, 2005), p. 13.

29 A first international photography exhibition in the southern hemisphere, it was a joint effort organized by Britain's Royal Photographic Society and the Linked Ring, with the American Photo-Secession Society.

30 Hayes, 'Southern Africa', p. 13; Grundlingh, 'South Africa', p. 244.

31 Jürgen Schadeberg, *Sof'town Blues: Images from the Black '50s* (Hurlyvale, South Africa, 1994); Anthony Sampson, *Drum, the Newspaper that Won the Heart of Africa* (Boston, MA, 1957); Mike Nicol, *A Good-Looking Corpse: World of Drum – Jazz and Gangsters, Hope and Defiance in the Townships of South Africa* (London, 1991); Paul Weinberg, 'Apartheid – A Vigilant Witness: A Reflection on Photography', in *Culture in Another South Africa*, ed. W. Campschreur and J. Divendal (London 1989).

32 Mining heir Jim Bailey revamped the magazine in 1951, geared it towards a black urban audience and installed Anthony Sampson as editor with the editorial board of Joe Rathebe, Dan 'Sport' Twala, Dr Alfred Xuma and Andy Anderson; *The Drum Decade: Stories from the 1950s*, ed. Michael Chapman (Scottsville, South Africa, 2001). *Drum* later expanded to other countries, including Nigeria, Ghana, Sierra Leone, Kenya, Uganda, Tanzania, Zambia and Zimbabwe – it was often banned, but is now widely regarded as one of the most influential illustrated magazines on the continent.

33 Peter Metelerkamp, 'Considering Coloniality in South African Photography', www.petermet.com; Schadeberg, *Sof'town Blues*.

34 Schadeberg, *Sof'town Blues*, p. 16.

35 Nicol, *A Good-Looking Corpse* (1991).

36 Jacky Heyns, *The Beat of Drum: The Story of a Magazine that Documented the Rise of Africa as Told by Drum's Publisher, Editors, Contributors, and Photographers* (Braamfontein, 1982); Nicol, *Good-Looking Corpse*.

37 See Nxumalo's account in Nicol's *A Good-Looking Corpse*, pp. 183–95; see also David Goldblatt's interview with Okwui Enwezor, 'Matter and Consciousness: An Insistent Gaze from a not Disinterested Photographer', in *Fifty-One Years, David Goldblatt*, exh. cat., Museu d'Art Contemporani de Barcelona, David Goldblatt et al. (Barcelona, 2001).

38 Kathleen Grundlingh, 'The Development of Photography in South Africa', in *Anthology of African and Indian Ocean Photography* (Paris, 1999), pp. 246–7; Hayes, 'Southern Africa', p. 13.

39 Omar Badsha, 'Preface', *South Africa: The Cordoned Heart* (New York, 1986), pp. xv–xvi. Peter Magubane described his banning: refused the right to attend gatherings, speak to more than one person at once, enter a school or press, enter a township without a permit, live in Johannesburg without a permit, or speak with another banned person. Photographers could not work because they could not receive credit for their pictures, nor take a picture of more than one person. Family, neighbours, employers were

40 It is crucial to note that many books and photographic publications produced from the 1950s through the 1980s, were only available to international audiences in response to resistance movements in the early 1980s that collaborated with artistic programmes abroad; Paul Weinberg, 'Apartheid – A Vigilant Witness'.

41 Magubane, *South Africa*, p. 7.

42 Weinberg, 'Apartheid', p. 62.

43 Magubane, *South Africa*, pp. 11–12.

44 Ernest Cole, *House of Bondage* (New York, 1967).

45 *Ernest Cole, 1940–1990* [video recording], The Schadeberg Movie Company (Blairgowrie, South Africa, 1999).

46 Cole, *House of Bondage*, p. 170.

47 Joseph Lelyveld, 'One of the Least-known Countries in the World,' in Cole, *House of Bondage* (New York, 1967), p. 19.

48 Ian Berry, *Living Apart, South Africa Under Apartheid* (London, 1996).

49 Derrick Price, 'Drum', in *Photography, A Critical Introduction*, ed. Liz Wells (3rd edn, 2004), p. 78.

50 Peter Metelerkamp, interview with David Goldblatt, September 1999, 'Considering Coloniality', p. 12.

51 Weinberg, 'Apartheid', p. 62.

52 Goldblatt and Enwezor, 'Matter and Consciousness'.

53 This first appeared in 1986 in *The Cordoned Heart*, and was later published separately, see David Goldblatt, *The Transported of KwaNdebele: A South African Odyssey* (New York, 1989).

54 David Goldblatt et al., *David Goldblatt, South African intersections* (Munich, 2005).

55 Weinberg, 'Apartheid', p. 63; Pierre-Laurent Sanner, 'Comrades and Cameras', *Anthology of African and Indian Ocean Photography* (Paris, 1999), pp. 253–7. Badsha and Weinberg collaborated with the cultural magazine *Staffrider* to create exhibitions for photographs, just as the magazine provided a forum for the work of artists, photographers, writers and poets.

56 Reprinted in Weinberg, 'Apartheid', p. 64.

57 Pierre-Laurent Sanner, 'Comrades and Cameras', in *Anthology of African and Indian Ocean Photography* (Paris, 1998), p. 256.

58 Other workshops were organized by the Brotherhood, the Centre for Documentary Photography, Dynamic Images and Vakalisa.

59 Sanner, 'Comrades', p. 256.

60 Peter McKenzie, *Staffrider*, v/2 (1989), quoted in Sanner, ibid., p. 254.

61 There were exceptions: Sue Williamson recalled that some photographers' work was included in art venues, including a show in Cape Town's Baxter Theatre, *Art for Peace*, and in 1987, *Artists Against Apartheid*; personal communication, 15 May 2007.

62 Sue Williamson, ibid.

63 Omar Badsha, ed., *The Cordoned Heart: Twenty South African Photographers* [Prepared for the Second Carnegie Inquiry into Poverty and Development in Southern Africa] (Cape Town, 1986).

64 Francis Wilson, *Cordoned Heart*, p. 110; Chris Ledochowski's work continues in new veins, for example, *Cape Flats Details: Life and Culture in the Townships of Cape Town* (Pretoria, 2003).

65 Interview by Wallace Mgoqi for the film *Crossroads*, produced by Lindy Wilson (Cape Town and London, 1978); Francis Wilson, *Cordoned Heart*, p. 42.

66 *Cordoned Heart*, p. 102.

67 André Odendaal et al., *Beyond the Barricades: Popular Resistance in South Africa* (New York, 1989), p 7.

68 Grundlingh, 'South Africa', p. 248.

69 Weinberg, 'Apartheid', p. 68.

70 Victor Levie, ed., *De Verborgen Camera: Zuidafrikaanse Fotografie aan de Censuur Ontkomen (The Hidden Camera: South African Photography Escaped from Censorship)*, trans. Robert Dorsman (Amsterdam, 1989), afterword.

71 There were photographers who worked in less overtly political ways through apartheid, but the opportunities for other subject matter became central to the concerns of activist photographers, who moved into new subject areas and approaches as apartheid began to collapse.

72 *PhotoSynthesis: Contemporary South African Photography*, exh. cat., South African National Gallery (Cape Town, 1997), preface ed. Marilyn Martin et al.; Omar Badsha founded the South African History Online in 1999 which maintains an outlet for documentary and political photography, see www.sahistory.org.za; Michael Godby, 'After Apartheid: 10 South African Documentary Photographers', *African Arts*, XXXVII/4 (2004), pp. 36–41, 94; Kathy Grundlingh, ed., exh. cat., *Lines of Sight: Perspectives on South African Photography* (Cape Town, 2001).

four: Painting, Printing and Photography

1 I am very grateful to Julie McGee and Jürg Schneider for their insights and comments on this chapter.

2 See Stephen F. Sprague, 'Yoruba Photography: How the Yoruba See Themselves', *African Arts*, XII/1 (1978), pp. 52–9, 107; Christopher Pinney, *Camera Indica: The Social Life of Indian Photographs* (London, 1997), pp. 72–107; Liam Buckley, 'Self and Accessory in Gambian Studio Photography', *Visual Anthropology Review*, XVI/2 (2001), pp. 71–9; Christraud Geary, *In and Out of Focus, Images from Central Africa 1885–1960*, exh. cat., National Museum of African Art (Washington, DC, 2002); Hulleah J. Tsinhnahjinnie, 'When is a Photograph Worth a Thousand Words?', in *Photography's Other Histories*, ed. Christopher Pinney and Nicolas Peterson (Durham, 2003); Deborah Poole, *Vision, Race and Modernity: A Visual Economy of the Andean Image World* (Princeton, NJ, 1997).

3 Poole, *Visual Economy*.

4 John Mack, *Madagascar, Island of the Ancestors* (London, 1986), pp. 56–9.

5 Christraud Geary, 'Views from Outside and Inside: Representations of Madagascar and the Malagasy, 1658–1935', in *Objects as Envoys: Cloth, Imagery and Diplomacy in Madagascar*, ed. eds. Christine Mullen Kreamer and Sarah Fee (Washington, DC, 2002), p. 164. The portraits were reproduced in a catalogue: *A Tale of Two Islands: Aspects of Anglo-Malagasy History and Culture*, ed. John Mack et al. (Antananarivo, 1998); Hemerson Andrianetrazafy, *La Peinture Malgache dès Origins à 1940* (Antananarivo, 1991); Mervyn Brown, *A History of Madagascar* (London, 1995).

6 Geary, 'Representations of Madagascar', p. 164; Andrianetrazafy, *Peinture Malgache*, p. 18.

7 Geary, 'Representations of Madagascar', p. 171; Andrianetrazafy, *Peinture Malgache*, pp. 20–23; James Sibree, *Madagascar and Its People: Notes of Four Years' Residence, with a Sketch of the History, Position, and Prospects of Mission Work amongst the Malagasy* (London, 1870), pp. 22–6.

8 William Ellis, *Three Visits to Madagascar during the Years 1853–1854–1856: Including a Journey to the Capital, with Notices of the Natural History of the Country and of the Present Civilization of the People* (London, 1858), pp. 395–6; Geary, 'Representations of Madagascar', p. 162; and Sibree, *Madagascar and its People*, pp. 238, 348. Royal residences on the continent often hold significant collections of objects given by foreign and European rulers. One soldier likened the stores of objects looted by British soldiers during the sack of the Asantehene's Palace in Kumase, to collections held by the British Museum.

9 Geary, following Ellis, has made the case that Ellis's own family photographs were of interest to the younger generations of Merina monarchs; they were also curious to see images of English architecture, the English queen's customs for receiving guests in her palace, and requested copies of the *Illustrated London News*; Geary, 'Representations of Madagascar', pp. 162–3.

10 William Ellis, *Madagascar Revisited* (London, 1867; reprinted New York, 1972), p. 35.

11 Geary, 'Representations of Madagascar', pp. 165–8; Christine Downer, 'King Radama II of Madagascar', *History of Photography*, XXIV/2 (2000), p. 185.

12 This painting is in the collections of the Palace at Antananarivo, and was reproduced in Geary, 'Representations of Madagascar', p. 168, and in Rolf Roth, *Madagascar: Land Zwischen den Kontinenten*, exh. cat., Linden Museum (Stuttgart, 1994).

13 Geary, 'Representations of Madagascar', p. 167; J. Geiser, based in Algiers, sold postcards of the exiled Queen Ranavalona III.

14 Andrianetrazafy, *Peinture Malgache*, p. 28.

15 Ibid. These few images evoke a number of research questions, and even as more possibilities for reviewing the connection between painting, photography and royal and elite patronage come accessible, the situation is still in flux at the time of press, following the coup in March 2009.

16 'Fine arts' such as painting and sculpture and distinguished from 'crafts' have long been considered relevant distinctions in European art history, predicated on economic factors under which artists worked. Such distinctions pervade museum and art training today in the West, but are necessarily helpful distinctions when considering the range of creative production on the African continent, including photography.

17 Among these were artists from west Africa trained in Europe, for whom we still know very little, including Esi Isabelita Hermona of Elmina (d. 1692), who went to Spain for school in 1649, and lived in Europe for more than 40 years, travelling extensively to study painters, and she also worked with Velázquez. There is also the ex-slave Attabora Kweku Enu (1742–1798), active in Britain and who worked with the first painter to the Prince of Wales; see Isaac S. Ephson, *Gallery of Gold Coast Celebrities 1632–1958* (Accra, 1969), pp. 1–2, 31.

18 Ola Oloidi, 'Defender of African Creativity, Aina Onabolu, Pioneer of Western Art in West Africa', *Africana Research Bulletin*, XVII/2 (Freetown, 1991), pp. 21–49.

19 Ibid., p. 23; Onabolu's notes on an interview with K. C. Murray, 1931, and lecture by Onabolu dated 1954.

20 Sylvester Ogbechie, 'The '30s in Lagos, Nigeria', in *Anthology of African Art: The Twentieth Century*, ed. N'Gone Fall (New York, 2002), pp. 168–74.

21 Oloidi, 'Onabolu'; Ola Oloidi, 'Art and Nationalism in Colonial Nigeria', *Seven Stories about Modern Art in Africa*, ed. Clémentine Deliss, exh. cat., Whitechapel Art Gallery (London, 1995), pp. 192–4, 317; Everlyn Nicodemus, 'Inside. Outside.', in *Seven Stories*, pp. 29–37.

22 Ola Oloidi, 'Art and Nationalism'.

23 Oloidi, 'Onabolu', p. 24, from the artist's personal notes, 1924.

24 Erin Haney, 'If These Walls Could Talk! Photographs, Photographers and their Patrons in Accra and Cape Coast, Ghana, 1840–1940', unpub. PhD thesis, University of London, 2004.

25 Respectively: Donald Simpson and Peter Lyon, *Commonwealth in Focus: 130 Years of Photographic History* exh. cat., Royal Commonwealth Society in association with the ICC of Australia Ltd and Queensland Art Gallery (Sydney, 1982), pp. 34–5; Haney, ibid.; the *Gold Coast Chronicle*, XV, 165, 11 August 1894 (Accra); Jürg Schneider, pers. comm., 6 July 2007; Allister Macmillan, ed., *The Red Book of West Africa* (1920; reprinted London, 1968), p. 116; Françoise Morimont, 'Herzekiah Andrew Shanu', in *Les Photographies de Kinshasa*, ed. N'Gone Fall (Paris, 2001), pp. 12–16.

26 Oloidi, 'Onabolu', p. 32.

27 Haney, 'If These Walls Could Talk', ch. 4.

28 Oloidi, 'Onabolu', pp. 27–8 from Onabolu's private papers, 1925.

29 Ibid., p. 39.

30 Ibid., pp. 39–42; from Onabolu's papers 'Important People', November 1920.

31 Ibid., p. 42, Onabolu papers, 5 February 1920.

32 I'm grateful to the Wulff and Wulff-Cochrane families of Accra, and the Ebiradze House family of Cape Coast, and Selena Axelrod Winsnes, Carina Ray and Nels Buch-Jespsen; Haney, 'If These Walls Could Talk'; Erin Haney, 'Film, Charcoal, Time: Contemporaneities in Gold Coast Photographs', *History of Photography*, XXXIV/2 (May 2010).

33 This is not unreasonable or naive, as there are a number of crayon portraits and other kinds of heavily retouched photographs from this era in Ghanaian family collections; yet it does not appear to be a photograph of the original painting.

34 For work on impermanence in archives, see Liam Buckley, 'Objects of Love and Decay: Colonial Photographs in a Postcolonial Archive', *Cultural Anthropology*, XX/2 (2005), pp. 249–70.

35 This portrait of Cooke is reproduced in Haney, 'Film, Charcoal, Time'.

36 Anne-Marie Bouttiaux-Ndiaye, *Senegal Behind Glass: Images of Religious and Daily Life*, exh. cat., Royal Museum of Central Africa (Tervuren, 1994).

37 Ibid., p. 14.

38 Marie-Hélène Boisdur de Toffol, 'The Souweres', in *Anthology of African Art: The Twentieth Century*, ed. N'Goné Fall (New York, 2002), p. 120; *Revue Noire, Mama Casset et les Précurseurs de la Photographie au Sénégal, 1950: Meïssa Gaye, Mix Gueye, Adama Sylla, Alioune Diouf, Doro Sy, Doudou Diop, Salla Casset* (Paris, 1994); Bouttiaux-Ndiaye, *Senegal Behind Glass*.

39 Til Forster and Benetta Jules-Rosette, 'Representation and Advertising', in *Anthology of African Art: The Twentieth* Century, ed. N'Gone Fall (New York, 2002), pp. 114–15; Michel Renaudeau and Michèle Strobel, *Peinture sous verre du Sénégal* (Paris, 1984).

40 Bouttiaux-Ndiaye, *Senegal Behind Glass*, p. 140.

41 This discussion of Bamba imagery comes from Allen F. Roberts and Mary Nooter Roberts, 'Mystical Reproductions, Photography and the Authentic Simulacrum', *A Saint in the City: Sufi Arts of Urban Senegal*, exh. cat., UCLA Fowler Museum of Cultural History (Los Angeles, 2003), pp. 43–67.

42 Roberts and Nooter Roberts, *Saint in the City*, p. 21.

43 Ibid., ch. 1.

44 Ibid., p. 43.

45 Ibid., pp. 63–7.

46 Prince Claus Fund et al., eds, *The Art of African Fashion* (The Hague, 1998); John Picton et al., *The Art of African Textiles: Technology, Tradition, and Lurex*, exh. cat., Barbican Art Gallery (London, 1995; repr. 1999).

47 Picton, *The Art of African Textiles*, pp. 9–31.

48 These are graphic symbols, some of which are of local Gold Coast origin; others are linked to Islamic calligraphy and appear in gold weights, wood sculpture and hand-printed on prestigious stamped *adinkra* cloth.

49 Haney, 'If These Walls Could Talk', ch. 5; pers. comm. and images, John Picton.

50 Marleen de Witte, *Long Live the Dead! Changing Funeral Celebrations in Asante, Ghana* (Amsterdam, 2001); Haney, 'If These Walls Could Talk'.

51 Picton, *Technology, Tradition, and Lurex*; Prince Claus Fund, *African Fashion*; Okwui Enwezor, ed., *The Short Century: Independence and Liberation Movements in Africa, 1945–1994*, exh. cat., Museum Villa Stuck (Munich, 2001).

52 Martha Anderson, Lisa Aronsen and Christraud Geary, who are researching J. A. Green, kindly attributed this image.

53 Nii O. Quarcoopome, 'Les Portraits Funéraires Akan', in *Ghana, Hier et Aujourd'hui*, exh. cat., ed. Christiane Falgayrettes-Leveau, Musée Dapper (Paris, 2003).

54 Tobias Wendl and Nancy du Plessis, *Future Remembrance: Photography and Image Arts in Ghana*, VHS, 55 minutes (1998); Sunday Jack Akpan produces portraits and genre figures sculpted in cement by working from photographs in the Anang region of south-east Nigeria, Susan Vogel, *Africa Explores: Twentieth Century African Art*, exh. cat. (New York, 1991), p. 101.

55 Wendl and du Plessis, *Future Remembrance*.

56 Haney, 'If These Walls Could Talk', ch. 4; de Witte, *Long Live the Dead*.

57 Margaret Thompson Drewal, 'Portraiture and the Construction of Reality in Yorubaland and Beyond', *African Arts*, XXIII/3 (July 1990), p. 48.

58 Johannes Fabian, *Remembering the Present: Painting and Popular History in Zaire* (Berkeley, CA, 1996).

59 Bogumil Jewsiewicki, *Chéri Samba: The Hybridity of Art = L'Hybridité d'un Art* (Westmount, Québec, 1995).

60 Pers. comm. with Atta Kwami, see forthcoming *Kumasi Realism, 1951–2007: An African Modernism* (London, 2010).

five: Intimate Views

1 This can be contrasted with the tone of the early important publications and venues of contemporary photography, including: *Revue Noire*'s numerous publications beginning in 1991, especially their 1998 exhibition *L'Afrique par elle-même* at the Maison Européenne de la Photographie, Paris, the 1998 volume *Anthology of African and Indian Ocean Photography* and also Clare Bell, ed., *In/Sight: African Photographers, 1940 to the Present*, exh. cat., Guggenheim Museum (New York, 1996). In Africa, the South Africa National Gallery (SANG) mounted the exhibition *Photosynthesis* in 1997 and *Lines of Sight* (1999) at Cape Town; the Bamako photography biennale and

accompanying catalogues, *Rencontres Africaines de la Photographie* began in 1994; the work of photographers has increasingly appeared in other biennales such as Dakar, and for a time in the South African Month of Photography. The Kunsthalle at Vienna showed *Flash Afrique! Photography from West Africa*, in 2001; *The Short Century* opened in Munich in 2001; *Fault Lines: Contemporary African Art and Shifting Landscapes*, ed. Gilane Tawadros and Sarah Campbell, showed at the Venice biennale in 2003; *Decade of Democracy: South African Art 1994–2004* at SANG in 2004; *Africa Remix: Contemporary Art of a Continent* began at Museum Kunst Palast, Düsseldorf in 2004, and in London joined other exhibitions of that city's 'Africa 2005' season; recently, the International Center for Photography mounted *Snap Judgments: New Positions in Contemporary African Photography* at the ICP in New York in 2006. Since 2005, monograph and group shows of photographers from Africa and its diasporas have flourished in Europe, the UK and the USA, exhibitions in Bamako, Dakar, and Cairo, Lagos, Luanda, Cape Town and Johannesburg among other African centres. The Paris-based Afriphoto has published and exhibited the work of African and Diaspora photographers since 2001. Presently, databases, blogs and artists lists online proliferate at an astonishing pace, see for instance the Arab Image Foundation; Iconothèque Historique de l'Océan Indien; the photographic archive of the mission at Basel, Switzerland; London's Royal Geographic Society; the archives and online projects of the Pitt Rivers Museum, Oxford; the Eliot Elisofon Photographic Archive at the National Museum of African Art, Smithsonian Institution (Washington, DC); and the Africana collection, Northwestern University, Chicago. Recent South African online venues and print journals are notably comprehensive in their international African coverage.

2 Since 1994, significant expansion in educational opportunities, international support, venues and community programmes for photographers resulted in new art schools, private galleries and biennales, although these still tend to attract photographers with some kind of financial means.

3 Gideon Mendel, *A Broken Landscape: HIV and AIDS in Africa* (London, 2001).

4 Fazal Sheikh, *A Camel for the Son* (2001).

5 Sarah Nutall, ed., *Beautiful/Ugly: African and Diaspora Aesthetics* (Durham, NC, 2006).

6 Yto Barrada, *A Life Full of Holes: The Strait Project* (London, 2005).

7 Barrada, *Full of Holes*; Nadia Tazi, 'The State of the Straits', *Afterall*, 16 (2007), pp. 91–8.

8 Texts from installation at Galerie Polaris for *Iris Tingitana*, *Guerilla Gardening in Five Dates*, and *The Botanist* (colour video, 20 minutes, 2007); I thank Yto Barrada and Bernard Utudjian for their assistance.

9 Mikhael Subotzky, www.imagesby.com/.

10 Subotzky, *Beaufort West* (London, 2008).

11 Jodi Bieber, *Between Dogs and Wolves: Growing Up with South Africa* (Stockport, England, 2007); www.jodibieber.com.

12 Randa Shaath et al., *Randa Shaath: Under The Same Sky, Cairo* (Rotterdam, 2002).

13 Gomis's images as seen in *Le Journal* were assembled in *Snap Judgments: New Positions in Contemporary African Photography*, exh. cat., Okwui Enwezor, International Center of Photography (New York, 2006).

14 Muluneh works in photojournalism, video, and runs DESTA for Africa in Addis Ababa; her newest work is *Ethiopia: Past/Forward* (Africalila, 2009).

15 David Goldblatt, *The Structures of Things Then* (Cape Town, 1998); Guy Tillim, *Jo-burg* series (Paris, 2004); Jo Ractcliffe, *Johannesburg Inner City Works* (2000–4), seen in *Snap Judgments*, Okwui Enwezor (2006); Andrew Tshabangu, *City in Transition*; Jean Brundrit, 'Homeport' (2000) and *A Walk Around the Block With Goliath* (2004).

16 Based on author's interviews with the artists, Lagos and London, for the exhibition *Depth of Field*, South London Gallery, March 2005.

17 Zarina Bhimji, *Out of Blue*, film (2001); and various photographs, light boxes, films and installations (1998–2006); see *Fault Lines: Contemporary African Art and Shifting Landscapes*, ed. Gilane Tawadros and Sarah Campbell (London, 2003), pp. 131–7; and in *Snap Judgments* (2006).

18 Allan deSouza, *Allan deSouza: The Lost Pictures* (New York, 2005); Allan deSouza, *Allan deSouza: A Decade of Photoworks 1998–2008* (New Delhi, 2008).

19 Theo Eshetu, *Trip to Mount Ziqualla*, film (Ethiopia, 2005).

20 Akinbode Akinbiyi in *Africa Remix: Contemporary Art of a Continent*, exh. cat., ed. Simon Njami, Hayward Gallery (London, 2005).

21 Emeka Okereke, 'Emeka Okereke, Unspoken Hero', *Collection Afriphoto*, 16 (Paris, 2007).

22 Ibid.; and author's interview with Emeka Okereke, 14 December 2007.

23 *Moshekwa Langa*, solo exhibition, Goodman Gallery (Johannesburg, 2005); *Snap Judgments*, pp. 258–65; 'Moshekwa Langa: In Conversation', in *Looking Both Ways: Art of the Contemporary African Diaspora*, ed. Laurie Ann Farrell, exh. cat., Museum for African Art (New York, 2003), pp. 93–113.

24 Author's interview with Jide Adeniyi-Jones, 8 January 2008 and 15 December 2007.

25 Jane Alexander, *Photobook* (Vlaeberg, South Africa, 1995).

26 Fatimah Tuggar, *Village Spells Series + Fusion Cuisine*, solo show, Galerie SAW (Ottawa, 2004).

27 Baladi's work is published in *Africa Remix, Snap Judgments*, and www.factum-arte.com/eng/artistas/lara/default_en.asp.

28 Harandane Dicko, Septièmes Rencontres Africaines de la

Photographie: Dans La Ville et Au-dela, exh. cat., ed. Simon Njami (Bamako, Mali, 2007), pp. 50–51.

29 Author's interview with Santu Mofokeng, 27 November 2007.

30 First seen at the Johannesburg Biennale (1997).

31 Santu Mofokeng, *Santu Mofokeng*, TAXI Art Books series, 4 (Johannesburg, 2001).

32 As part of his work for the Ruth First prize project, 2007.

33 Author's interview, ibid., 27 November 2007.

34 Author's interview with the artist, Lagos, 5 December 2004; London, 29 March 2005 and 19 December 2007.

35 Residency 2006 with Mairie de Paris and Cité Internationale des Arts.

36 Author's interviews with Odunsi, 29 December 2007, 30 December 2007, 1 May 2008.

37 Erika Nimis, 'Contemporary Photography in Africa', Africa Now! Emerging Talents From a Continent on the Move, ed. Marina Galvani, exh. cat., World Bank (Washington, DC, 2008).

38 Elizabeth Harney, 'Exhibitions, Apertures and Imaginaries, Lessons from Snap Judgments', in *Nka, Journal of Contemporary African Art*, 22–23 (Spring–Summer 2008), pp. 28–37; review of Snap Judgments by Erin Haney and Erika Nimis, *African Arts*, XL/1 (Spring 2007), pp. 92–3.

39 I am especially grateful for the insights and conversations with Jennifer Bajorek, Elizabeth Harney, Akinbode Akinbiyi, Zaynab Odunsi, Erika Nimis and Joni Brenner among many others.

Select Bibliography

Afriphoto, http://afriphoto.com/index.asp

Afrique in visu, http://afriqueinvisu.org/

Alloula, Malek, *The Colonial Harem* (Minneapolis, 1986)

Anthology of African and Indian Ocean Photography (Paris, 1999)

Arab Image Foundation, www.fai.org.lb/

Badsha, Omar, ed., *The Cordoned Heart: Twenty South African Photographers* (Prepared for the Second Carnegie Inquiry into Poverty and Development in Southern Africa) (Cape Town, 1986)

Barrada, Yto, *A Life Full of Holes* (London, 2005)

Bell, Clare, ed., *In/Sight: African Photographers, 1940 to the Present*, exh. cat., Guggenheim Museum, New York (1996)

Bensusan, A. D., *Silver Images: The History of Photography in Africa* (Cape Town, 1966)

Bigham, Elizabeth, 'Issues of Authorship in the Portrait Photographs of Seydou Keïta', *African Arts*, XXXII/1 (1999), pp. 56–67, 94–5

Bonetti, Maria Francesca, and Guido Schlinkert, *Samuel Fosso*, exh. cat., Calcografia (Rome, 2004)

Buckley, Liam, 'Objects of Love and Decay: Colonial Photographs in a Postcolonial Archive', *Cultural Anthropology*, XX/2 (2005), pp. 249–70

Bull, Marjorie, and Joseph Denfield, *Secure the Shadow: The Story of Cape Photography from its Beginnings to the End of 1870* (Cape Town, 1970)

Cambridge University Library: Royal Commonwealth Society Collection, www.lib.cam.ac.uk/rcs_photo_project/homepage.html

Cole, Ernest *House of Bondage* (New York, 1967)

Contemporary Visual Art in South Africa, www.artthrob.co.za

David, Philippe, *Inventaire Général des Cartes Postales Fortier* (Paris, 1986–8)

——, L'Association Images et Mémoires, www.imagesetmemoires.com/index2.html

Edwards, Elizabeth, and Janice Hart, eds, *Photographs Objects Histories: On the Materiality of Images* (London, 2004)

Edwards, Elizabeth, *Anthropology and Photography, 1860–1920* (New Haven, CT, 1992)

——, *Raw Histories, Photographs, Anthropology and Museums* (Oxford, 2001)

Elisofon, Eliot, Photographic Archives, The National Museum of African Art, Smithsonian Institution, Washington, DC; see online at www.nmafa.si.edu/research/archives.html

Enwezor, Okwui, *Snap Judgments: New Positions in Contemporary African Photography* (Göttingen, 2006)

——, ed., *The Short Century: Independence and Liberation Movements in Africa, 1945–1994*, exh. cat., Museum Villa Stuck, Munich (2001)

Fall, N'Gone, ed., *Les Photographies de Kinshasa* (Paris, 2001)

Geary, Christraud, 'Different Visions? Postcards from Africa by European and African Photographers and Sponsors', *Delivering Views: Distant Cultures in Early Postcards*, ed. Christraud Geary and Virginia-Lee Webb (Washington, DC, 1998)

Geary, Christraud, *Images from Bamum, German Colonial Photography at the Court of King Njoya, Cameroon, West Africa, 1902–1915*, exh. cat., National Museum of African Art, Smithsonian Institution, Washington, DC (1988)

——, *In and Out of Focus, Images from Central Africa 1885–1960*, exh. cat., National Museum of African Art, Washington, DC (2002)

Godby, Michael, 'Excavating Memory: Collage as a Strategy for the Recovery of History in the Work of Cecil Skotnes, William Kentridge, and Willie Bester', in *Nka, Journal of Contemporary African Art*, 6–7 (Summer–Autumn 1997), pp. 38–43

Goldblatt, David, et al., *Fifty-One Years, David Goldblatt*, exh. cat., Museu d'Art Contemporani de Barcelona (2001)

Grantham, Tosha, ed., *Darkroom: Photography and New Media in South Africa, 1950 to the Present*, exh. cat., Virginia Museum of Fine Arts, Richmond (2009)

Grundlingh, Kathy, ed., *Lines of Sight: Perspectives on South African Photography*, exh. cat., South African National Gallery, Cape Town (2001)

Hartmann, Wolfram, with Patricia Hayes, and Jeremy Silvester, eds, *The Colonising Camera: Photos in the Making of Namibian History* (Cape Town, 1998)

Howe, Kathleen Stewart, *Excursions Along the Nile: The Photographic Discovery of Ancient Egypt*, exh. cat., Santa Barbara Museum of Art, California (1993)

Iluminando Vidas, Fotografia Moçambicana 1950–2001, Ricardo Rangel & the Next Generation, www.iluminandovidas.org/

Killingray, David, and Andrew Roberts, 'An Outline History of Photography in Africa to ca. 1940', in *History of Africa: A Journal of Method*, XVI/1 (1989), pp. 197–208

Landau, Paul S., and Deborah D. Kaspin, 'Empires of the Visual: Photography and Colonial Administration in Africa', in *Images and Empires, Visuality in Colonial and Postcolonial Africa*, ed. Paul Landau and Deborah Kaspin (Berkeley, 2002), pp. 141–71

Levie, Victor, ed., *De Verborgen Camera: Zuidafrikaanse Fotografie aan de Censuur Ontkomen (The Hidden Camera: South African Photography Escaped from Censorship)*, trans. Robert Dorsman (Amsterdam, 1989)

Magnin, André, ed., *Seydou Keïta* (Zurich, 1997)

Magubane, Peter, *Magubane's South Africa* (New York, 1978)

Maison Africaine de la Photographie, www.pro2m.net/fotoafrica/article.php3?id_article=24

Matt, Gerald, with Thomas Miessgang, and Wien Kunstahalle, *Flash Afrique!*, exh. cat., Kunsthalle Wien (2001)

Mirzoeff, Nicholas, ed., *The Visual Culture Reader* (London, 2002)

Monti, Nicolas, *Africa Then* (New York, 1987)

Mundus, Gateway to Missionary Collections in the United Kingdom, www.mundus.ac.uk/

Newbury, Darren, *Defiant Images: Photography and Apartheid South Africa* (Pretoria, 2009)

Nickel, Douglas R., *Francis Frith in Egypt and Palestine: A Victorian Photographer Abroad* (Princeton, NJ, 2004)

Nimis, Erika, *Photographes d'Afrique de l'Ouest: L'expérience Yoruba* (Paris, 2005)

——, *Photographes de Bamako de 1935 à nos jours* (Paris, 1998)

Northwestern University. Melville J. Herskovits Library of African Studies. Winterton Collection, www.library.northwestern.edu/africana/winterton/index.html

Odendaal, André, et al., *Beyond the Barricades: Popular Resistance in South Africa* (New York, 1989)

Oguibe, Olu, 'Photography and the Substance of the Image', in *In/Sight: African Photographers, 1940 to the Present*, exh. cat., Guggenheim Museum, ed., Clare Bell (New York, 1996), pp. 231–49

Pankhurst, Richard, 'The Political Image: The Impact of the Camera in an Ancient Independent African State', in Elizabeth Edwards, *Photography and Anthropology, 1860–1920* (New Haven, CT, 1992)

Peers, Simon, *The Working of Miracles: William Ellis: Photography in Madagascar, 1853–1865* (London, 1995)

Perez, Nissan N., *Focus East: Early Photography in the Near East (1839–1885)* (New York, 1988)

PhotoSynthesis: Contemporary South African Photography, exh. cat., South African National Gallery, Cape Town (1997)

Pinney, Christopher, *Camera Indica: The Social Life of Indian Photographs* (London, 1997)

——, and Nicolas Peterson, eds, *Photography's Other Histories* (Durham, 2003)

Poole, Deborah, *Vision, Race and Modernity: A Visual Economy of the Andean Image World* (Princeton, NJ, 1997)

Rencontres Africaines de la Photographie, Bamako, Mali, *Dans la Ville et Au-delà: Bamako 2007, VIIes Rencontres Africaines de la Photographie*, exh. cat., Bamako Festival of Photography, Paris (2007)

——, 6th edn, 2005, Bamako, Mali, *Un Autre Monde, VIes Rencontres Africaines de la Photographie*, exh. cat., Bamako Festival of Photography, Paris (2005)

——, 5th edn, 2003, Bamako, Mali, *Rites Sacrés/Rites Profanes, VES Rencontres Africaines de la Photographie*, exh. cat., Bamako Festival of Photography, Paris (2003)

——, 4th edn, 2001, Bamako, Mali, *Mémoires Intimes d'un Nouveau Millénaire, IVES Rencontres Africaines de la Photographie*, exh. cat., Bamako Festival of Photography, Paris (2001)

——, 3rd edn, 1998, Bamako, Mali, *Ja Taa = 'Prendre L'Image': 3e Rencontres Africaines de la Photographie*, exh. cat., Bamako Festival of Photography, Arles (1998)

Roberts, Allen F., and Mary Nooter Roberts, 'Mystical Reproductions, Photography and the Authentic Simulacrum', *A Saint in the City, Sufi Arts of Urban Senegal*, exh. cat., UCLA Fowler Museum of Cultural History, Los Angeles (2003), pp. 43–67

Ryan, James R., *Picturing Empire: Photography and the Visualization of the British Empire* (London, 1997)

Schadeberg, Jürgen, *Sof'town Blues: Images from the Black '50s* (Hurlyvale, South Africa, 1994)

Seye, Bouna Medoune, *Mama Casset et les Précurseurs de la Photographie au Sénégal, 1950: Meïssa Gaye, Mix Gueye, Adama Sylla, Alioune Diouf, Doro Sy, Doudou Diop, Salla Casset* (Paris, 1994)

Shaath, Randa, et al., *Randa Shaath, Under The Same Sky: Cairo* (Rotterdam, 2002)

Sheikh, Fazal, *A Camel for the Son* (2001)

Shumard, Ann, *A Durable Memento: Portraits by Augustus Washington, African-American Daguerreotypist*, exh. cat., National Portrait Gallery, Washington, DC (1999)

Simpson, Donald, and Peter Lyon, *Commonwealth in Focus: 130 Years of Photographic History* (Victoria, Australia, 1982)

Southern Sudan Photo and Object Collections at the Pitt Rivers Museum, Oxford, http://southernsudan.prm.ox.ac.uk/index.php

Sprague, Stephen F., 'Yoruba Photography: How the Yoruba See Themselves', *African Arts*, XII, no. 1 (1978), pp. 52–9, 107

Stanford University, California, 'South of the Sahara, Contemporary and Historical African Photographs', compilation of online sources at http://library.stanford.edu/depts/ssrg/africa/photographs.html

Subotzky, Mikhael, *Beaufort West* (London, 2008)

University of Southern California: Mission 21/Basel Mission Image Archive, http://bmpix.org/bmpix/controller/index.htm

Vansina, Jan, 'Photographs of the Sankuru and Kasai River Basin: Expedition Undertaken by Emil Torday (1876–1931) and M. W. Hilton Simpson (1881–1936)', in *Anthropology and Photography*, ed. Elizabeth Edwards (New Haven, CT, 1992), pp. 193–205

Viditz-Ward, Vera, 'Photography in Sierra Leone 1850–1918', *Africa*, LVII/4 (1987)

Wendl, Tobias, and Heike Behrend, *Snap Me One! Studiofotographen in Afrika*, exh. cat., Münchner Stadtmuseum (1998)

Wendl, Tobias, and Nancy du Plessis, *Future Remembrance: Photography and Image Arts in Ghana*, VHS, 55 minutes (1998)

Acknowledgements

This project sprang from a series of inquiries into photography over a long while, beginning in the village of my great-grandfather's photo studio to Minneapolis, Accra, London, and other places. My work in London and Ghana was generously and incisively shaped by John Picton, to whom I owe an enormous personal and intellectual debt. I am also exceedingly grateful to John Parker, whose enthusiasm for and love of teaching via photographs, as well as his intricate knowledge of Accra, has encouraged this project. In Accra, I have benefited greatly from the kindness, wisdom and diverse interests of George Hansen, Alexander P. K. Lutterodt, Theodora Naa-abia Chinery, Sammy Danquah, Ben Dowuona, Charles Owusu, Freddie Wulff, the Abraham family, the Wulff-Cochrane family, Salaamatu Dormenyu-Brown, Mrs Dorothy Barnor, Michel Doortmont and Carina Ray; in Lagos, Zaynab Odunsi, Toyin Sokefun-Bello, Kelechi Amadi-Obi, Uche James-Iroha, Amaize Ojeikere, Emeka Okereke, Don Barber, and Bisi Silva. In London and beyond, I have learned much from conversations with Charles Gore, Elsbeth Court, Elizabeth Edwards, Atta Kwami, Gus Casely-Hayford, Akinbode Akinbiyi, and Jide Adeniyi-Jones.

Part of this project began during my postdoctoral fellowship at the National Museum of African Art, Smithsonian Institution, especially the tremendous collection of the Eliot Elisofon Photographic Archive. I would like to acknowledge the assistance and encouragement of Christine Mullen Kreamer, Christraud Geary, David Binkley, Janet Stanley, Katherine McKee, Andrea Nichols, Bryna Freyer, Alice Howard, Karen Brown, and special thanks for critical insights from Allyson Purpura, Jessica Martinez, and Xavier Courouble. I am very happy to acknowledge the generous provision of images and expertise of Amy Staples, Kareen Morrison, and the wise eyes of Franko Khoury. Thanks also go to Wilma Medeiros, Flor Pena, Sita Reddy, Carol Johnson, Sue Williamson, Jenn Law, John Peffer, Tosha Grantham and Sylvester Ogbechie. For their insights, critical reckoning, and friendship, I owe a great deal to Julie McGee, Erika Nimis, Jürg Schneider, Dabney Hailey, Elizabeth Harney and Jennifer Bajorek.

This work, of course, could not have been possible without the goodwill of the institutions and artists who generously shared their images or assisted in securing them for this book. They include Uche James-Iroha, Zaynab Odunsi, Babajide Adeniyi-Jones, Patricia Hickling, members of the Ebiradze House, the Lutterodt family, Harandane Dicko, Emeka Okereke, Akinbode Akinbiyi, Allan deSouza, the Talwar Gallery, Yto Barrada, Galerie Polaris, Gideon Mendel, Gille de Vleig, Omar Badsha, Ben Maclennan, Chris Ledochowski, David Goldblatt, Lesley Lawson, Peter Magubane, Luanne, Dave Meyer-Gollan, Aida Muluneh, Michael Subotzky, Santu Mofokeng, Phillip Kwame Apagya, Fazal Sheikh, John Picton, Mary Nooter Roberts and Allen F. Roberts, Don Cole and the Fowler Museum of Cultural History, University of California at Los Angeles, the Leslie Wulff-Cochrane family, Carina Ray, Selena Axelrod Winsnes, Heike Behrend, Liam Buckley, Dieudonné Agaounga, Erika Nimis, Robert Bell and the Wisbech and Fenland Museum in Cambridgeshire, Tristan Bréville and the Musée de la Photographie of Port-Louis, Mauritius, David Easterbrook and the Winterton Collection of East African Photographs, Melville J. Herskovits Library of African Studies, Northwestern University, the Rare Books and Special Collections Library, The American University in Cairo, Samuel Fosso, and Jean Marc Patras Gallery, Roland Belgrave and Bernard J Shapero Rare Books, Wilson Centre for Photography, Duncan Clarke, Elizabeth Whitelaw and CAAC – Pigozzi collection, Margaret Thompson Drewal, The National Museum of African Art, Smithsonian Institution, Christraud Geary, and the Van-Leo and Angelo Boyadjian Photograph Collection of the Rare Books and Special Collections Library at the American University in Cairo. Thank you.

I'd also like to thank those who granted me permission to reproduce their images: El Hadj Adama Sylla, Paul Weinberg, Robyn Keet and Africa Media Online, Barbara Frey Näf and the Basel archive mission-21, Kenis Lutgard Dutrelepont, Mathilde Leduc-Grimaldi and the Royal Museum of Central Africa, Tervuren, the King Baudouin Foundation, the George Eastman House- International Museum of Photography and Film, Carol Johnson and the Library of Congress, Linda Briscoe and the Gernsheim Collection of the Harry Ransom Humanities Research Center, The University of Texas at Austin, the Smithsonian Institution Libraries, the Israel Museum in Jerusalem, and Anti-Slavery International. The research for part of this work was provided for by the Overseas Research Students Award Scheme; the University of London Central Research fund; a bursary from the School of Oriental and African Studies, University of London; a Predoctoral Research Fellowship, 2003, and a Postdoctoral Fellowship, 2004, both through the National Museum of African Art, Smithsonian Institution, Washington, DC. For support of the publication of images, I am very grateful to Tom Gibian and to Emerging Capital Partners, a private equity group investing across Africa, and have contributed generously to this work.

I would especially like to thank Vivian Constantinopoulos at Reaktion for her patience and critical eye, and for the breadth of knowledge and valuable insights by Peter Hamilton and Mark Haworth-Booth.

My family merits a special note for their support and encouragement: Ellen and Tony West, Jan Haney, Kirk Haney, and Lora and Gabriel Mains: thank you. Finally, I dedicate this book to Markus Goldstein, whose exuberant generous intelligence and good humour sustained me, and to our daughter Luka and son Jasper, both of whom came along and kept things lively during the writing of this book.

Photo Acknowledgements

The author and publishers wish to express their thanks to the following sources of illustrative material and/or permission to reproduce it:

Courtesy Babajide Adeniyi-Jones: 97; courtesy Akinbode Akinbiyi: 95; The American University in Cairo (© Rare Books and Special Collections Library): 44; courtesy Anti-Slavery International: 57; by permission of Archives Mission 21/Basel: 8 (BMA QS-30.029.0012), 40 (Mission E-30.29.048), 85 (BMA QD-32.008.9190); author's photograph: 88; courtesy Omar Badsha: 63; courtesy of Mrs Dorothy Barnor: 69; courtesy Yto Barrada and Galerie Polaris, Paris: 91; courtesy Heike Behrend: 47; from Anne-Marie Bouttiaux, *Senegal Behind Glass: Images of Religious and Daily Life* (New York, 1984): 76; Tristan Breville: 18; collection A. Brunnschwelier and Co.: 81; photo courtesy Liam Buckley: 46; courtesy CAAC – The Pigozzi collection, Geneva, © Seydou Keïta: 42; collection Duncan Clarke-Adire: 28; courtesy the artist (Allan deSouza) and Talwar Gallery: 94; courtesy Harandane Dicko: 98; courtesy of Salaamatu Dormenyu-Brown: 83; George Eastman House (International Museum of Photography and Film), Rochester, New York: 12; Foreign and Commonwealth Office Library, London: 11; © 2009 Samuel Fosso, courtesy Jean Marc Patras Gallery, Paris: 45; collection Fowler Museum of Cultural History, University of California at Los Angeles: 80; from Gustav Fritsch, *Die Eingeborenen Süd-Afrikas ethnographisch und anatomisch beschrieben* (Breslau, 1872): 14; courtesy Christraud Geary: 54; family collection Elmina Ghana: 6; © David Greenblatt: 60; courtesy of Patricia Hickling: 10; Israel Museum, Jerusalem: 5; courtesy the artist (Uche James-Iroha): 101; from *The Journal of the African Society*, XIII/49 (1913): 70; © Lesley Lawson: 64; courtesy Chris Ledochowski: 61; Levy and Lepage collection, Paris: 4; Library of Congress, Washington, DC (American Colonization Society collection): 7, 27, 30, 38; collection of APK Lutterodt family: 9; courtesy Ben Maclennan: 62; courtesy Peter Magubane: 59; from Paul Marty, *Etudes sur l'Islam au Sénégal* (Paris, 1917): 78; from Gideon Mendel, *Broken Landscape: HIV and AIDS in Africa* (London, 2001): 89; courtesy Santu Mofokeng: 17, 99; Musée Royal de l'Afrique Centrale, Tervuren, Belgium: 13 (Stanley Archives 5195), 77 (EO.1988.35.18); photography Museum Port-Louis, Mauritius: 18; reproduction courtesy of the National Museum of African Art, Smithsonian Institution, Washington, DC: 87 (Henry John Drewal and Margaret Thompson Drewal Collection, courtesy the photographer and the Eliot Elisofon Photographic Archives – EEPA 1992-028-02945); National Museum of African Art, Smithsonian Institution, Washington, DC (Eliot Elisofon Photographic Archives): 1 (Nigerian Photographic Album, EEPA 2000-003-0042), 21 (EEPA Postcard Collection – Zanzibar series 190, number 24), 22 (Madagascar Photographic Album – EEPA 2000-004-0018), 25 (Ghana Photographic Album – EEPA 1995-0018-0041), 26 (Ghana Photographic Album – EEPA 1995-0018-0002), 29 (West Africa Postcard Album – EEPA 1992-004-052), 31 (EEPA Postcard Collection MG 20-9), 32 (West Africa Postcard Album – EEPA 1992-004-118), 33 (EEPA TZ PCA), 34 (EEPA Postcard Collection – SA 20-84), 35 (EEPA Postcard Collection – SA 20-92), 36 (African Postcards – EEPA 2002-0006), 37 (EEPA 1995-180000), 39 (West African Photographic Album – EEPA 1995-0017-0020), 41 (W. H. Himbury Photographic Album – EEPA 1995-0024-0031), 51 (EEPA Postcard Collection – CG 5-52), 52 (EEPA Postcard Collection – CF 16-6), 53 (EEPA Postcard Collection – CG 35-5), 55 (Emile E. O. Gorlia Collection – EEPA 1977-0001-152-03), 56 (EEPA Postcard Collection – CG 38-8), 68 (EEPA Postcard Collection – MG 15-8), 84 (W. H. Himbury Photographic Album – EEPA 1995-0024-0043); National Museum of African Art, Smithsonian Institution, Washington, DC: 82 (The Wilbert and Irene Petty Collection – 2008-5-50 Franko Khoury); courtesy Erika Nimis: 48; Northwestern University, Evanston, Illinois: 23 (Melville J. Herskovits Library of African Studies – Winterton Collection of East African Photographs); courtesy Zaynab Odunsi: 100; courtesy Emeka Okereke: 96; courtesy of John Picton: 81, 86; private collections: 15, 74; courtesy of Mary Nooter Roberts and Allen F. Roberts: 79; from Louis A. Roussin, *Album de l'ile de la Réunion: recueil de dessins représentant les sites les plus pittoresques et les principaux monuments de la colonie* (Saint-Denis, Ile de la Reunion, 1860): 19; © Jürgen Schadeberg: 58; from Guebre Selassie, *Chronique du Régne de Ménélik II, Roi des rois d'Ethiopie* (Paris, 1930): 24; courtesy Bernard J. Shapero Rare Books, London: 3; courtesy Fazal Sheikh: 90; photo reproduced with the permission of the Smithsonian Institution Libraries: 14; from Henry M. Stanley, *Cinq années au Congo 1879–1884: voyages-exploration-fondations de l'état libre du Congo* (Paris, 1885): 50; courtesy of Mikhael Subotzky and the Goodman Gallery: 92; reproduced by permission of El Hadj Adama Sylla: 43; The University of Texas at Austin (Harry Ransom Center) Photography Collections: 16; courtesy Gille de Vleig: 66; by permission of, and ©, Paul Weinberg and Africa Media Online: 65; from *The Life and Journals of the Rev. Daniel West . . .* (London, 1857): 6; Wilson Centre for Photography, London: 2; courtesy Selena Axelrod Winsnes and the Leslie Wulff-Cochrane family: 71; Wisbech & Fenland Museum, Wisbech: 20, 67; courtesy Freddie Wulff family: 72,73; courtesy Leslie Wulff-Cochrane family and Carina Ray: 75; photo courtesy Yarak: 6.

Index

Numbers in *italic* refer to pages on which illustrations are reproduced.